Mobile Orientations

Mobile Orientations

An Intimate Autoethnography of Migration, Sex Work, and Humanitarian Borders

NICOLA MAI

The University of Chicago Press
Chicago and London

The University of Chicago Press, Chicago 60637
The University of Chicago Press, Ltd., London

Published 2018

27 26 25 24 23 22 21 20 19 18   1 2 3 4 5

ISBN-13: 978-0-226-58495-9 (cloth)
ISBN-13: 978-0-226-58500-0 (paper)
ISBN-13: 978-0-226-58514-7 (e-book)
DOI: https://doi.org/10.7208/chicago/9780226585147.001.0001

Library of Congress Cataloging-in-Publication Data

Names: Mai, Nicola, author.
Title: Mobile orientations : an intimate autoethnography of migration, sex work, and humanitarian borders / Nicola Mai.
Description: Chicago ; London : The University of Chicago Press, 2018. | Includes bibliographical references and index.
Identifiers: LCCN 2018008600 | ISBN 9780226584959 (cloth : alk. paper) | ISBN 9780226585000 (pbk. : alk. paper) | ISBN 9780226585147 (e-book)
Subjects: LCSH: Male prostitutes—Europe. | Sex workers—Europe. | Foreign workers—Europe. | Male prostitution—Europe. | Sexual orientation—Europe. | Europe—Emigration and immigration. | Prostitution—Europe. | Human trafficking—Europe.
Classification: LCC HQ119.4.E85 M35 2018 | DDC 306.74/3094—dc23
LC record available at https://lccn.loc.gov/2018008600

CONTENTS

Preface / vii
Acknowledgments / xvii

INTRODUCTION / 1

ONE / Intimate Autoethnography / 20

TWO / Engaging Albanian (and Romanian) Masculinities / 33

THREE / Selling *Comidas Rapidas* in Seville / 53

FOUR / Boditarian Inscriptions / 74

FIVE / Burning for (Mother) Europe / 91

SIX / The Trafficking of Migration / 106

SEVEN / Love, Exploitation, and Trafficking / 124

EIGHT / Interviewing Agents / 142

NINE / Ethnofictional Counter-Representations / 167

CONCLUSION / Challenging Sexual Humanitarianism / 188

Appendix: Research Projects and Filmography / 199
Notes / 201
References / 205
Index / 219

PREFACE

> No, I did not decide, what was I going to do? My family is suffering in Nigeria and I have no papers, what else can I do? They should give us papers instead of fining clients! It is only going to make things more difficult for us than they are already. They should give us work if they want us to stop doing this!

Joy said this all at once when I asked whether she felt she had made her own decision to work in the sex industry.[1] Immediately before, I had asked whether she had been forced to work in the sex industry, which she had also denied. These two questions were the start of a survey of five hundred (migrant and nonmigrant) sex workers I undertook in France between March 2014 and March 2015.[2] The survey was part of a research project to understand the effects in France and the United Kingdom of "sexual humanitarianism," a concept I have introduced to analyze the impact on migrant sex workers of policymaking and social interventions based on their assumed vulnerability to trafficking and exploitation. The concept of *sexual humanitarianism* refers to the global emergence of a neo-abolitionist epistemology that legitimizes targeted forms of control and protection of social groups defined as vulnerable in relation to their sexual orientation and behavior.

Joy's words perfectly embody the epistemological dissonance at the core of this book: the dissonance between the complexity of migrant sex workers' experiences of agency and the ways in which that complexity tends to be ignored by antitrafficking policies and interventions. Throughout my experience of researching the sex industry, I faced the axiomatic sexual humanitarian belief that the majority of migrants working in the industry were victims of trafficking.[3] The fact that this did not coincide with migrants' own experiences of sex work prompted me to investigate further, resulting in almost twenty years (and counting) of research and, ultimately, in the book you are reading now. My ability to tap into the complexity of people's involvements in the sex industry developed only gradually. At the very beginning of my research, I entered the field with precisely the stereotypical assumptions that I challenge in this book. I somehow "knew" that there had to be a problem behind people's involvement in the sex industry. I spent the following twenty years "unlearning" those assumptions (hooks 1995, 157) with the help of a lot of people who were patient enough to explain and show their working and migratory lives to me.

Since the beginning of my doctoral studies in 1997, I have talked to many migrants working in the sex industry. I have met them through specialized services, sex work organizations, and independently, in the context of different research projects.[4] While undertaking such projects, I addressed them primarily as workers, and asked nonmoralizing and nonpathologizing questions while also addressing the real stigmatization and exploitation they encountered in their working and social lives. My research on the relationship between migration and the sex industry started with three years of fieldwork in Albania between 1998 and 2001. My original focus on heterosexual experiences of sex trafficking in Albania gradually expanded to include female, male, and transgender migrants working in the sex industry in a variety of origin and destination contexts, including Belgium, France, Germany, Greece, Italy, Morocco, Romania, Spain, the Netherlands, Tunisia, and the United Kingdom.

In none of those places, with the partial exception of the initial phase of my first fieldwork in Albania (1998-2001), did I encounter the prevalence of victimhood that is generally presented as self-evident by political, academic, and nongovernmental actors advocating the criminalization of clients and the abolition of prostitution as the best ways to fight sex trafficking. On the contrary, the majority of the people I met—including minors (adolescents between the ages of fourteen and seventeen) and third-party agents[5]—explained to me the different ways in which they had decided to work in the sex industry. A minority told me that they had embraced sex work enthusiastically and that they found it emancipatory or liberating. An even smaller minority considered themselves victims of trafficking and exploitation. But the vast majority referred to what they did as work. No, not "sex work," and definitely not "a job like any other." Just "work"—no small matter, given the relevance of the dimension of labor for understanding why people work in the sex industry, and given how little this dimension is acknowledged within sexual humanitarian research and representations.

In my Albanian fieldwork during the early postcommunist years, I witnessed young women and men working in the sex industry according to intensely patriarchal patterns of economic and emotional domination (Mai 2001a). Later in that fieldwork I had the opportunity to observe the fluidification and renegotiation of those relationships in relatively more consensual terms. I decided to further examine this process of fluidification by studying the subjectivities of young men from Albania and Romania who were involved in the sex industry as both sex workers and third-party agents. In the years that followed, as my entry points into the nexus of migration and the sex industry multiplied, I started to meet a majority of nonvictims. At the same time, I gradually gained the confidence of people who had at first presented to me as "victims." As a result, a more diverse range of experiences became visible to me.

Historically, prostitution has been framed by policymaking and ideological approaches that range along a spectrum between prohibition and regulation. These approaches emerged in relation to different feminist understandings of women's ability to exert their agency in the context of patriarchal oppression. Since the early 1990s, liberal feminists' recognition of women's agency when consenting to sell sex has been challenged by neo-abolitionist feminists, who understand prostitution as "paradigmatic of a system of male power" and seek its abolition by removing the demand for sexual services (O'Neill and Scoular 2008, 13). This shift is best represented by the global resonance achieved by the "Swedish model," a globally hegemonic, neo-abolitionist epistemology and policymaking framework which equates sex work with violence against women, and which introduces the parallel decriminalization of sex workers and criminalization of male clients as an ideal instrument to fight trafficking (Skilbrei and Holmström 2013).

Liberal feminists first mobilized the contemporary concept of *trafficking* in the late 1990s to understand and fight new, migration-related forms of exploitation emerging within the sex industry. The concept was later appropriated by neo-abolitionist feminists in the context of the negotiation of the 2000 UN Palermo Protocol (Ditmore and Wijers 2003). Resulting from a negotiation between opposing feminist sensibilities and coalitions, the protocol defines trafficking as "the threat or use of violence or other types of coercion, of abduction, of fraud, of deception, of the abuse of power or of a position of vulnerability, or of the giving or receiving of payments or benefits to achieve the consent of a person having control over another person for the purpose of exploitation" (UN General Assembly 2000, 2). From the perspective of migrant sex workers, there are two main and interrelated problems with this definition. First, in the absence of any "neutral" understanding of what constitutes coercion and exploitation in the sex industry, this definition of trafficking allows a considerable degree of arbitrary discretion, which often translates into antimigrant and antiprostitution interventions and policies (O'Connell Davidson 2005, 73). Second, the fact that the victim's consent to being exploited according to the vague and broad terms of the Palermo Protocol mentioned above is considered irrelevant exacerbates further the degree of arbitrariness with which migrant and nonmigrant sex workers are targeted by sexual-humanitarian interventions and policies. Liberal feminists' early concerns about the possible co-optation of antitrafficking legislation by antimigrant and antiprostitution law-enforcement efforts were corroborated by later evaluations of antitrafficking initiatives, which showed that the rights and livelihoods of sex workers tended to be considered expendable "collateral damage" in the fight against organized crime (GAATW 2007). The resulting increase in migrant and nonmigrant sex workers' socioeconomic vulnerability is part and parcel of the neo-abolitionist epistemology and its overall aim to eradicate prostitution as a form of violence against women. By failing to grasp the complex ways in which migrant (and nonmigrant) sex workers understand exploitative sexual transactions as different from trafficking, sexual humanitarianism's neo-abolitionist epistemological focus remains distant from the lives and complexities of the people it proposes to help. Therefore it systematically misses its target and exacerbates people's vulnerabilities—as drones have systematically failed to spot the difference between civilians and fighters in Afghanistan and Iraq. The focus of "militarized" and "carceral" humanitarian interventions remains too far from the complexity of reality to apprehend the difference between victims of trafficking and migrants trying to live their lives by making difficult decisions constrained by limited opportunities (Bernstein 2010).

These considerations are key to the increasing involvement of humanitarian rhetoric and dynamics in the global government of migration and sex work. Sexual humanitarianism plays a strategic role in the global onset of forms of governance based on the production of strategic moral panics that exaggerate the extent of trafficking (Mahdavi 2014). The relevance of moral panics about trafficking to global geopolitical governance is most evident in the yearly Trafficking in Persons Report (TIP). Produced in 2001 by the George W. Bush administration, the TIP made access to crucial US development funds conditional on the adoption of antitrafficking and antiprostitution laws. It resulted in the worldwide adoption of neo-abolitionist and repressive policies that further criminalized and marginalized sex workers, within the United States and globally (e.g., Lerum, McCurtis, Saunders, et al. 2012; Cheng 2010, 201–2). Against these unilateral forms of epistemological and other forms of violence, this book brings the complex experiences of migrants to the center of global debates on the relationship between migration, sex work, and trafficking. For instance, all of the Nigerian women who participated in the survey in France in 2014–15—including the 38 percent who felt they had not decided on their own to work—identified economic problems and lack of legal status as the two constraints under which they sold sex. These considerations highlight the necessity to transcend the (false) free/forced and victim/agent dichotomies that structure sexual humanitarian notions of trafficking and modern slavery, and to focus on the different forms of socioeconomic vulnerability generated and exacerbated by neoliberal policies if we want to understand the specificity of exploitation in the sex industry (O'Connell Davidson 2013). I elaborate on this necessity throughout the book. The false dichotomies shaping sexual humanitarianism are grounded in the neo-abolitionist conflation of *choice*, seen as an apolitical and ahistorical expression of *free will*, and agency, the capacity to act within socioeconomic and moral constraints—which all sex workers (just like everybody else) have (Shah 2014, 198). It is in order to challenge this neo-abolitionist, simplistic, and neoliberal conflation of choice, free will, and agency, that in this book I theorize the notion of *decision* in relation to the concept of *mobile orientations*, which expresses migrant sex workers' complex and evolving experiences of agency and exploitation.

There is a very close relationship between sexual humanitarianism and neoliberalism, an economic theory based on the belief that freeing markets and trade from state and other forms of social and political control inherently enhances human well-being (Harvey 2005, 2), which translates to the understanding and governance of social phenomena according to market logics, values, and priorities. In this book, I refer to the concept of *moral gentrification* to analyze the Global North's imposition on the rest of the world of privileged and profitable moralities that are grounded in both neo-abolitionist and neoliberal ideologies. These ideologies reflect neither the socioeconomic constraints nor the related priorities and needs that frame migrant sex workers' agency. The Global North is not a geographical expression; it is the diffused geopolitical center from which neoliberal policies and politics produce desirable and undesirable individuals and groups in underprivileged and affluent countries alike. In this respect, the concept of moral gentrification expresses different scalar experiences of the convergence between conservative moralization and sexual humanitarianism in neoliberal times. At a global level, the term frames the ways in which sexual humanitarianism legitimizes the globalization and mainstreaming of neo-abolitionist policies and neoconservative moralities through the strategic conflation of sex work and trafficking, which obfuscates the fact that many migrants work in the sex industry to avoid being exploited in other labor sectors (Amar 2009). At a local level, the concept of moral gentrification expresses the moralizing agenda that is often implicit (and sometimes explicit) in the active gentrification of desirable properties and areas where sex workers live and work in order to "reclaim" them for mainstream and highly profitable commercial and residential use.

The successful export to France of the Swedish model in 2016 is an exemplary case of globalized moral gentrification in sexual humanitarian times. The survey I undertook in France in 2015 aimed to understand what people selling sex in France thought about the proposal by François Hollande's Socialist government to criminalize clients. The proposed law, which aimed to fight trafficking and modern slavery by reducing the demand for commercial sex through the criminalization of clients was passed at the Assemblée Nationale on 6 May 2016. Ninety-eight percent of the surveyed sex workers, both migrants and nonmigrants, were against it. Significantly, all of the Nigerian women who participated in the survey were strongly against the criminalization of clients, which they felt would make it even more difficult to repay their debts. As I explain in the book, many Nigerian women could only afford to access mobility and migration by consenting to "bounded" experiences of exploitation in the sex industry (Mai 2016b). It was only when those terms were not respected that the antitrafficking instrument available to them made sense; otherwise, they preferred to honor the debt they had agreed to in order to live and work in Europe. These concerns highlight further the gap between sexual-humanitarian and migrants' understandings of agency and exploitation, which I explore throughout the book. They also show how the neo-abolitionist priorities that shape sexual humanitarian policies and interventions exert forms of epistemological violence that end up being complicit with the brutal enforcement of anti-migration and antiprostitution policies, by obliterating migrants' ability to consent to "indentured" forms of mobility "inhabiting a middle zone between human trafficking and labor migration" (Parreñas 2011, 7).

The main aim of this book is to explore the contrast between the ways migrants understand and experience their own agency and exploitation and the ways in which the latter are understood and targeted by sexual-humanitarian moralities, policies, and interventions. In order to understand this interplay, I elaborate the notion of "biographical borders": standardized, discursive repertoires according to which migrants can get their rights recognized (and avoid deportation) by humanitarian institutions and organizations (Mai 2014). Throughout the book I review the ways in which humanitarian categories such as "unaccompanied minor" and "victim of trafficking" fail to frame the complexity of migrants' desires, needs, and priorities, as well as their understandings of their own agency and exploitation. For instance, while analyzing young migrants' multiple movements between (and within) different countries in the European Union, I distinguished two main mobility patterns, characterized by different degrees of agency. Minor mobility is characterized by young migrants' agentic ability to understand and navigate the psychological, economic, and sociocultural dimensions that shape their journeys, through which they aim to achieve pragmatic and attainable objectives. On the other hand, errant mobility is characterized by an unresolved passage to adulthood that generates an undetermined psychological and social liminality, and utopian and unrealistic migratory projects whose unavoidable failure is repeated at each new destination. The concepts of *minor* and *errant mobility* are useful to understand the different degrees of agency characterizing young people's migratory projects and their experiences of selling sex. By "migratory project" I refer not only to actual geographical displacement but also to the wider discursive processes and practices of cultural consumption through which prospective and actual migrants imagine themselves with respect to the new, individualized, and transnational sociocultural environments, lifestyles, and material cultures brought together by the convergence of globalization and neoliberalism (Mai 2005).

Migration tends to be explained primarily in terms of economic motivations, push/pull factors between sending and receiving regions, transnational networks, and the impact of migration industries (e.g., Castles and Miller 2009; Hernández-León 2008). However, the role of imagination in the formulation and enactment of people's migratory projects has not been sufficiently explored (Mai 2001b; Koikkalainen and Kyle 2015). What is lacking, and what this book aims to provide, is a theoretical and evidence-based conceptualization of the sociocultural, economic, and historical factors that frame people's decisions to migrate in order to embody their desired and imagined subjectivities. To understand the ways in which commodification, individualization, and the globalization of mobility affect the imagination and enactment of migrants' migratory projects, I elaborate the concept of *mobile orientations*: socially established alignments of objects, mobilities, and models of subjectivity that frame migrants' capacity to act. This concept, which draws on Sara Ahmed's (2006) theory of orientations, acknowledges the increasing resonance of objects in people's subjectivities in commodified and individualized late-modern times. At the same time, the "mobile" aspect of orientations highlights the importance of mobility in migrants' identities and subjectivities, reflecting how being mobile has become a key, late-modern discourse that reproduces social distinction and exclusion (Skeggs 2004, 50). The concept of mobile orientations challenges the conflation of "choice" and agency operated by the neo-abolitionist ideology powering sexual humanitarianism. It highlights how people's capacity to act is expressed through decisions that are embedded within "contextual and relational" dynamics rather than according to abstract and ethnocentric notions of choice (Ham 2017, 17). Migrants' agency is framed in this book as a socioculturally situated capacity for action that allows people to inhabit and perform norms in different ways, rather than as an ahistorical ability to resist constraints (Mahmood 2005, 9).

The mobile orientations of migrants emerge from the encounter between local cultures and the globalization of commodified youth culture that expresses the individualized models of subjectivity prevailing in the Global North. In order to analyze and explain the unfolding of migrants' mobile orientations across contradictory social roles and subjectivities at home and abroad, I use the geometrical concept of the *fractal*, a form of regularity emerging through the repetition of highly irregular patterns. The concept of the fractal allows me to talk about how migrants both reproduce and challenge normative sexual and gender roles in their cultures of origin and destination. In the process, new patterns of normativity and transgression emerge, allowing migrants to express contradictory moralities, priorities, and needs. By working in the sex industry, they can afford, economically and morally, to be both successful, individualized consumers by selling sex abroad and dutiful sons, daughters, husbands, or wives according to hegemonic sexual and gendered roles at home. This fractal engagement with the sex industry allows migrants to respond to the contradictory ways in which they are subjectified in times of neoliberal globalization. The concept is also useful for understanding the tacit and embodied, rather than verbalized, ways in which migrants working in the sex industry negotiate their subjectivities across different cultures, priorities, and needs.

My research on the relationship between migration and the sex industry was characterized by transformative encounters with informants whose lives and knowledge allowed me to understand the complexity, similarity, and difference of our mobile orientations. This book reappraises my research experiences through an intimate, autoethnographic lens which aims to convey the affective, performative, and intersubjective dimensions through which knowledge emerged through different and interconnected fieldwork projects. Following Hoefinger (2013, 72), I define my autoethnographic approach as intimate because most of the knowledge informing this book emerged through "authentic intersubjective time" during which informants and I exchanged affects, information, and perspectives. As autoethnography is an approach focusing on the personal experience of the researcher to understand and analyze wider social dynamics, *Mobile Orientations* presents concepts, theories, and data as they emerged during the development of the research process and my relationships with other research participants, whether they were informants, friends, or both. As a consequence, concepts and data are often and purposely disseminated across different chapters analyzing interconnected, multisited fieldwork periods, rather than being presented cohesively in thematic units.

In order to account for the affective, performative, and intersubjective dimensions of knowledge production, besides adopting an intimate autoethnographic approach, I also developed a participative, creative, methodology based on filmmaking. I was greatly inspired by Jean Rouch's ethnofictions, which included research subjects as active producers and performers of their own representations, transcending the distinction between fiction and nonfiction, participation and observation, knowledge and emotion. My main intentions in approaching the genre of ethnofiction are to convey the complexity of migrants' life and work trajectories, and to use filmmaking to represent and reproduce both the process of knowledge production (research interviews and ethnographic observation) and the socio-anthropological truth of migrant sex workers' complex decisions and priorities, which deeply question sexual humanitarianism. The process of filmmaking is an integral part of the book's intimate, autoethnographic approach, reflecting the synergy between my research and my interest in ethnographic filmmaking. Some chapters result from a strategic assemblage of interviews, ethnographic observation, and accounts of filmmaking to present the different methods, relations, and contexts through which knowledge arose between my informants and me.

Both my films and my writing show that most migrants decide to work in the sex industry in order to fulfill their mobile orientations, have a better life, and escape the forms of exploitation they meet in other jobs. Sexual humanitarian rhetoric obfuscates the complex mix of opportunities and constraints framing their agency. By conflating migrant sex work with trafficking, and by merging the latter with previously separate legal categories, such as forced labor and modern slavery, according to the logic of "exploitation creep" (Chuang 2014), sexual humanitarianism legitimizes restrictive and criminalizing measures that exacerbate migrants' vulnerability to exploitation. This book aims to break this vicious circle by bringing migrants' own understandings and experiences, as well as their complex decisions and trajectories, to the center of academic and public debate.

ACKNOWLEDGMENTS

As I started drafting the acknowledgments for this book, which builds on twenty years of life and work experience, I soon realized that if I were to mention all those who had helped me through the process, this section would be longer than the book itself! I ask forgiveness in advance from the people I will inevitably be unable to include here but who helped me along the journey to understanding the issues and dynamics I examine in this book. In this respect, my first and most important thank you goes to the many sex workers whose knowledge and support has guided me all these years. Although I lost touch with some of you as our migration journeys took us in different directions, I will never forget you. This book is dedicated to you, your hopes and struggles, with the hope that one day you will finally get all the rights you need and deserve.

Looking back at the long journey that led to this book feels like reappraising the whole of my academic career so far, as the research experiences analyzed here stretch as far back as the very beginning of my PhD dissertation on Albanian migration to Italy in 1998. I would not have been able to find my bearings in Albania back then without the help and guidance of Rubin Celaj and Skender Fifo. Thanks for your insight into Albanian sexualities, for your assistance in organizing interviews, and for making me aware of the presence of male Albanian sex workers in Greece and Italy in the first place. I also owe a huge debt of gratitude to Selami Brahaj, who greatly assisted me in arranging and undertaking difficult and strategic interviews. Thanks also to Stefania Servidio for giving me the opportunity to direct the development project through which I learned so much about Albania and myself.

In Italy, I am especially grateful to Giancarlo Spagnoletto, Antonella Inverno, and Giusy d'Alconzo for their friendship and support. We shared incredible moments and our exchanges (and laughs!) will be with me forever. Thanks also to Save the Children Italy and the International Organization for Migration in Rome for their logistical and financial support. In Greece, a very big thank you goes to Constantine Giannaris for his friendship and for his insight into male migrant sex workers' lives. I am also very thankful to Pierre Sintes and Krini Kafiris for being there for me at a life-changing (and crazy) moment. I am very much indebted to Prof. Russell King for his guidance during the postdoctoral research on the social inclusion and exclusion of Albanian migrants in Italy and Greece, and to the Leverhulme Trust for having funded that research.

I would not have been able to deliver the project entitled *Migrant Workers in the UK Sex Industry* without the help of the many colleagues and friends who supported the project with their work and advice. First and foremost, the team of researchers who undertook interviews and ethnographic observations: Kate Hardy, P. G. Macioti, and Thierry Schaffhauser. A big thank you goes also to the members of the project's advisory board, who supported me through very challenging times right at the beginning of the project and throughout its implementation: Rosie Campbell, Linda Cusick, Justin Gaffney, Bill Jordan, James Mannion, Maggie O'Neill, Anthony Pryce, and Catherine Stephens. Thanks also to Mary Hickman, director of the Institute for the Study of European Transformations (at London Metropolitan University, hosting the project), for her trust, support and guidance. A very big thank you goes to Madeleine Kingston, whose administrative skills and commitment have been a driving force throughout the project. I am very grateful to the Economic and Social Research Council for having funded the research and its dissemination, and for their understanding and flexibility. I would also like to thank the members of the Haringey Council for their confidence and for having funded the research on migrant sex workers assisted by the Sexual Health on Call (SHOC) project. A very big thank you goes to Tiziana Mancinelli and Heidi Hoefinger, who undertook most of the interviews with migrants; to Rosie Campbell for her invaluable insight on project evaluation and sex work more generally; and to Michelle Farley, SHOC's director, for her support. Georgina Perry, thank you for your friendship, passion, and knowledge; you have been a source of inspiration all these years.

I am very grateful to all the talented actors that played in *Normal* so generously. Selami Brahaj, Matthew Crawley, Annie Lebura, Bobi Rostas, Rebecca Roots, and Tonia Sotiropoulu, it was fantastic working with you! I am also grateful to Giles Foreman for having allowed me to learn about acting direction and to participate in his inspiring classes. A very special thank you goes to Charlotte Worthington for having believed in my potential as a filmmaker and for having produced *Normal*. Huge thanks also to Titus Kojder for his generous and talented work as an editor, which made the film more engaging and dynamic.

In France, I am very grateful to the IMéRA Institute of Advanced Studies at Aix Marseille University, and to the A*MIDEX Foundation for their generous financial support of the early and final stages of the *Emborders* project and for their flexibility, without which my films *Samira* and *Travel* would never have seen the light of day. A special thank you goes to Brigitte Marin for having believed in my work from the start and for her friendship and support. Thanks also to Isabelle Arvers for her beautiful friendship and for all of her effort to discuss, promote, and disseminate *Samira* and *Travel*. I am very grateful to Cedric Parizot for having included me in the *AntiAtlas of Borders* project right from the beginning; we had a fantastic time, intellectually and otherwise. At IMéRA, special thanks go to Emmanuel Girard Reydet for his support, and to Samuel Bordreuil for his insightful comments. I am very thankful to Calogero Giametta, who worked as a postdoctoral researcher for the *Emborders* project, for all his hard work, for his trust, and for our fruitful exchanges. A big thank you goes also to Sylvie Mazzella and the Mediterranean Laboratory of Sociology at the Maison Mediterranéenne des Sciences de l'Homme for having wholeheartedly hosted and supported the *Emborders* project.

My films *Samira* and *Travel* would not have been possible if many generous, creative, and committed people had not supported their production. I am hugely indebted to Jacques Sapiega, director of SATIS, the Department of Sciences, Arts and Audio-Visual Techniques of Aix-Marseille University, and the team of students that helped me direct and finalize *Samira*: Teddy Pierru, Thomas Bernal, Franck Bruckner, Flora Graillot, Gaetan Tessier, Theo Pizard, and the rest of the team. I will never forget your generosity and professionalism, and the fun we had together. A very special thank you goes to Karl Sarafidis, the actor playing Karim/Samira, whose talent and commitment brought the character to life and made the film possible. I am very indebted to the Bus des Femmes association for their fantastic support for the undertaking of the *Emborders* research and the production of *Travel*: France Arnaud, Pénélope Giacardy, Vanessa Simoni, and Audrey Smolen-Koné. Thanks also to Marine Thisse for her support for both the *Emborders* project and the production of *Travel*. My gratitude and admiration go to Esse, Esther, Gift, Gina, Kate, Margaret, Pat, and Queen for their generous participation in the writing and making of *Travel*, and for their courage in expressing their life experiences through the story of Joy. It was an incredible privilege to work with you, and our adventure has a special place in my heart. Thanks also to Celine Bressieux, Sarah Marie Maffesoli, Cadyne Senac, and Marie Claire Vallaud for playing their roles in the film and for their knowledgeable contributions to its content. I am hugely indebted to Clément Dorival and the Anamorphose team (Tristan Clamorgan, Jean-Baptiste Mees, Hadrien Bayard, Jean-Michel Perez, Clémentine Giovanetti, and Leïla Porcher) for their incredible generosity, talent, and commitment to the production of *Travel*. The nights spent shooting the film in the heart of the Bois de Boulogne will stay with me forever. Thanks also to Bruno Ulmer for the opportunity to be part of the process that led to his film *Welcome Europa*, even though we did not see eye to eye about the relationship between ethnographic truth and documentary filmmaking in the end.

I also want to praise Doug Mitchell, Kyle Wagner, and the editorial team at the University of Chicago Press for their support and advice throughout the publication process. I am very grateful to the anonymous referees for their insightful and constructive reviews. A very big thank you also to Merl Storr for her thorough editing and manuscript preparation work.

I am very grateful to my friends Helen Crowley, David Napier, and Susan Ossman, who read early drafts of the book and helped me to focus on the aspects and issues that made it to its final version. Thanks also to Clare Hemmings for her feedback on the book proposal and her support during the early phases of the publication process.

A big and special *grazie* goes to my parents for their support through all these years, and particularly to my mother, Marzia Bergamaschi, for having always believed in my abilities and for putting up with the extended periods of seclusion that accompanied the writing of the book.

Finally, I am hugely indebted to my partner, John Groves, who wholeheartedly supported me and believed in me throughout the many ups and downs I encountered along the journey that led to the publication of this book.

INTRODUCTION

Crossing Sexual-Humanitarian Borders

"You think so because you are French!" Samira told me (slightly) angrily when I said as a joke that I saw no real man in front of me.[1] She was wearing a frock and full makeup while claiming to be a real man like her father. That night, like most nights, she was selling sex *en femme* in Marseille. She replied quickly to my protest that I was not French but Italian, saying, "I know that you are Italian, but you are like the French. . . . Your parents accept that you are queer, right?"

I replied, "Yes, but it took a while, you know? With my mother, it was easier, but with my father, it took almost thirty years."

We were standing against the wall at the corner where she usually sold sex. "Whatever!" she objected. "I am not like that. I am a real Algerian man, just like my father. In my family a man is a man; a woman is a woman. When I am Karim, I go with women; when I am Samira, I go with men. You will never see me go with a man when I am Karim! I am not like those whores over there, you know?"

By then I had already decided that Samira was going to be the protagonist of the first ethnofiction in *Emborders*, an art-science project analyzing the effectiveness and scope of humanitarian initiatives targeting migrant sex workers and sexual minority asylum-seekers. To get their rights recognized by humanitarian institutions and organizations, migrants perform their life histories according to standardized discursive repertoires that constitute biographical borders between deportation and access to social support, legal documentation, and work (Mai 2016a). The *Emborders* project combined ethnographic observation and filmmaking to analyze and represent how humanitarian biographical borders respond to migrants' experiences of subjectivation, agency, and exploitation.

There is an intrinsically ambivalent relation between humanitarianism and borders. Rights emerged historically as a governmental instrument of domination, offering people an ambivalent basis for their subjection and emancipation (Souter 2008). In contemporary, late-modern times, this structural ambivalence has been amplified by a "moralising reorientation of politics towards the suffering of the victims of political struggles" (Whyte 2012, 20–21), which has coincided with the emergence of new kinds of humanitarian borders, governance, and interventions. The intensification and diversification of globalized migrant flows, the implementation of restrictive migration policies, and the onset of humanitarian forms of governance all converge to invest the social protection of vulnerable migrant groups with new functions of control (Agier 2011; Webber 2012). At the same time, the neoliberal reorganization of state sovereignty and labor mobility results in the proliferation and heterogenization of borders, regulating flows of goods and workers according to the interests of an increasingly globalized form of capitalism (Mezzadra and Neilson 2013). As a result of these dynamics, contemporary times are characterized by the global proliferation of new, humanitarian socio-legal spaces that act as bordering devices and within which governmental, nongovernmental, and academic actors produce strategic forms of knowledge about vulnerable migrant groups in relation to the "temporality of unfolding crises" (Walters 2010, 152).

In the Global North, sexuality and gender have increasingly become humanitarian repertoires through which racialized barriers to mobility are inscribed on migrants (Ticktin 2011). As essentialist discourses of gender equality and sexual liberation become "avatars of both freedom and modernity" (Butler 2008, 2), they can legitimize neoliberal forms of "democratic" governance through the strategic production of moral panics in relation to sexuality and gender (Fassin 2010). I have developed the concept of sexual humanitarianism to analyze how fixed and sexuality-related notions of vulnerability operate as migration-control mechanisms. By focusing on the sexual salience of humanitarian migration control, the concept analyzes how groups of migrants are strategically problematized, supported, and intervened upon by humanitarian institutions and NGOs according to vulnerabilities that are supposedly associated with their sexual orientation and behavior.

Sexual humanitarianism's moral imperative to "rescue" victims of sex trafficking often becomes entangled with the enforcement of restrictive labor-migration policies and controls, exacerbating migrants' vulnerability to exploitation in line with racial, ethnic, and class-based hierarchies (Chapkis 2003). My work draws on critical studies of the category of the trafficked "victim," which strongly indicate the need to transcend the dichotomy between "free" and "forced" in studies of the nexus between migration and the sex industry, in order to make visible women's migratory agency (Doezema 1998; Andrijasevic 2010; Ham 2017). My work also engages with studies of the sexualized and gendered "livelihoods" (Shah 2014) and forms of "indentured mobility" (Parreñas 2011) through which migrants and nonmigrants selling intimate and sexual services negotiate agency in contemporary neoliberal times.

This book problematizes sexual humanitarianism as a strategic vector of neoliberalism in five main ways. First, sexual humanitarianism normalizes the everyday exploitability and precarization of labor engendered by neoliberal policies because it grants humanitarian protection only to exceptional and extreme forms of gender- and sex-related exploitation. Second, sexual humanitarianism's prevailing neo-abolitionist ideology represents sexual transactions according to the economic fundamentalist mantra of supply and demand, neglecting the complexity of the libidinal, socioeconomic, and intersubjective dynamics involved. Third, sexual humanitarianism's sexual and gender politics play a strategic role in framing antitrafficking as a legitimate object of investment for multinationals, which increasingly use campaigns against sex trafficking as part of their branding, effectively laundering their own involvement in similar exploitative practices in other employment sectors (Bernstein 2016). Fourth, by legitimizing the surveillance and control of migrant sex workers on the basis of their supposedly inherent vulnerability, sexual humanitarianism operationalizes neoliberal governance through the punitive containment of their marginality, which ignores and exacerbates the underlying socioeconomic insecurities and inequalities it enforces (Wacquant 2009). Fifth, sexual-humanitarian, "end-demand" antitrafficking campaigns, by blaming individual customers and criminal networks for trafficking, cast governments as "heroes offering compassion and support" while deflecting from their direct responsibilities for instituting restrictive labor migration regimes that create the conditions for forced labor and "perpetuate a market for people smugglers and traffickers" (O'Brien 2016, 220).

Mobile Orientations analyzes the complicity between sexual humanitarianism and neoliberalism by engaging with a range of interrelated case studies. The chapters that follow reflect the fact that most migrant sex workers decide to work in the sex industry to escape the exploitation they face in the "straight jobs" available to them (Mai 2013). By concealing how such decisions respond to forms of labor exploitability engendered and exacerbated by neoliberalism, sexual humanitarianism is deeply implicated in the globalization, normalization, and enforcement of moralities and policies that express the privilege of the Global North. Moreover, by shifting the representational terms of the "humanitarian media complex" toward a neo-abolitionist representation of all migrant sex workers as victims of trafficking, sexual humanitarianism transcends the world of policymaking and social interventions to encompass the production of influential films that straddle the boundaries between documentary and fiction, and set the terms of global debate on these issues (Lindquist 2010). The "spectacular rhetoric" characterizing neoliberal epistemology (Hesford 2011) translates into moral panics about migrant "sex slaves" that strategically amplify the magnitude of the issues they raise (Weitzer 2007). Documentary and fictional filmmaking that spectacularizes migrant (and nonmigrant) sex work as sex trafficking and modern slavery plays a key role in the moral gentrification of the world according to priorities reflecting moral sentiments and humanitarian priorities that are privileges of the Global North. To account for the implication of documentary films, antitrafficking campaigns, and other representations in the workings of sexual humanitarianism, I draw on Lauren Berlant's critique of "national sentimentality" as "a rhetoric of promise that a nation can be built across fields of social difference through channels of affective identification and empathy" (2001, 53). I argue that the sexual and representational politics of sexual humanitarianism attempt to create a new global sentimentality which, paraphrasing Berlant, I define as a rhetoric of promise that a global humanity can be built across fields of social difference, through the production and dissemination of fictional and moralized notions of victimhood that ultimately prevent people from the Global North from acknowledging their own increased exploitability and precarity.

In order to understand the specific ways in which migrants' sexual orientation and behavior are problematized within sexual humanitarian dynamics, I introduce the term *sex-gendered* to indicate how people understand and represent themselves in relation to the interlinked dimensions of sexuality and gender. The term *sex-gendered* both follows and challenges Iris Marion Young's (2002, 427) suggestion that we should transcend the sex/gender distinction because it potentially reifies the distinction between nature (sex) and nurture (gender). While acknowledging the necessity of transcending this potential reification, the distancing dash in the term *sex-gendered* retains the potential to address the ways in which selves are specifically and intersectionally gendered and "sexed" at the same time (Probyn 1993).

The story of Samira, which opened this chapter, illustrates how migrants embody and understand sexual-humanitarian biographical borders and other sex-gendered repertoires in relation to their own unfolding and transforming lives. Karim, the Algerian refugee who worked as Samira at night, was an ideal research subject for the *Emborders* project. He belonged to two key categories of migrants targeted by sexual humanitarianism: sex workers and sexual minority refugees.[2] I was first introduced to him by people who were working for a harm-reduction project supporting sex workers in Marseille. When I met him on the doorstep of his flat in central Marseille in June 2012, Karim was selling sex as Samira. He was almost forty years old. During the many ethnographic moments that I shared with him in the two years that followed, he told me his incredible story of biographical, humanitarian, and geographical border-crossing. His experience embodies and explodes the intersection of sex-gender, class, and ethnicity in the shaping of people's identities, their subjectivities, and the forms of geographical and social mobility they can access.

Defining Selfrepresentations

While listening and talking to Samira, I was fascinated by the way her story both resonated with and jarred against humanitarian biographical borders. Karim leaves Algeria when his breasts start to develop as a result of his taking hormones. He gets hormones from the transsexual sex workers—his only reference for his own sex-gendered "difference"—that he meets while wandering his city of origin.[3] Karim decides to leave Algeria for Italy, where he starts selling sex alongside fellow Algerian transsexuals in Naples. Samira describes those years as exciting and glamorous: "I was not like now, you know? I was gorgeous! Italian men were crazy about me, you should have seen the clients I had, the clothes I wore . . ."

But as life moves on, Karim wants to start saving money and "make something of his life." He moves to France, where he learns that there are better chances of being regularized as a refugee if he seeks asylum as an "Algerian transsexual," a category officially recognized in France as a social group deserving of asylum under the 1951 UN Refugee Convention. Ten years later, Karim is granted asylum in France as Samira, "thanks to his breasts," which he presents as having allowed him to defend his asylum application as a transsexual whose life is at risk if he is deported back to

Algeria. In the process, Karim represents his life according to a standardized biographical border: a teleological and normative narrative originating from the Global North, which frames his complex sexual and gender identification in stereotypically "transsexual" terms of being a woman trapped "in the wrong body" (Stone 1992, 152).

He keeps selling sex and living in France, first in Paris and then in Marseille, where he moves in order to be "closer to Algeria." This move is the beginning of a gradual process of reinscription within Algerianness and heteronormativity, which concludes ten years later. As his father lies dying in a French hospital, Karim has his breasts surgically removed, presents himself to his father as a "man," and is reinstated as his son. Later he marries a French-Algerian lesbian woman in order to get a new passport, allowing him to return to Algeria to assume his new role as male head of the family. This is when I meet him selling sex in central Marseille, with the aid of fake breasts. "It's much better like this," he tells me one night. "I can attach them and get rid of them when I want. If I wore them during the day people would spit at me."

The unfolding of Samira's life trajectory between different biographical borders and priorities in relation to evolving opportunities for humanitarian protection and regularization strongly evokes Stuart Hall's (1996, 3) anti-essentialist definition of identity as "strategic and positional." Identities, and related forms of subjectivity, do not exist in unified and coherent forms, but are continually reconstructed over time and performed in social interactions, according to the strategic needs and priorities of the group or individual deploying them. A performative and relational understanding of identity is predicated on the recognition of the intrinsic—if not ontological–heterogeneity of subjectivity. It acknowledges how subjectivities are always heterogeneous and contextual, "articulated in relation to specific problems and solutions concerning human conduct" (Rose 1996, 28).

The contradictory assemblage and juxtaposition of multiple subjectifying scripts characterized Samira's understanding of her life history as well as its representation for others. Corresponding to the poststructuralist approach outlined above, I use the concept of "selfrepresentation" to describe how identities and subjectivities emerge through the constant interaction between subjects and the social worlds they inhabit. My conceptualization of selfrepresentation subsumes and transcends the difference between social and individual representations, since discourses framing particular models of personhood also frame how the surrounding social world is understood and experienced (Moore 1994, 51). The absence of the distancing dash between *self* and *representation* is meant to underline the complex and simultaneous interplay between social representations and their internalization, mediation, or rejection at an individual level. This interplay is a crucial aspect of the constant making and remaking of the self in relation to the social world, and vice versa: "a reification continually defeated by mutable entanglements with other subjects' histories, experiences, self-representations; with their texts, conduct, gestures, objectifications" (Battaglia 1995, 2).

The poststructuralist understanding of subjectivities as intrinsically heterogeneous, constructed, and contextual evokes the epistemological dilemma of how to understand the relationship between the subject's discursive interpellation and its autonomy. The scholarly conversation between Foucault and Butler on the theoretical sustainability of the existence of prediscursive subjects that "disrupt the regulating practices of cultural coherence imposed by a regulatory regime" (Butler 1999, 178) resumes this dilemma. The possibility of prediscursive and presocial subjects and materialities intersects with the founding epistemological enigma of all social sciences—the relation between individual autonomy and social normativity—as well as the foundational philosophical enigma of the relation between ontology and epistemology, being and knowing. Following Clare Hemmings' (2012) reappraisal of Elizabeth Probyn's theorization of experience, I conceptualize experience as a result of the dynamic intersection of affective, ontological, and epistemological dimensions, and as a strategic nexus for understanding people's apprehension of themselves and the world they inhabit. An important implication of this conceptualization is that our ontological experience of objects, subjects, and the affects and attachments linking them is intrinsically connected to epistemological self-representations. It is only by apprehending these two dimensions together onto-epistemologically that we have a chance of understanding social phenomena in their complexity and historical relevance.

Researching migrant sex workers' experiences of agency means engaging with the regimes of selfrepresentation and subjectification that are part and parcel of the sexual-humanitarian onto-epistemology. It means identifying the sexual stories that frame the experiences and subjectivities of migrants, which emerge from the wider social and historical settings that they intersect by migrating. The concept of "sexual story" developed by Plummer (1995) highlights the historical and sociological relevance to late-modern social dynamics of the production, dissemination, and consumption of particular sexual scripts. Plummer's conceptualization has two main implications that are strategic for the aims of this book. First, as a particular sexual story—such as the "coming out" story—is circulated recursively across a variety of social settings, the distinction between fiction and reality becomes less relevant as "fiction becomes faction," which occurs because the story's social and political resonance challenges scientific and other authorities. Second, the circulation and consumption of sexual stories is always embedded in social change through the production of an "interpretive community of support" that makes these stories socially audible and believable at a specific historical conjuncture (Plummer 1995, 166).

These storytelling dynamics highlight the emancipatory potential of the circulation of sexual stories that assert the rights of marginalized minorities, such as the LGBT community in the case of the "coming out" story. However, if we follow Allison Jobe (2008) in considering "sexual trafficking" an emerging sexual story, a much less emancipatory picture emerges: migrant (and nonmigrant) sex workers, who are undoubtedly marginalized minorities, are denied rather than given rights in the name of their presumed vulnerability, a state of affairs sanctioned by an international, neo-abolitionist "interpretive community of support." This neo-abolitionist community—which includes most organizations, authorities, institutions, and multinationals invested in the fight against trafficking—plays a key role in the mainstreaming and "institutionalization" of sexual humanitarianism at both global and local levels through its privileged "consultative access" to political and policymaking actors (Weitzer 2007, 459).

One of the main aims of this book is to counter the fixity of the sexual-humanitarian onto-epistemology by bringing in the lived complexity of migrant sex workers' lives. Again, Samira's contradictory selfrepresentations are an ideal example. While listening to her telling her sexual story, I was often reminded of the contextual and dynamic ways in which ethnic identities, class relations and sex-gendered roles (and practices) are assembled into a person's sense of belonging to national moral communities (Lambevski 1999). For instance, the claim to be "only active" (i.e., penetrating) in sexual encounters with clients was a strategic selfrepresentation by Albanian and Romanian sex workers as belonging to their national and moral communities, against the passivity and immorality of their "queer" Italian clients (Mai 2004a). In the same way, Samira seems to associate her Algerianness—"I am a real man like my father"—with a heterosexual (and heterosexist) sex-gendered demarcation. This retroactive and normativizing repositioning is best embodied in her motto, "I sleep with men when I am Samira and with women when I am Karim," which frames her as different from "those queers and whores over there." Most importantly, this heteronormative reframing is in direct contradiction with the "Algerian transsexual" biographical border she mobilized when she applied for asylum in France, according to which she was a "woman trapped in a man's body."

Mobile Orientations

Samira's life history is an exemplary case study of the "relational and contextual" nature of agency (Ham 2017, 17). Her switching of selfrepresentations reminded me again and again that agency arises out of the ways humans are assembled historically, rather than from any essential property of the subject (Rose 1996, 186–87). These considerations are important for the aims of this book: migrants' understandings of agency and exploitation are embedded within existential priorities and needs that evolve alongside their migratory projects. What used to be a risk can become an opportunity, and vice versa, as migrants decide implicitly or explicitly to take risks and opportunities according to where they are in relation to their desired life trajectories.

To enable an adequately complex analysis of migrant agency, I have introduced the concept of "mobile orientations" to refer to the socioculturally available alignments of objects, mobilities, and discourses that allow migrants to embody and perform a desired subjectivity (Mai 2017). The concept of mobile orientations aims to account for the inextricable role of materiality and mobility in the emergence of migrants' subjectivities and migratory projects. These subjectivities and projects are marked by the convergence of individualization and "objectualization," i.e. the "increasing orientation towards objects as sources of the self, of shared subjectivity . . . and of social integration" (Knorr Cetina 1997, 9). These considerations highlight the importance of consumption within migrants' selfrepresentations, as well as the need to analyze how migration and related experiences of agency emerge in relation to the possibility of becoming successful sex-gendered beings by accessing associated materialities and mobilities.

To understand this complex interplay, I draw on Phillips' (2006) reappraisal of Deleuze and Guattari's notion of *agencement*. I translate *agencement* as "agencing" rather than "assemblage," to underline its original reference to a heterogeneous and dynamic arrangement that enables a specific experience of becoming. This notion of "becoming" refers to the way Deleuze and Guattari's work offers opportunities to address the affective, material, and corporeal dimensions and everyday events through which sex-gendered subjectivities emerge "at the molecular level, through and across bodies and objects" (Osgood 2014, 198). I also draw on Sara Ahmed's (2006) phenomenological notion of "orientation," which refers to specific sociocultural alignments of objects, narratives, bodies, gender/sex roles, and mobilities that can become the space for action of specific subjectivities. At the center of the concept of mobile orientations is the awareness that no agency precedes the agencing arrangement, or vice versa. Rather, mobile orientations are heterogeneous alignments that emerge socially as the context framing migrants' capacity to act through *agencing decisions* that reflect their priorities and needs.

Mobile orientations frame agency as the capacity to act within, rather than against, the contradictory constraints and opportunities for subjectivation engendered by the globalization of neoliberal policies and politics. The concept draws on Saba Mahmood's (2005, 18) definition of agency as a socioculturally situated capacity for action that is always created and enabled by specific relations of subordination. It highlights the "existential" urgency and quality of people's decisions to migrate in order to feel that they are "going somewhere" by reaching "a space that constitutes a suitable launching pad for their social and existential [selves]" (Hage 2009, 97–98), where they can hope to become the women and men they have been subjectivized into according to the contradictory scripts of individual self-realization and self-sacrifice they encounter in their everyday lives. This is the case with young migrants who risk their lives to cross the Mediterranean in the hope of embodying their desired subjectivities as successful, individualized consumers abroad while remitting to their families at home, which I analyze in chapters 2 and 5. It is also the case with Joy and the other female, Nigerian migrant sex workers mentioned in the preface, who endure "bounded exploitation" (Mai 2016b) in the short term in the name of a better future for themselves and their families.

It is beyond the scope of this introductory chapter to elaborate further on the theorization of migrant agency. Here I would like to emphasize the contextual and sex-gendered salience of people's mobile orientations and the agencing decisions they make by returning to Karim's case. Karim's trajectory reminds us powerfully that to make sense for migrants, academics, and policymakers alike, agency has to be viewed as a socioculturally situated capacity for action that allows people to both resist and comply with constraints and norms. Once he migrates, Karim experiences selling sex in Europe as enabling and liberating, because it provides him with the possibility of embodying Samira. This is a version of himself that is in continuity with his selfrepresentation and experience as "effeminate" in Algeria while also responding to the socioeconomic consequences of his expulsion from his family. The first, "outbound" phase of his life is characterized by his desire to flee homophobia in Algeria by "becoming woman," which translates into moving abroad and applying for asylum in France as an "Algerian transsexual."

At the same time, the sexual stories and sex-gendered roles framing Karim's mobile orientation remain anchored to a heterosexist and homophobic framework within which he needs to keep being "just like his father" while selling sex as Samira abroad. As Karim's life evolves, and his family addresses him as its new male head, his mobile orientation becomes "inbound" and veers toward "becoming man" according to the sex-gendered roles and stories available in Algeria. This is when he decides to convert his French refugee passport (which does not allow him to return to Algeria) into a regular French passport by marrying a French (lesbian) woman. His decisions to migrate, sell sex abroad, apply for asylum as an Algerian transsexual (woman) and then return home as a heterosexual man highlight the contextual, positional, and dynamic nature of agency.

The Contours of Intimate Autoethnography

While Samira was talking about her decision to leave Algeria to "be herself," my thoughts kept going back to my adolescent self and the genealogy of my agencing decision to migrate to the United Kingdom. I too was made to feel effeminate by some of my peers. I also felt that I had to go abroad to "be myself." That was an agencing decision that was unquestionable for me: I just "knew." At an age when "being gay" suddenly became all I thought I was, I found narrative and visual scripts in British films, pop music, and novels that made me feel that only by going "there" could I be myself. That was my mobile orientation at that time: becoming gay in the United Kingdom.

I remember reading Italian newspapers merely to find news about the United Kingdom. I was inspired by Boy George, Jimmy Somerville, and Marc Almond. I was fascinated by the courage and defiance with which groups such as ACT UP and OutRage! were challenging the invisibilization of the HIV/AIDS epidemics and the stigmatizing marginalization of LGBT people and communities. I felt (and I still feel) that their battles were my battles—that by getting closer to London, I could find a voice to express what I felt about being gay at that political and historical juncture. The political struggles of the Thatcher years interested me; the Italian scenario bored me. I was born in the wrong country, by mistake, I thought. I felt English inside, and I thought that English people were more open—that they would understand me better. Most importantly, I felt that I could be either Italian and straight, or English and gay. In my imagination and projection of myself into the future, there was no possibility of a third space between those options. I had to go and participate in a material and cultural economy that gave me hope of being myself, whatever that meant. I left for London as soon as I could.[4]

As I reappraised my mental notes from my ethnographic encounters with Samira, my thoughts often went back to my adolescence. I had been in a similar state of mind for a long time. But in many other ways, I came from a different planet, one characterized by much more pluralist and accepting sex-gendered selfrepresentations. I did experience homophobia, but I was never presented with even the threat of being kicked out of my family and home. I was not persecuted socially. I was respected and loved by my classmates and friends. In my mother's family there was an ongoing intellectual conversation about homosexuality, mainly in relation to the towering figure of Pier Paolo Pasolini and his function as an organic intellectual within the Italian Communist Party, which was the hegemonic political formation in my family, city, and region of origin.[5] I remember how my mother cried when he was murdered; it was a mourning we all shared. So, yes, I guess in comparison with Samira, I was "French" after all.

As my own subjectivity is a central methodological tool in my research on the nexus between migration and the sex industry, I have increasingly written up my research findings in the format of autoethnography. This is a writing and research approach that systematically explores the researcher's personal experience to analyze wider social, cultural, and political meanings and understandings (Ellis, Adams, and Bochner 2010). In doing this I carry out a double operation. I first write myself into the emotional and cognitive texture of my research experience, in order to then write myself out of that texture and analyze the specificity of the dynamics I seek to study. Since I became familiar with ethnography not long after its self-reflexive turn, this comprehension was a starting point for me, enabling me to avoid the navel-gazing hermeneutic dilemma of "the comprehension of the self through the detour of the comprehension of the other" (Ricoeur 1969, quoted in Rabinow 1977, 5).

Autoethnography has become a common genre of ethnographic writing in a range of disciplines. Different ethnographic approaches have been characterized by (and classified according to) different relationships between the "auto" personal dimension of the writer and the "ethnographic" social and cultural dynamics being engaged with. "Analytical autoethnography" is a genre of autoethnographic writing that aims to connect self-reflexivity and the "narrative visibility of the researcher's self" to the "dialogue with informants beyond the self" and the "commitment to theoretical analysis" (Anderson 2006, 378). In line with my theoretical understanding of migrants' subjectivities as embedded within the agencing arrangement of mobile orientations—and with my use of ethnographic filmmaking as a research methodology—I conceptualize autoethnography as an assemblage. More specifically, I operationalize autoethnography as a strategic assemblage of modes of representation (interviews, ethnographic observation, documentary filmmaking) produced through the study of a time and place in the history of my professional life as a researcher, in order to "foreground, through juxtaposing multiple accounts one against the other, an uneasy, unstable relationship between the writer and the self she writes about" (Denshire and Lee 2013, 11).

I define my autoethnographic approach as intimate for two main reasons: because it draws on personal and intersubjective processes as heuristic and hermeneutic tools, and because it focuses on sexual practices, migration-related stigmatizing factors (e.g., the lack of legal migration status, or the impossibility of returning home as an achieving migrant), and affects that are generally embedded in the private dimension of people's lives. In many cases, as I explain in more detail in the next chapter, I use my "erotic subjectivity" as a strategic instrument of research (Kulick and Wilson 1995) to both elicit and challenge hegemonic selfrepresentations. For instance, I sometimes proactively disclosed my homosexuality to male and female research subjects, so as to negotiate a safe intersubjective space for those who felt threatened by homophobia and "whore stigma" (Pheterson 1993). Less often, when the intersubjective circumstances made it appropriate, I used humor or flirting to challenge male and female research subjects whose stories, subjectivities, and orientations were less "straight" than those they were presenting to me. Provoking my research participants during ethnographic encounters often allowed me to better understand the workings of sexual-humanitarian biographical borders by exploring the fissures and disjunctions between the selfrepresentations they mobilized in relation to different situations and approaches.

Ethnofictional Research

After I started to research the relationship between migration and the sex industry, I had the privilege of meeting extraordinary people, and of participating in the intimate, intersubjective, and affective co-construction of their narrated lives in the context of ethnography and interviewing. Throughout my career as a sociologist and ethnographer, I have felt frustrated with academic writing as a way to fully convey the embodied, sensuous, affective, performative, and intersubjective dimensions of knowledge production. I remember feeling that I could only discuss my affective and intersubjective approach to knowledge production during the time reserved for questions after a formal talk, or more often when a talk was followed by drinks in convivial, informal settings. Besides using intimate autoethnographic writing, I decided to respond to this frustration by developing participative and filmmaking-based methodologies inspired by the principles of "ethnofiction" (Rouch 2003) and "ethno-mimesis" (O'Neill 2011). Both of these include migrants as active producers and performers of their own interpretations, transcending the distinction between fiction and nonfiction, participation and observation, knowledge and senses.

My intention with the genre of ethnofiction is to convey the complexity of migrants' life and work trajectories, to protect their identities, and to share with viewers the affective and sensuous dimensions of ethnography and knowledge production more generally. This resulted in the production of my *Sex Work Trilogy* and the *Emborders* diptych, in which I explore different experiences of migrant sex work by using different cinematographic and research methods. The *Trilogy* includes *Comidas Rapidas—Fast Bites* (Mai 2010, five minutes),[6] about young Moroccan and Romanian men selling sex in Seville; *Mother Europe* (Mai 2011, five minutes), about young Tunisian men selling sex and performing love (i.e., selfrepresenting as potential fiancés) to female tourists in Sousse; and *Normal* (Mai 2012, forty-eight minutes), about the experiences of six migrants (women, men, and transgender people) working in Albania, Italy, and the United Kingdom as sex workers and third-party agents. The first film in the *Emborders* diptych, *Samira* (Mai 2013, twenty-seven minutes), tells Karim's story. The second *Emborders* film is *Travel* (Mai 2016, sixty-three minutes), which tells the life history of Joy, a Nigerian migrant woman who obtained asylum as a victim of trafficking and subsequently continued to sell sex in the Bois de Vincennes in Paris.

In the first two films in the *Trilogy*, the research subjects are active participants in the making of the film, and they present their stories and realities directly. However, their visibility is mediated by filmic choices such as filters and superimpositions, both to protect their identities and to express their marginalization and stigmatization. I discuss these stylistic and filmic choices, which are ethnographically and heuristically relevant, in chapters 3 (*Comidas Rapidas*) and 5 (*Mother Europe*). In *Normal* and the *Emborders* diptych, I take the traditional ethnofictional approach of directly involving research participants in filmmaking further, using actors to respond to ethical, epistemological, and cinematographic challenges.

Contemporary times are characterized by the saturation of public debates with sexual-humanitarian representations that frame migrant sex workers as either victims or perpetrators of trafficking. By using actors to play real research participants, I am able to reproduce faithfully how they challenged these stereotypical selfrepresentations before my eyes during research interviews and ethnographic observations, which were not recorded so as to allow them to express themselves without fear of being exposed. In this respect, I use actors and ethnofictional filmmaking to get closer to the truth: to represent and reproduce both the process of knowledge production (research interviews and ethnographic observation) and the socio-anthropological truth of migrant sex workers' complex decisions and priorities, which deeply question sexual-humanitarian discourses. I discuss the methodological and filmic implications of my "fictional turn" in ethnofiction in more depth in chapter 9. Suffice it to say that the documentary status of *Normal, Samira,* and *Travel* does not reside in the "consubstantial" coincidence between the research participant and the person performing her, but in the factual, affective, and performative adherence to the socio-anthropological truth of the people and dynamics being represented. This truth would have been alienated by the imposition of a camera on real interview and ethnographic situations.

Organization of the Book and Chapter Outline

There is a strong, organic relationship between my writing and my filmmaking, both of which draw on migrants' experiences of agency and exploitation to challenge hegemonic sexual-humanitarian representations. In this book I present an autoethnographic reappraisal of the encounters and situations through which ethnographic knowledge emerged. In the chapters that follow, I show how concepts and ideas were generated through observations, discussions, and events that unfolded during interviews, fieldwork, and participative ethnographic filmmaking. The chapters consist of organic assemblages of stories, voices, observations, and analyses, reproducing the intersubjective process of knowledge production as it unfolded in real life.

One of the main aims of the book is to weave together the different, interconnected fieldwork sites through which I undertook a "multisited ethnography" (Marcus 1995) of the interplay between agency, mobility, migration, and sex work in neoliberal times. The sites considered by the book either belonged to the European Union (France, Italy, Romania, Spain, the Netherlands, the United Kingdom) or were culturally, economically, and geopolitically linked to it (Albania, Tunisia) because of the intersection between postcolonial dynamics, the expansion and consolidation of the European Union, and the influence of transnational media consumption. In order to highlight comparability across the research sites considered in this book and in my research more generally, I refer to Peggy Levitt and Nina Glick Schiller's concept of the "transnational social field" as a "set of multiple interlocking networks of social relationships through which ideas, practices, and resources are unequally exchanged, organized, and transformed" (2004, 1009). Although the book deals with a range of cases and settings, these can be seen as belonging to two well-established and intersecting transnational social fields and migration spaces: one between the European Union and Eastern Europe, and the other between the European Union and (North/sub-Saharan) Africa. As a result, the sites considered in this book share—albeit from unequal power positions—cultural repertoires, sex work dynamics, sex-gendered selfrepresentations, migration processes, and geopolitical dynamics that make their realities highly comparable. This book therefore jointly analyzes different but comparable experiences of intimate and sexual transactions, including tourism-related forms of "intimate labour" in Tunisia (Boris and Parreñas 2011); informal male and female sex work in Greece, Italy, and Spain; and more structured and routinized situations in the Netherlands and the United Kingdom.

Throughout the book, I distinguish the specific forms of informality, professional identification, and precariousness that characterize these different experiences of sex work and intimate labor. I address these experiences as broadly belonging to the "sex industry," rather than using the concept of "sexual commerce" (Shah 2014, 15), for two main reasons. First, the sex industry—just like the "straight"[7] sectors that absorb migrant labor, such as agriculture, construction, hospitality, care, and fishing—includes services, practices, and establishments that, although characterized by different degrees of formality, are integral to a sector of economic activity that tends to be relatively regular and routinized, particularly in the settings investigated by this book. Second, the term *sex industry* reflects the parallel "mainstreaming" of the commodification of sexuality and the expansion of the sexual services sector in the context of neoliberal globalization, although they still coexist with strong dynamics of social marginalization and stigmatization (Brents and Sanders 2010).

This introductory chapter has presented the main dimensions and methodological tools of my research on the relation between migration and the sex industry, as well as sketching a genealogical outline of my heuristic subjectivity. Chapter 1 further explores my subjective positioning and presents in more detail the methodological implications of my intimate, autoethnographic approach. It focuses on the strategic nature of this approach for understanding the emergence of the mobile orientations and agencing decisions encompassing migrants' subjectivities and mobilities.

Chapter 2 presents the results of my first intersubjective and autoethnographic engagements with Albanian (and Romanian) masculinities in Italy and Greece. It analyzes the discourses and practices through which young migrant men both reproduced and challenged the heteronormative and homophobic way in which the relation between masculinities and sexual conduct was negotiated at home.

Chapters 3 and 4 explore the engagement of young male migrants, including minors, in multiple and itinerant forms of mobility, with reference to Moroccan migrants in Spain and Romanian migrants in Amsterdam. Their priorities and needs, as well as their understandings of their own agency, are compared with those informing sexual-humanitarian interventions. Chapter 3 focuses on "errant" mobilities that are characterized by migrants' experiences of loss in relation to their mobile orientations. It discusses the invisibilization of migrant minors and young people selling sex in Seville by referring to the stylistic choices adopted throughout the making of *Comidas Rapidas*, my short film about the tearoom trade at Seville's main bus station. Chapter 4 presents more agentic forms of "minor" mobility, characterized by the "boditarian"—that is, embodied, tacit, and underprivileged—experiences of ownership of the commodified terms of late-modern subjectivity among young Romanian men selling sex in Amsterdam.

Chapter 5 draws on original research with "professional fiancés" working in the tourist sex industry in Tunisia. Drawing on my autoethnographic experience as a tourist who unexpectedly became a researcher, the chapter problematizes in different ways the presumptions about the vulnerability and exploitability of local people within public and academic debates concerning "sex tourism." Chapter 5 also analyzes the making of *Mother Europe*, the second film in my *Sex Work Trilogy*, which is about a young Tunisian "professional fiancé" performing love to female tourists. The film explores the material and sociocultural dimensions as well as the politics of visibility that frame the encounter between tourism and intimate forms of labor in Tunisia.

The large majority of migrants working in the UK sex industry are neither forced nor trafficked. Immigration status and restricted access to the labor market are the most important factors shaping their agencing decisions to work in the sex industry, which is often a way for migrants to avoid the unrewarding and exploitative conditions they meet in other sectors. Their understandings of agency and exploitation in sentimental and economic terms are intimately interwoven; they cannot be read, let alone intervened in, according to the reductive, free/forced dichotomies engendered by the sexual-humanitarian onto-epistemology. These are the combined main findings of *Migrant Workers in the UK Sex Industry*, the research project I directed between 2007 and 2009, and also of the evaluation of services for migrant sex workers that I directed in the London Borough of Haringey between 2010 and 2011. Chapters 6 and 7 analyze these findings and their impact on policymaking and public debates in the United Kingdom. They also discuss the resistance that the research findings met among institutions and organizations that target all sex workers as potential victims of trafficking. The two chapters analyze how findings that were dissonant with the sexual-humanitarian onto-epistemology resulted from an intimate autoethnographic method that adopted irony as a strategic affective and heuristic approach. They do so by discussing the politics of representation and visibility that characterize migration, the sex industry, and trafficking, and by presenting some of the main heuristic and stylistic choices adopted in *Normal*, the third film in my *Sex Work Trilogy*.

The personal and professional relations between male third-party agents and female sex workers are highly fluid and ambivalent, even when they are characterized by dynamics of domination and oppression. Drawing on original and unique research material—interviews with thirty-three male third-party agents from Albania and Romania—chapter 8 questions the usefulness of profiling male agents as "traffickers" for understanding their diverse life and work experiences in the sex industry. The experiences of early postcommunist Albanian agents who managed sex work through violence (and ended up in jail) are compared with the more consensual and fluid management techniques adopted by Albanian and Romanian agents in later postcommunist times. The chapter shows that the sex-gendered subjectivities, interpersonal relations, and roles that agents embody reflect ambivalences and contradictions mirroring those faced by the women they manage. These shared ambivalences and contradictions are embedded in the deep socioeconomic and geopolitical transformations taking place in the societies of origin and destination of migrants working in the sex industry. The chapter also discusses the implications of these intersubjective dynamics and socioeconomic transformations for antitrafficking interventions, which should acknowledge that migrant and nonmigrant sex workers, including minors and people working under the management of third-party agents, can and do consent to work in the sex industry in order to fulfill their mobile orientations.

In chapter 9, I discuss the methodological implications of my filmmaking, with particular reference to experimental ethnofictions as strategic, political/artistic interventions within the sexual-humanitarian onto-epistemology. The chapter shows how my films *Normal*, *Samira*, and *Travel* seek to reproduce the socio-anthropological truth of the people and dynamics they address, and the intersubjective relations and affects through which knowledge emerges. At the same time, the three films' ethnofictional approach challenges the criteria of authenticity and credibility that characterize sexual-humanitarian research, documentary filmmaking and interventions.

How does the theorization of subjectivity and agency as embedded in mobile orientations help us to understand the nexus between migration, sex work, and exploitation? The conclusion offers a final appraisal of the way migrants working in the sex industry both reproduce and challenge sexual-humanitarian selfrepresentations as they try to fulfill their mobile orientations. At the same time, it analyzes how the "global sentimentality" produced by sexual humanitarianism around the issues of trafficking and "modern slavery" becomes complicit with neoliberal politics and policies by concealing the increased labor precarization and exploitability they engender in the Global North and the rest of the world.

ONE

Intimate Autoethnography

Affective and Intersubjective Knowledge

"So what are you doing here, exactly?" Fatjon asked. We had met in Piazza della Repubblica, one of the main male sex work joints in central Rome.

"I am working at the university," I replied evasively.

He went on ironically, "Oh yeah? And what is your job?"

"I am writing a book about how young men fucking queers for a living manage to remain men while doing what they do," I replied, less hesitantly.

"And they pay you for that?"

"Yes."

"And do they pay you well?"

"Not too bad," I admitted, embarrassed.

"You have a very good job, man, and I think I can help you," was his enthusiastic reaction.

Fatjon was a nineteen-year-old male sex worker (among many other things) from Albania. He became my first informant, thanks to his intellectual curiosity and the shared intimate, affective, and intersubjective platform that enabled knowledge to happen to us, together.

In framing knowledge as something that happens to and between people, I draw on the work of Veena Das (1998, 192), who underlines the affective and intersubjective nature of anthropological knowledge production. The notion of intersubjectivity is particularly strategic for understanding how agency is embedded in mobile orientations for two main reasons. First, it frames subjectivities as socially interdependent and as emerging through dialogue and "human relations with material and natural things" (Jackson 1998, 6). Second, it acknowledges the role played by sex-gendered and other selfrepresentations in people's understandings of themselves in relation to the social worlds they live in.

Researching sex-gendered subjectivities and mobilities requires a degree of self-reflexivity to bypass the "official" selfrepresentations that allow people to protect themselves from moralizing, criminalizing, and pathologizing assumptions (and interventions) during interviews and fieldwork. Affective and intersubjective dynamics played a strategic role in the emergence of the data and concepts presented in this book. In order to understand the complexity of people's mobile orientations and agentic decisions, I often used affective transactions and intersubjective dynamics as a privileged observation site from which to question selfrepresentations, particularly when interview narratives were contradicted by ethnographic evidence.

From a posthuman perspective, affect is a strategic concept to understand the "pre-personal" way in which energy and other intensities can orient bodies, objects, and subjects, bypassing socially embedded emotions and subjectivities (Massoumi 2002). However, the transmission of intensities can only work by being reinscribed within and between subjects through "affective practices" that are socially rooted (Wetherell 2013)—a consideration that problematizes the supposed "subjectless" nature of affect. Hence the concept of affect is used in this book in the context of the socially embedded practices within which affect resonates and "makes sense" between people. In this chapter, as well as in those that follow, affective consonances and "dissonances" (Hemmings 2012) provide strategic toolkits that allow me to identify and analyze the intersubjective dynamics characterizing the events and encounters that punctuated my fieldwork. Drawing on the traditional sociological focus on empathy as an affective repertoire to connect with other people, I use a wider affective palette, including irony and revulsion, to describe how I came to meet and interact with the people whose narrated and lived lives made my research happen.

In some cases, pain and empathy were the main affective and intersubjective platforms on which knowledge happened between research participants and me. In some circumstances, particularly in cases that presented aspects of subjection to force and trafficking, I asked people to abstain from talking about the details of particularly traumatic events and situations in their lives for four main reasons. First, I did not want to upset them by revisiting distressing memories. Second, I wanted to keep the focus of the interview on their migration and work experiences. Third, I wanted to avoid "overaffecting" the intersubjective process of knowledge generation with pain and suffering, in order to potentially allow more pluralist and heterogeneous selfrepresentations and stories to surface. Finally, I wanted to protect myself from upsetting details and traumatic stories that I felt I would not be able to contain emotionally or psychologically. More often, I tried to elicit irony as the main affective current underlying the intersubjective dynamics through which knowledge happened. As I show in chapters 6 and 7, irony has been a powerful strategic affect in my work, enabling knowledge and eliciting selfrepresentations that often exceed normative sex-gendered practices and sexual-humanitarian discourses.

Doing Intimate Autoethnography

Intersubjective intimacy—a close association and relationship with informants and other research participants—was a privileged context through which knowledge happened throughout my autoethnographic observations. Heidi Hoefinger (2013, 8) conceptualizes "intimate ethnography" as a self-reflexive, egalitarian mapping of the shared emotional and social relations between researcher and participants within the negotiation of intimacy and friendship. Drawing on this notion, I operationalize the intimate dimension as a strategic epistemological and methodological suture point between intersubjectivity and autoethnography. The resulting notion of intimate autoethnography acknowledges the nature of knowledge production as co-constructed by intersubjective relations between observing and observed subjects. At the same time, it builds on critiques of the potential "banal egotism" (Probyn 1993, 80) of self-reflexive ethnography, which can paradoxically participate in the reproduction of coherent and separately observable selves and others (Rabinow 1977).

In methodological terms, the practice of intimate autoethnography means negotiating a reflexive, affective, and intersubjective connectedness with the people and spaces defining the field of observation. It means acknowledging the research aims, objectives, and questions when entering the field, while at the same time embodying this connectedness with the people, situations, and places being observed. When everything goes well, this embodied awareness translates into an affectively and sensuously connected intersubjective presence that enables people in the field to open up about themselves and their lives. When stigmatization and criminalization frame fieldwork, omissions and lies become precious, if sometimes enigmatic, indicators of silenced discourses and practices that can be better observed during ethnography.

Throughout my research on the sex industry, I have never felt fundamentally different from the people I have researched. We have "simply" been given different selfrepresentations, opportunities, and resources in life. I think that this intimate awareness helped me to be with people and share their spaces and time in ways that often made me seem part of the social tapestry I was observing, while maintaining my role as observer and researcher. In all of the contexts analyzed in this book, I carried out ethnographic observation by "deeply hanging out" (Geertz 2001, 107) in sex work places and by establishing direct contact with sex workers. I think immersing oneself critically and selectively in the material culture, spaces, and practices being analyzed, and then writing about them while affects, discourses, and relations are still fresh in the memory of the researcher, is an essential requirement at the beginning of fieldwork and a precondition for making knowledge happen. Isn't that the only way to understand things ethnographically? But then again, how deeply should we "hang out" if we are to remain ethically and methodologically appropriate? Where must we draw the line between professional and personal intersubjective investment? I try to respond to these questions through theoretically and methodologically relevant examples throughout this book.

Often I became close to people who were just as intrigued by me as I was by them. Our encounters became pivotal points in the development of my work and punctuate the presentation of my findings in this book. The intimate connection with the people and field under observation sometimes exposed me to completely unexpected affective and intersubjective dynamics, which enabled me to better understand what is being transacted in commercial sex. For example, in July 2004, as I was sitting in a hustler bar in Seville, a sixty-year-old customer approached me, mistaking me for one of the boys. I felt both flattered and embarrassed by the misunderstanding, and tried to find a sensitive way to extricate myself from the situation. In the meantime, he started asking me the "classic" questions about why I was there and suggested he could help me by giving me a job as an assistant in his florist's shop. I could tell he liked me a lot. "This is not a job for a guy like you," he continued with his chat-up routine. "I can see that you are intelligent. Maybe you can complete your studies here in Spain?" I had told him in my broken Spanish that I was Albanian and that I had had to drop out of my university degree in engineering back in Tirana when my father lost his job and I had to support my family. Another hustler-bar classic. Having listened innumerable times to the "survivalist" discourses justifying involvement in sex work exclusively as an "economic necessity"—about which I say more in the next chapter—I knew exactly what to say. So did he: the "rescue narrative" is sometimes part and parcel of a client's intersubjective investment in the transaction. The interesting and surprising thing for me, and the reason I mention it here, was how much I was affected by this seduction dynamic. As I was being addressed as a subject of desire and care, a part of me was excited, titillated, flattered. It worked—or rather, I could see how it worked, revealing what else was on offer besides the obvious money.

Tampering with Preferred Selfrepresentations

In many cases, working together with associations, services, and organizations supporting sex workers enabled my introduction into the field as a credible and safe interlocutor—that is, not a client or police officer. Wherever I undertook research, I first liaised with the main associations and organizations intervening in the lives of sex workers and/or young migrants, and then interviewed key practitioners and representatives. Although many of these associations were actively involved in the fight against trafficking, none of them adopted a neo-abolitionist approach toward sex work. This allowed a fruitful critical exchange and synergy between research and practice. In a second phase, I contacted people working in the sex industry directly, in order to allow them to tell me stories they would not expect to tell in a context of social intervention. This has been a key methodological aspect of my research and has allowed me to tap into a wider variety of selfrepresentations than is usually accessible through social interventions alone.

Interviews with practitioners were usually conducted at the premises of the organization they worked for, while sex workers were interviewed in discreet public or private places of their choice. In the beginning, I recorded all interviews with practitioners and most interviews with migrants working in the sex industry. With time and experience I decided not to record interviews with migrants, since many people were in irregular and stigmatized situations and felt threatened by being recorded. Instead I took written notes and transcribed them immediately afterwards. This offered the double advantage of allowing participants to feel safe when disclosing intimate details about their private lives (particularly issues regarding their migration status and involvement in sex work), while encouraging me to be more attentive to the content and to the intersubjective and ethnographic context of interviews as they happened.

As an ethnographer trying to elicit and value emic concepts to understand social phenomena,[1] I decided to use the expression *sex work* for two main reasons. First, it captures how people working in the sex industry understand what they are doing when they sell sex: they are working. Second, it demarcates my research from neo-abolitionist scholarship, which refuses to recognize the possibility that people might consent, and therefore decide to work in the sex industry on the basis that there is no distinction between free and forced prostitution (Barry, 1995; Farley, 2004; Jeffreys, 1997; Raymond, 2004). I also use the term *prostitution* to refer to the phenomenon of sex work and the way it is framed in public discourse, but I do not use the stigmatizing term *prostitute* to refer to sex workers. Of course, I did not use the phrase *sex work* while undertaking fieldwork or interviewing, in order to avoid imposing preexisting terms and categories onto the research relationship and subject. I simply asked research participants how they would describe what they did for a living. Most of them said they worked.

When interviewing or engaging in ethnographic observation, I tried to detect and challenge the foundational, neoliberal dichotomy and moralized narratives that sexual-humanitarian rhetoric applies to people who sell sex: either that they are "forced," or that they have simply "chosen" to do a job "like any other" (Doezema 1998). Both terms of this dichotomy impede a nuanced and emic appraisal of migrants' experiences of migration and sex work. The "forced" discursive strategy is consistent with current sexual-humanitarian hegemonic trends toward the victimization of migration and sex work (i.e., the increasing framing of migrant sex workers as victims). It allows research subjects to selfrepresent in ways that potentially avoid deportation as well as (some of) the stigma associated with voluntary engagement in sex work. On the other hand, the "free" discursive set can be seen as potentially overemphasizing the agentic dimension of people's mobile orientations, which can obfuscate how they may also consider that they have been exploited in relation to specific aspects of their involvement in the sex industry (working conditions, etc.) and/or feel shame and anxiety about what they are doing.

As discussed in the previous chapter, sexual stories are narrative repertoires that allow previously private and stigmatized dynamics to enter the public arena by reproducing specific plots of suffering and survival (Plummer 1995). Stories about coming out, sexual addiction, and sex trafficking can be seen as recasting the intrinsic heterogeneity and complexity of people's mobile orientations, histories, and subjectivities according to teleological and moralized "biographical illusions" (Bourdieu 1986) that reflect and frame hegemonic hierarchies of values and moralities at any given historical moment. The sexual-humanitarian onto-epistemology understands all migrant (and increasingly also nonmigrant) sex workers as victims of trafficking. In doing so, it shapes the hegemonic, sex-gendered selfrepresentations that currently frame the relationship between migration and sex work.

These dynamics have methodological relevance. Research subjects often mirrored the "free" or "forced" selfrepresentation repertoires in their "narrativization" (Najmabadi 2013, 268) of themselves in interviews, which was often contradicted by the way they embodied those narratives during ethnographic observation. While listening to participants' selfrepresentations in interviews, I was frequently reminded of Judith Butler's (1999) theories of performativity and Stuart Hall's (1996) conceptualization of subjectivity as relational, performative, and contextual. Particularly at the beginning of an interview, I could hear strong echoes of the fixed, normative biographical borders circulated by sexual humanitarianism in the ways people selfrepresented according to stereotypical notions of freedom, necessity, and constraint. These became much more nuanced after intimate, intersubjective rapport had been established.

During interviewing and ethnography, I would often start by working with the preferred selfrepresentations offered by subjects and would then try to critically challenge them in order to elicit more complex understandings and interpretations. For instance, early on during my very first fieldwork with male sex workers, I became aware of the need to be careful with the explanations and narrations given by subjects, as these were usually consistent with psychological defensive strategies. I only tried to challenge people's preferred selfrepresentations when I felt that our intersubjective relationship and their self-confidence made it viable and appropriate. In the few circumstances where people became uncomfortable or anxious in the process, I apologized for the provocation and repeated that the interview could be interrupted at any moment and that consent for my use of interview material was entirely at their discretion. In other situations, I encouraged interviewees to continue talking freely about themselves in whatever way they felt appropriate, and apologized for having interfered. More rarely, I decided unilaterally to stop the interview by initiating a casual conversation on different and less sensitive topics.

Another strategy to subvert preferred selfrepresentations was to use my own erotic subjectivity to establish intersubjective rapport and trust. I did so differently in relation to the different sex-gendered selfrepresentations at work in different fieldwork situations and settings. In some circumstances I mentioned my own homosexuality openly, as a way to reassure young men and women that it was OK to talk about their involvement in stigmatized activities such as sex work and sex with other men. My aim was to make them more comfortable about being interviewed on their working experiences. In many instances, mobilizing my erotic subjectivity played a key role in establishing an intimate, intersubjective context within which sexual-humanitarian biographical borders and preferred sex-gendered self-representations could be both adopted and challenged. For instance, many female participants were able to talk a little more about the nuances of agency and victimization they felt while selling sex. Young migrant men selling sex on the streets of Athens and Rome found it easier to talk about their understanding of "what it means to be a man" in a heterosexist and homophobic context that framed selling sex as "fucking queers" (which I discuss in more depth in the next chapter). Sometimes, the negotiation of my erotic subjectivity in the intimate, intersubjective space created by the interview allowed relevant contradictions to emerge, as I became unexpectedly and unilaterally "sexualized" by male participants who had initially selfrepresented as strictly heterosexual (Walby 2010). In these cases, I noted the revealing contradiction (in my mind) and negotiated an ethical and polite refusal by pointing out that such feelings often emerged as an outcome of the intimacy created by the interview—which was also a way to gently remind participants that this was the point of our encounter.

In a heterosexual context, my homosexuality (whether I made it explicit or not) often allowed me to negotiate a third role between those of client and time-waster: the "harmless" queer researcher. This was particularly evident one day in a Soho brothel. I was interviewing Tracy, a twenty-seven-year-old Lithuanian woman, who kept stopping and resuming the interview between clients. I was amazed at her boundary skills: she always seemed to remember where we had left off, while I had to concentrate on many different things so as distract myself from what was going on in the next room, which meant I often lost track. Each time Tracy came back, we had to squeeze into a small sofa. Her body rubbed against mine, she was half-naked, and I must have looked at her. It was after the third work break that she told me she noticed I had been looking. She was complaining about the fact that many clients only wanted to take a free peek through the door and then run home to masturbate. She claimed to know exactly who was going to do that from the way they moved as they came up the stairs to the flat, which we could observe on the CCTV monitor in the room. Her comments were hilarious. As I expressed my solidarity in looking down on people who stole free peeks, she said, "I know, it's really not fair, but it happens a lot, and people don't think they are doing what they are doing. Just like with you. I saw you were looking at my tits, but I thought it was OK as I know you like men." I did not know what to say; I was so embarrassed about having been seen as looking. But Tracy had the healthier reaction. She laughed at my embarrassment and carried on with the interview.

The information gathered during ethnography was often much more significant than that emerging from recorded interviews, as it allowed people to show the life circumstances that framed their mobile orientations and embedded agencing decisions in a "tacit" but equally (if not more) informative way (Decena 2011). Asking sex workers to "tell the truth" and narrate their lives in a biographical form can create a dimension of permanence and highlight behaviors that only fit with people's acceptable and moralized selfrepresentations (Nencel 2005). In many cases, lies, omissions, and silences spoke more loudly than what was said—especially when the latter included stereotypical discourses that framed sex work as a "job like any other" or exclusively as an "economic necessity," which can become the only ways to protect and fashion one's selfrepresentation in morally acceptable terms.

While trying to elicit and understand the complex experiences of agency and exploitation framing people's mobile orientations, I tried to minimize lies, omissions, and silences by introducing an ironic sensibility into the interview. I did this by speaking about my own queerness and by joking about lies being an acceptable way to answer my questions. A standard preinterview introductory chat would typically include something like this: "This must not be difficult for you, so please feel free to tell me what you want or don't want to talk about, or to lie without explaining anything if you feel more comfortable." In many cases this preparatory, ironic line opened up the discursive possibilities in ways that minimized lies, silences, and recourse to destigmatizing official narratives. The real challenge and opportunity when analyzing narrated lives is to treat embedded silences and narratives as potential omissions, providing an insight into what the subject might be unable (or unwilling) to acknowledge and verbalize (Giami 2001). However, interpreting silences as omissions can be a dangerous operation in research, as it can lead the researcher to presume to know what the interviewee "really" wants to say, even when the opposite—or nothing at all—is actually being said. It is only by measuring the silences imposed by normative sexual stories and selfrepresentations against the lived contradictions emerging from ethnographic observation that silences, omissions, and grand narratives can be legitimately interpreted. I will clarify these strategies and dynamics with two examples.

Although Tracy claimed not to use any drugs and to be very good at negotiating the roles of the "good wife" at home (her husband "did not know") and the "bad girl" in Soho, I could not help but notice that she was high on cocaine during the interviews. This probably explains why she could remember the interview topics between clients so effortlessly and might offer an insight into a potential difficulty in reconciling the different parts of herself she claimed to be managing well:

> I like it as well like this, that it is so separate. I have my own space and my own money. Here I am a bad girl, . . . while at home I am a virgin, so to speak. It is true that I am quite traditional, though. I mean . . . I would never go to clubs and bring men home the way girls do here. . . . At the same time, I am traditional my own way . . . because look at what I do! [Laugh]. . . . The truth is that I am myself in both places, both at home and here. . . . It's just different parts. . . . At the same time, it is quite difficult to keep up and live with all the lying. . . . My family does not know anything, of course! And only a couple of friends know.

Nonetheless, interpreting Tracy's cocaine habit as a response to a difficulty in reconciling different parts of herself would be quite arbitrary and would risk confirming stereotypical, pathologizing and stigmatizing associations between sex work and substance misuse (Benoit, McCarthy, and Jansson 2015). Interviewees' tension between different aspects and versions of their selves is completely in line with the understanding of subjectivities as inherently contradictory and heterogeneous. However, the coexistence of contradictory social, moral, and economic dimensions proved to be both a predicament and an opportunity for some young migrants selling sex, and emerged from the life histories of other research participants.

Hegemonic and sex-gendered sexual-humanitarian selfrepresentations are often deployed and officially preferred by migrant sex workers because they are "safe" in relation to potential exposure to stigma and deportation. However, such selfrepresentations seldom help them to build a psychologically and morally sustainable understanding of their complex experiences of agency and exploitation (Giordano 2014). In chapters 3 and 4 I explore how the ability to reconcile the contradictory, sex-gendered selfrepresentations of young male migrant sex workers is a key factor in the distinction of mobility patterns characterized by different degrees of agency. Here I would like to underline that the inability to master contradictory sex-gendered selfrepresentations was a source of great suffering for some interviewees and in a few cases was also identified by them as a reason for taking drugs. The following account from Altin, a twenty-two-year-old Albanian living in

Athens, shows how young migrants selling sex can experience a lot of anxiety and a sense of fragmentation in relation to their sexual orientation and their self-perception as viable, masculine moral beings.

> I should not use cocaine, I got into a lot of trouble because of it. . . . I have lots of debts, and I am here [in a hustler bar] also to pay up. . . . But when I use it, everything becomes clear to me. . . . Everything makes sense; it is like the pieces of a puzzle finally all fit. . . . You know, coming here in Athens, everything changes, the way you see things, what you do. . . . It is difficult sometimes. . . . I don't talk with my family any more; they are back in [another Greek city], not here in Athens, but I think they heard something about what I do. . . . You know, I go with men . . . for money. . . . I am also like that ["gay'] a bit, . . . but I cannot live with this; where I come from it is shameful. . . . I lived with a Greek [man] for a while. . . . But in the end it did not work out because I could not make my mind up and he got bored.

Tracy's and Altin's accounts reveal the complexity of subjective investments, moralities, and trajectories that characterize migrants' involvement in the sex industry and their complex, inextricable experiences of agency and vulnerability. They provide a glimpse into the discursive labyrinth framing their selfrepresentations and experiences, which are characterized by the silencing intersection of multiple stigmatizations and moralizations. Navigating these complex selfrepresentation dynamics is strategic for understanding the workings of mobile orientations, whose agencing decisions respond to the contradictory sex-gendered roles and subjectifications coming from globalized and more traditional and local repertoires.

Embedded Research Evidence

Since 1998 I have conducted six research projects investigating the deployment of sexual humanitarianism in relation to different groups of migrants that are constructed as vulnerable and targeted as such by social interventions in several EU countries. The projects I directed were characterized by strong collegial participation and were carried out by interdisciplinary research teams. In all of the projects I directed, I adopted self-reflexive and observational interview methodologies, acknowledging the intersubjectivity between researcher and researched as a key methodological dimension of knowledge production. While conducting such projects, I often adopted an innovative methodological combination of ethnographic observation, semistructured interviewing, and participatory approaches. In accordance with the democratic tenets of participatory research, which promote "recognition, participation and inclusion in the production of knowledge and public policy" (O'Neill 2010, 21), I included organizations and services supporting sex workers in an advisory role and sex workers as researchers whenever this was relevant to the issues being investigated.

My research findings show that by working in the sex industry, most young migrant men and women, including minors, are able to express their agency by trying to avoid the exploitative conditions they meet in the other sectors of employment available to them (Mai 2011). They also show that most migrants working in the sex industry are not trafficked, while identifying the socioeconomic and psychological factors that strongly contribute to their vulnerability in socioeconomic and individual terms (Mai 2013). My finding that only a minority of migrant sex workers' are trafficked does not stand alone but is grounded in an established and increasing body of ethnographic scholarly work, which Musto (2013, 261) dubs "critical trafficking studies," showing that the neo-abolitionist equation of migrant (and nonmigrant) sex work with trafficking does not match reality (e.g., see Agustin 2007; Bernstein 2007a; Blanchette and da Silva 2012; Cheng 2010; Cheng 2011; Doezema 2010; Ham 2017; Hoefinger 2013; Kempadoo and Doezema 1998; Kempadoo, Sanghera, and Pattanaik 2005; Marcus, Horning, Curtis, et al. 2014; Musto 2016; Parreñas 2011; Shah 2014; Zheng 2014).

The epistemological and methodological approaches outlined above are key to understanding why my research findings go against the "wild guesses and conflated meanings" (Cusick, Kinnell, Brooks-Gordon, et al. 2009) that are routinely produced as evidence in the context of the globalization of sexual-humanitarian onto-epistemology. Existing macro-level claims exaggerating the extent of trafficking within the sex industry and establishing a causal link between the regulation of prostitution and an increase in trafficking (e.g., Cho, Dreher, and Neumayer 2012), are made on the basis of inconsistent data and definitions across noncomparable settings (Weitzer 2014). The fact that a minority, neo-abolitionist, "carceral" sensibility has managed to turn the global debate on the nexus between migration and the sex industry away from available evidence and toward a scenario of endemic sex trafficking is a problematic sign of the neoliberal times we live in (Bernstein 2010).

Typically, neo-abolitionist research conflating sex work with trafficking and exaggerating the prevalence of trafficking to meet its political goals tends to extrapolate "vast captive slave markets from individual cases found *ex situ* through rescue institutions or rapid assessments of police and social service workers" (Marcus, Sanson, Horning, et al. 2016, 48). Like a closed onto-epistemological circuit, such research cannot but implement heuristic categories of victimization that justify the funding of the research and social intervention projects that host it. However, pursuing different *in situ* ethnographic entry points into a social group—particularly when the group is engaging in stigmatized and criminalized activities—provides the researcher with the wider plurality of positions and experiences that marks the difference between a scientific analysis and an activist pamphlet. My adoption of this pluralistic, participative, and ethnographic approach to engage with migrant sex workers' emic understandings and experiences of agency and exploitation is the main reason why my findings diverge from hegemonic, neo-abolitionist and sexual-humanitarian research on migration and the sex industry. Overall, my research findings show that migrants express their mobile orientations through their agencing decisions to migrate and work in the sex industry, which respond to the constraints on social mobility they encounter in their countries of origin and destination.

The chapters that follow provide more detailed examples of how my intimate autoethnographic method highlights a plurality of socioeconomic trajectories and subjective investments, debunking the neo-abolitionist claim that trafficking is the reality for the majority of sex workers (Mai 2009b). My aim in this chapter was to focus on the methodological approach adopted throughout my research before presenting the different research settings through which my findings and conceptualizations emerged. More specifically, I wanted to explain how an intimate, autoethnographic approach involving sex workers as intersubjective participants in the knowledge-generation process was strategic for understanding the complexity of their mobile orientations and embedded agencing decisions. In the next chapter I present the first ethnographic research through which I engaged with the relationship between migration and the sex industry, which focused on the sex-gendered selfrepresentations and livelihoods of young men selling sex in Rome.

TWO

Engaging Albanian (and Romanian) Masculinities

Invisibilized Sexualities

The very beginning of my intimate, affective, and intersubjective engagement with the field was meeting Fatjon in April 2002. It was on Piazza della Repubblica, the main male sex work strip in central Rome, a scenic roundabout just a few hundred meters from Termini railway station. I will never forget that evening. I had been circling the topic and the piazza for several weeks, trying to understand more about the places and context of male sex work in Rome and looking for a way in. My main initial contact and source of information was a friend of mine, an Albanian gay activist who was then in Rome seeking asylum on the basis of sexual orientation. I supported his case with my expert witness report, the first of many. As a result of the teamwork mobilized around his case, and because of his circumstances, Neritan obtained humanitarian protection. This was excellent news, not only for him but more broadly too, as his was one of the first cases to recognize the specific vulnerabilities of sexual minority refugees in Italy. During this process I got to know people working for a progressive NGO addressing the rights of marginalized migrant groups in Rome. They became my friends, and they provided me with both preliminary information about the field and strategic contacts.

The first time Neritan told me there were lots of young Albanian men selling sex to other men on the streets and squares of Athens and Rome, I thought he was pulling my leg. I had been living in Albania for about a year, and had been overwhelmed by the prevailing homophobia and patriarchal values. Sexuality, let alone homosexuality, was an unutterable topic in professional and other public conversations. My curiosity was piqued by the contradiction between the invisibility and stigmatization of homosexuality in Albania, and the public visibility of young men selling sex on the street. My first hypotheses to make sense of this contradiction addressed the relationship between geographical and moral boundaries and were informed by the seminal work of Gloria Anzaldúa (1999) and Lionel Cantù (2002) on the multiple ways in which sexuality, migration, and border-crossing are involved in the emergence of new sex-gendered subjectivities, practices, and orientations. How do young male migrants selling sex reproduce and queer the contradictory selfrepresentations and practices they encounter? How do they make sense of their masculinities? Do geographical and state borders highlight interruptions or continuities? What new, sex-gendered selfrepresentations emerge in the process? Such questions kept popping into my mind, and I had to pursue them.

My curiosity was also fueled by my own ethnographic and personal experience as an Italian homosexual man in Albania. I was the coordinator of four youth centers while living there between 1998 and 2001, and I had decided not to be indiscriminately "out"—the last thing I needed was to be delegitimized and stigmatized on homophobic grounds. When entering Albania, I reentered a closet I had left just a few years before, which reminded me of the (partial) repression and silencing I had endured as a young man in Italy. The interplay between the reproduction of my own experiences of sexual repression and stigmatization and the way it was mirrored in the lives of young, Albanian migrant men fired my interest in this topic. All of this happened while I was in Albania to undertake a doctoral study of the role played by Italian media in the imagination and enactment of migration, which gave me a vantage point on the transformation of young people's identities in postcommunist times.

My doctoral studies examined life histories of migration, along with prospective and actual Albanian migrants' experiences of watching television. I studied how the visual and narrative scripts—that is, selfrepresentations—disseminated by Italian media elicited individualized aspects of and relations to the self that had not found expression in Albania's recent communist past. In order to examine the role of Italian media in attracting Albanian migrants to Italy, I lived and worked in Albania for almost three years, directing an international cooperation program funded by the Italian government. In March 1997 Albania had teetered on the verge of civil war as a consequence of the collapse of pyramid selling schemes informally endorsed by the ruling Democratic Party and encouraged by the neoliberal deregulation of the Albanian banking system advocated by the International Monetary Fund and World Bank. The project I was directing aimed to provide a rapid response to the socioeconomic difficulties and mass migration that followed these events. My position involved setting up and managing social and cultural centers for youth in four Albanian towns (Tirana, Durrës, Berat, and Gijrokastër) in partnership with a local association, the Albanian Youth Council.

Italian television played an important role in the emergence of a transnational sensibility and imaginary within which new, individualized, and "migratory" Albanian youth identities emerged. On the one hand, through the consumption of Italian television, Albanians associated Italy with a utopian and disempowering understanding of the West as a universe of freedom and easily attainable material plenty. On the other hand, Italian television provided narrative and visual scripts according to which alternative—that is, individualized and consumerist—lifestyles and subjectivities could be imagined in the Albanian context. In other words, Italian television disseminated selfrepresentations within the Albanian social landscape that framed the emergence of new mobile orientations in relation to new migratory projects. By "migratory project" I mean not so much physical/geographical displacement, but the wider discursive processes and practices of cultural consumption through which prospective young migrants imagine themselves as subjects with reference to supervening social needs at home (Mai 2005).

By watching Italian television, young Albanians imagined themselves as different kinds of women and men in relation to a material and socioeconomic environment that had failed them at home. In this respect migration can be understood as a condition of subjective displacement, away from the selfrepresentations that have previously shaped subjectivity in relation to transforming needs, priorities, and possibilities (Pœrregaard 1997). However, this process of subjective displacement was ambivalently embedded in young Albanians' migratory projects. My doctoral work explored the ways in which, for many, migrating to Italy (and later to other foreign destinations) was a way to resolve the contradictions between their late-modern desire to experience new, individualized aspects of their selves, and their more socially established and hardship-bound roles as loyal sons and daughters sacrificing their lives for the survival of the family unit (Mai 2001b). The predicament which most young Albanians faced in their everyday lives is confirmed in this exchange with Ida, an eighteen-year-old participant in a focus group I organized in Durrës in March 1999:

IDA: Well, all I am saying is that *within ourselves live two different persons*: one is our relatives, who lived in a very different period from the one we are living today, and the other is us, who live in this world today. One person says: do like this. The other says: do like that. *We are always confronted with these two persons*. The rules our parents gave us, . . . well, these rules do not apply now the world is not the same and we are not the same. Very often we are forced to face two opposite possibilities, like they said and like we want, and we have to choose between these two different persons; this is the main problem: who to choose? Our parents or us?

NICOLA: Who do you think the most important person of the two is?

IDA: To find a middle way . . . this is the main thing.

NICOLA: How is this new person? What are the most important differences?

IDA: The most important differences . . . she wants to have fun, to stay with friends, have new experiences, study abroad to see new cultures, . . . see things she has never seen before . . .

NICOLA: Where did this new person come from? These new ideas, these different possibilities, where did you see them?

IDA: Well, I think it was a general change that came with the time; television of course was very important . . . but also many other things. Many friends were abroad and then returned. They tell you about the way life is there, and this makes such an impression on you that it generates a new person inside yourself, who wants to do the same thing they related. But then you have to find a compromise in order not to break up with parents and with the way life still is here in general.

I have italicized Ida's reference to her experience of being confronted with two different persons in order to highlight the contradictory models of personhood that characterized the subjectification of young people in postcommunist Albania. In the late 1990s, young Albanians were torn between the desire to "find themselves" according to the individualized and consumerist late-modern selfrepresentations of youth identity available on the Italian mediascape, and the fear of "losing themselves" in relation to the family-bound models of personhood hegemonic in Albania (Mai 2002). Their migratory projects could be seen as responding to their emerging need to recreate abroad a situation of "ontological security"—that is, "the confidence that most human beings have in the continuity of their self-identity and in the surrounding social and material environments of action" (Giddens 1991, 92), which had been shattered by the dramatic socioeconomic transformations framing the emergence of their mobile orientations at home.

In later postcommunist times, Albanians' initial cultural construction of Italy as an ideal place to articulate mobile orientations that challenged the lifestyles and models of personhood prevailing at home clashed with their stereotypical marginalization and exclusion as undesirable others in Italy. I investigated the impact of this marginalization on Albanian migrants' experiences, with particular reference to media selfrepresentations, during a postdoctoral project analyzing the social and economic inclusion and exclusion of Albanians in Greece and Italy. I was responsible for examining the experiences of employment, housing, and community structures and networks of Albanian migrants in Italy. I undertook eighteen months of fieldwork in Italy, and went regularly to Athens to compare results with the project's Greek team.

Albanian migrants' status within the Italian mediascape changed quickly, from "political refugees" in March 1991 to "economic migrants" just six months later. From then until the mid-2000s, Albanians were the most heavily stereotyped group in representations of migration-related events in Italy. Particular reference was made to their involvement in the trafficking and sexual exploitation of women, and in thefts and burglaries of a particularly ferocious nature. This ruthless stigmatization had its roots in Italy's "projective disidentification" (Grotstein 1981) and reprojection onto Albanian migrants of its own perceived backwardness and inadequacy in relation to EU integration and national governance, both of which came into question at the same time as Albanians were becoming a significant migrant group in Italy (Mai 2003). These dynamics of mirroring and othering reflected a cultural construction of Albanian migrants consistent with a regime of "differential integration" that produced more easily deportable and therefore exploitable labor (Castles 1995). At the same time, the research findings highlighted that Albanian migrants had been able to emancipate themselves from the conditions of social exclusion and marginalization enforced by the media and other social forces, and to successfully integrate with Italian society (Mai 2005; 2008).

The selfrepresentations circulated by Italian media of Albanian men and women as involved in trafficking were powerful agents of marginalization. They engendered stigmatizing prejudices that made it very difficult for Albanians to access adequate housing and non-exploitative working conditions. The desire to understand the basis of this powerful stigmatization was another reason that I became interested in the relationship between migration, sex work, and trafficking. In the context of my postdoctoral research on Albanian migration, I started to focus on the negotiation of gender, sexuality, and subjectivity through the migration process, with particular reference to international (female and male) sex work. I was further encouraged to engage with this topic by becoming one of the representatives in Albania of Arci, a broad umbrella of progressive Italian associations, which supported LGBT rights both in Italy and internationally. At the same time, I also became involved in an International Organization for Migration pilot program for the voluntary return from Italy of Albanian female victims of trafficking, which aimed to facilitate their social reintegration. Both of these roles provided me with unique opportunities to understand the sex-gendered forms of normativity and subjectivity at work in Albania. Wherever I looked, I noticed that the very visible presence of young Albanian men selling sex in Italy and Greece was not addressed by policymaking or academic debates on the nexus between migration, gender, and sexuality. Hence I decided to analyze their cultural construction of masculinity and their experiences of migration and sex work.

That evening in April, as I was walking around the piazza, I finally heard three guys speaking Albanian. It was the opportunity I had been waiting for, and I took it. I went up to the youngest of the three, who was smoking a cigarette, and asked if he had a light. I remember being embarrassed as I tried to negotiate a nonclient presence in a social and spatial setting that had historically been defined by same-sex prostitution. Everything I said took me back to the client position, which I did not want to occupy. For instance, when I said, "I'll take my jacket off, as it's getting a bit warm," Fatjon replied, "Can't you wait until later?" with a cheeky grin on his face. I guess I blushed, and I remember laughing the embarrassment away. All this took place in front of the two other young men, who claimed to be from Kosovo and Macedonia. However, I knew they were all from Albania because of their accents. I decided not to "come out" as an Albanian speaker, as that would have completely altered the relations between us. Whereas in Albania my ability to speak Albanian was welcomed as a sign of respect for "our culture," in Italy it often called into question the authenticity of my Italianness, as few Italians spoke Albanian in the late 1990s. Consequently I was often constructed as some kind of government spy or police infiltrator, which sometimes pushed people away. Here, I decided to avoid being seen as a potential Albanian mostly in order not to expose the three young men to the fear of being stigmatized according to the homophobia prevailing "at home."

But pretending not to understand what they said proved challenging. Not knowing what to do, and having been on my feet for a while, I asked if it would be OK to sit with them. And the most extraordinarily normal thing happened. Albanians pride themselves on being hospitable, the sacredness of hospitality (*mikpritja*) being one of the most celebrated aspects of their sense of national identity and morality. When I asked to sit down, we were in the corner of a set of steps that felt a little more private than the rest of the square. To my surprise, the three young men behaved as if I had asked to sit down in a formal family setting: they all stood up at once and gestured toward the side. "By all means! Do sit down with us!" they all said. I had to smile. It was then that I first felt that handling relations in the field would not be as difficult as I had feared. And it wasn't.

While I sat and smoked, they kept talking, in Albanian, about me, trying to figure out whether I was a client or not, and what I was doing there if I was not. I had to keep pretending I did not understand, but it became increasingly difficult. After about five minutes the "Macedonian" inadvertently "outed" me by asking his friend for a light. I automatically started to search my pocket. I stopped as soon as I realized that I could be found out and dissimulated by scratching my leg. But it was too late. He immediately told the other two, "The Italian understands Albanian." They ridiculed him. He insisted, "I am telling you, he understands, I can tell."

So I turned to them and said in Albanian, "Yes, I do understand. I used to live in Albania and I learned it over there."

The "Macedonian" was triumphant: "I told you!" The "Kosovar" became suspicious and left.

Fatjon looked at me, full of admiration, his eyes shining. "You are Italian and you speak Albanian?" he asked.

"Yes, I lived in Tirana for almost three years," I replied.

"That's really cool!" he said enthusiastically. And then, as if he felt that he had given himself away, he added, "You were lucky tonight, as I was going to pretend to go with you and then mug you!" But his tone was not aggressive, and his eyes were still shining. We both laughed.

Fatjon

When I first met him, Fatjon was nineteen years old. He was from a city in northern Albania that lies very close to the Montenegrin border. In early postcommunist times, his father had been able to make some money by smuggling goods over that border. This was hardly exceptional behavior in postcommunist Albania, where citizens were starting to build their social identities specifically through acquiring and consuming "forbidden" foreign goods as a strategy to constitute a selfhood against a regime and its rules, laws, and values (Humphrey 1995, 55–66). However, unlike most of his peers, at the age of thirteen Fatjon joined his cousins in southern Italy and ended up working as a pusher, selling mainly hashish and marijuana. Nowadays he lived independently from his family, selling sex and stealing with some of the other young people hanging around the piazza. It was very easy to be with Fatjon, at least for me. He had a great sense of humor and a lively and creative intelligence. When I told him what I was doing, as mentioned in the introduction, his first reaction was to volunteer help in exchange for money. But money was not our real currency. It was our mutual curiosity that underpinned our intersubjective relationship and made knowledge happen between us, which is why he offered to be my research assistant, and I readily accepted. I guess he did it to earn a few euros, but also to have the chance to understand a little more about himself and the world he was living in.

Right from the start it became clear that Fatjon's curiosity had to be kept under control. "I think I know what you want," he said. "You want to talk to those who are not sure. . . . Those who are a bit queer, isn't it?" He was right. But then he added, "I'll help you, but I want twenty euros for each person I bring you, and I want to listen to the interview recordings." The first condition was easy to agree to; the second was completely unacceptable, and I refused. He insisted, but I was not having it, especially as I could sense from the start that he was a bit of a bully on the scene and that listening to interviews might offer him the chance to try to control other people. Only later in our friendship did I understand that, for Fatjon, being involved in the research was mostly a chance for self-discovery.

Fatjon put me in touch with four young men and minors selling sex, aged between sixteen and twenty-four, all Romanian. Romanians were the prevailing group on the piazza at the time; by the early 2000s, most young Albanian men had left the male sex work scene, reflecting the fact that most Albanian migrants had integrated into Italian society (Mai and Paladini 2013). Seeing Fatjon and establishing a relationship with these first interviewees allowed me to negotiate a viable presence on the piazza and in other places of male sex work. In Rome, these include the area around Termini railway station and Valle Giulia, a section of the Villa Borghese gardens in front of the art gallery. In my remaining months in Rome, I diversified my entry points into the male sex work scene by obtaining new contacts from the NGO I was in touch with, meeting people during fieldwork, and networking from Fatjon and other contacts. By the time I left Rome, I had interviewed twenty young men selling sex: three from Albania, the others from Romania.

Fucking Queers

Young migrant men sell sex by night around Termini central station, an area of Rome that has historically been marked by socioeconomic and sexual liminality, and by the practice of male sex work. Park's notion of "moral regions"—"detached milieus in which vagrant and suppressed impulses, passions and ideals emancipate themselves from the dominant moral order" (Park and Burgess 1967, 43)—is particularly helpful for defining how stigmatized, sex-gendered livelihoods and criminalized behaviors are territorialized (and tolerated) within delimitated urban contexts. During the day, young migrant men mix with the crowds of tourists and inhabitants. The contrast between the grandeur of the archaeological monuments and other tourist sights, the affluence of the shops and restaurants, and the marginalization of the young migrant men selling sex provides the latter with relative invisibility, at least to the untrained observer. This is essential for the two main livelihood strategies composing the personal "economies of makeshift" (Lee 2012, 26) that they pursue in this moral region: sex work at night and pickpocketing during the day.

As I hung around the places and scenes of male sex work in Rome, I noted the coexistence of previous strata of marginality and migrancy: the Pasolinian, peri-urban *borgatari* and southern Italian internal migrants of the 1960s and '70s;[1] the North African migrants of the '80s; and Albanians and Romanians, the latest wave of young men looking for a better life. While I hung around on Piazza della Repubblica and chatted with young migrant men selling sex, my mind often wandered to the other roadside pick-up places for deskilled jobs in similarly irregular, but "straight," sectors—for example, agriculture and construction—which I had often come across just a few hours earlier in the context of the broader postdoctoral research on the social inclusion and exclusion of Albanian migrants. All of these pick-up places were sites marked by the constant renegotiation of informal economies and makeshift livelihoods across different historical periods in the development of the capitalist economy.

Before the arrival of international migrant laborers, the Piazza della Repubblica roundabout and other pick-up places for workers had been populated by local *borgatari* and internal southern migrants in the context of postwar industrialization and nation-building. However, unlike the Mumbai street corners explored by Svati Shah (2014), Piazza della Repubblica is not a place where sex is traded tacitly alongside morally acceptable and "straight" livelihoods; historically, it has been dedicated exclusively, albeit informally, to (male) sex work. This oxymoronic coexistence of informality and routinization, which I describe as fractal in chapter 4, is by no means exceptional. The forms of sex work present in the settings I researched were relatively routinized and regular in nature; that is why I consider *sex industry* a more apt phrase than *sexual commerce* to indicate the sexual transactions explored in this book.

Notwithstanding their different ethnic and sociocultural backgrounds, contemporary migrant sex workers seemed to have three main things in common. First, they were seeking fast-track economic gain in order to afford their selfrepresentations both as traditional male breadwinners (by remitting money home) and as proficient and individualized late-modern consumers. Second, the emergence of their mobile orientations in neoliberal times was entangled with the proliferation of irregular makeshift economies and increasingly precarious (and criminalized) livelihoods, including pickpocketing and selling sex. Third, when engaging in male sex work, they would demarcate themselves from their (homosexual) clients by selfrepresenting as exclusively active (penetrating) in sexual intercourse. They described this work as "fucking queers."

The relation between sexual practices and masculinities should be seen as historical and contextual, rather than fixed and timeless. For instance, most researchers on the history of homosexuality, influenced by Michel Foucault, agree that it was only in the second half of the nineteenth century that the concept of homosexuality emerged in the West as a specific identity associated with a category of desire linked to sexual orientation. In his analysis of how sexuality became a primary locus of personal identification and social control in modern times, Foucault looked back to the Greco-Roman world to trace different articulations of the relationship between morality, identity, and sexual practices. In particular, his analysis of Athenian homoeroticism emphasizes that, whereas in modern times sexual identities are defined confessionally and introspectively on the basis of the subjects' sexual orientation ("I desire, therefore I am"), amongst the Greeks they were defined performatively, on the basis of the distinction between active and passive sexual roles ("I do—and I am seen to be doing—therefore I am") (Foucault 1990, 30). According to this understanding of ancient Greek mores, it was socially acceptable for men to have sex with other men as long as they remained men—that is, as long as they respected the dividing and normative line between the "active" subjects of sexual activities, adult free men, and their "passive" partners: women, boys and slaves.

It is beyond the purpose of this chapter to enter into a more exhaustive discussion of Foucault's analysis of ancient Greek sexual mores, which I explore in more detail in my early work on Albanian young men's cultural constructions of masculinity (Mai 2004). Here I would like to underline that contemporary hegemonic (in the Global North), confessional attitudes toward sexual practices are arguably informed by the continuity of ancient performative understandings, as Faubion (1993) suggests in the case of modern Greece. Sasho Lambevski expands the focus of these considerations and argues that all Balkan and Mediterranean societies share "a particular configuration of patriarchy, misogyny and homophobia" (1999, 403), and that the different (i.e., performative) ways in which homosexualities are constructed and experienced in such societies must be acknowledged. Ancient and modern experiences of masculine identity, as well as the relations to the self with which they are consistent, should not seen as mutually exclusive, but as coexisting contradictorily and ambivalently in present times. Huseyin Tapinc's (1992) analysis of the four main models of homosexual relations found in contemporary Turkish society provides an important example. The second model of homosexual relations identified by Tapinc—that between the masculine and penetrative "heterosexual," and the feminine and penetrated "homosexual"—captures the contradictory ways in which the young migrant men I met in Rome framed and experienced their sex-gendered subjectivities in relation to homosexuality and selling sex to other men. When I asked them what they were doing on Piazza della Repubblica, their official, sex-gendered selfrepresentation was unequivocal: they were (straight men) fucking queers.

The "fucking queers" discursive framework allowed young migrant men to selfrepresent as straight: the queer is the person who is penetrated, not the one who penetrates. However, things were not so simple. This prevailing performative understanding of the masculine as sexually active often coexisted with a modern, confessional understanding of homosexuality in relation to the subject's sexual orientation, regardless of whether one adopts an active or passive role during sexual intercourse. In postcommunist countries, the modern homosexual paradigm was first introduced in association with criminalizing and pathologizing medico-legal discourses in communist times. In North African and other postcolonial societies, the very same "modernizing" and pathologizing framework was introduced during the process of colonization (Massad 2007). In both contexts, this early confessional understanding of sex between men (and women) in terms of homosexuality was subsequently complemented by the late-modern globalization and commodification of "gay" identities, subjectivities, and lifestyles, which were in a relationship of both continuity and "rupture" with previous sex-gendered regimes (Altman 1996). Nowadays, in young migrants' countries of origin, men who have sex with men are addressed by different selfrepresentations that frame the relation between masculinity and homosexuality according to contradictory social roles and individual identities. These originate both from their own historical, social, and cultural scenarios and from foreign moral and cultural landscapes, whether the latter are accessed through migration or media.

In general, the "fucking queers" discourse was firmly embedded in preferred selfrepresentations that justified young men's involvement in the sex industry exclusively according to the "survivalist" terms of economic necessity. Within the range of possibilities available to minors and young migrants, selling sex "officially" occupies the lowermost position in terms of masculine heterosexual respectability. It jeopardizes the credibility of the heterosexual male subject—unlike stealing and drug-smuggling, which are linked to role models such as the pusher, the gangster, and the thief, and were sometimes seen as more compatible with preferred selfrepresentations as "straight." The hierarchical positioning of different strategies of survival according to perceived levels of heterosexual, masculine respectability is illustrated by the following exchange with Arben, an eighteen-year-old Albanian man living in Rome who occasionally sold sex.

NICOLA: So, what do you do for a living?

ARBEN: Well, I steal . . . I do things . . .

NICOLA: Like what?

ARBEN: Well, I usually pickpocket . . . at the station, . . . at night; . . . I steal things in houses.

NICOLA: Alone?

ARBEN: Well, sometimes alone, sometimes in a group; . . . sometimes it goes well, sometimes not. . . . I even ended up in jail.

NICOLA: And what about this place here, . . . I mean fucking queers.

ARBEN: Eh, I do it, . . . everybody does it. . . . I started doing like all the others, . . . for money; . . . it is not the kind of life that I would like doing, . . . but it is the life I was given.

NICOLA: What do you do more often, steal or sell sex?

ARBEN: I would rather steal, and I do it more often. . . . I think it is better; . . . if you sell sex you are over, you are not a man any more; . . . it is better to go to jail than to become a queer.

NICOLA: What does it mean for you to become a queer?

ARBEN: It is different from here. . . . in my country it is the greatest shame not only for me; . . . I mean if I become a queer then all of my family loses its honor; . . . if I sell sex, . . . as it happened to many people here, . . . you begin by being a man and then you end up like them. . . . One week you have no money, somebody offers you a lot of money to fuck you, . . . what can you do? . . . Then you do it again and again, and then you end up liking it; . . . this is why I decided to steal; . . . it is better. I sell sex only when I have to . . . and as a man.

NICOLA: What does it mean for you to be a man?

ARBEN: It means staying the way you were born, . . . not to be fucked like a woman, . . . to fuck like a man. . . . Better to go to jail . . .

Arben's words illustrate how selling sex becomes an important livelihood among a very restricted range of possibilities. These possibilities are ordered hierarchically according to the perceived threat they pose to young men's heterosexual respectability and also in relation to other pragmatic considerations having to do with degrees of illegality. However, each individual interprets these official hierarchies according to his own priorities and experiences, and in relation to his preferred sex-gendered selfrepresentations. While some regard sex work as preferable to stealing because it is not a criminal act, for others the masculine considerations take priority.

Most young migrants insisted that "economic necessity" and the difficulty of finding a job in the formal and informal labor markets were the only reasons behind their involvement in sex work. Altin, aged twenty, explained this in his own words in our first meeting, in the presence of two fellow Albanians in Rome:

> Look, it is very simple: . . . for example, tonight it is eight days since I last worked, and I have got no money at all. . . . If now a queer comes and offers me fifty euros if I fuck him, . . . what can I do? I have no money. . . . When I have money, I tell them to fuck off; . . . when I don't, they give me fifty euros and in half an hour everything is over.

However, in many cases this was often an initial and officially preferred selfrepresentation. As the fieldwork unfolded, and relationships of trust and friendship emerged, the same people who had previously defended their heterosexual, masculine status by deploying the "fucking queers" and "economic necessity" discourses in peer talk revealed a more complex and ambivalent relation between their preferred, sex-gendered selfrepresentations and their involvement in sex work.

People's preferred selfrepresentations were often a point of departure rather than arrival in the intersubjective, affective, and intimate dynamics through which research knowledge happened in the field. Often the evidence I gathered through participant observation allowed me to challenge the selfrepresentations emerging from formal interviews. In the excerpt that follows, Eduard, a twenty-four-year-old Romanian man living in Rome, claims to be selling sex exclusively to survive and send money home, while also enjoying a less survivalist and more "hedonistic" lifestyle.

NICOLA: Do you send some money home to your family?

EDUARD: Well, I send €200 each month to my mother. It is quite a lot for her. . . . Now she has a better life; . . . she does not have to worry too much about the money.

NICOLA: Does this make you feel better about yourself?

EDUARD: Of course, man; . . . that is the reason why I am here. . . . [His voice becomes deeper and his face sadder.]

NICOLA: But you said that you came here to have fun.

EDUARD: But that was more in the beginning; . . . now it is a bit more complicated. . . . When I feel nostalgic about my mother and about Romania, I go to the disco and drink. . . . And then I phone them. . . . It hurts, man, it hurts. . . . I haven't seen them for a long time, . . . almost three years.

NICOLA: Why did you wait all this time, . . . the documents?

EDUARD: No, no, now I can go when I want. . . . It is just that with the money I spend to go home I can help my mother for two or three months.

NICOLA: But you spend a lot of money each month on drinks and fun stuff, come on now, . . . and then you don't have the money to go home . . . There is something a bit contradictory here, no?

EDUARD: [Smiles.] But I cannot stay here without food, . . . or drinks, . . . or going out at night, no?

NICOLA: Well, it seems like you are not really depriving yourself of these things, . . . come on . . .

EDUARD: You know how it is. . . . I have to eat out as I can't cook; . . . the mobile, . . . the clothes, . . . and then I have to go to the disco. . . . If you meet a girl, you have to show her you have the money, no? Especially if she is Italian, they are very racist, and for them to go out with you is like going out with a beggar.

This excerpt from Eduard's interview shows the gap between migrant sex workers' selfrepresentations of their decision to sell sex in terms of "economic necessity" and their aspiration to, and enjoyment of, more consumerist and individualized lifestyles. It also shows the intersubjective dynamics through which knowledge happens in the interstices between interviewing and ethnographic observation. By challenging Eduard's initial and preferred selfrepresentation, I gained an insight into the intricacy of his mobile orientation, which was arranged at the junction of contradictory selfrepresentations and regimes of experience: the dutiful son remitting money home, the desirable young man dating Italian women, and the conspicuously successful consumer in the eyes of his peer group, among others.

As previously mentioned, another strategy to subvert preferred selfrepresentations was to use my own erotic subjectivity as a research tool. By flirting jokingly during interviews or while doing fieldwork, I actively participated in eliciting an erotic and ironic "affective atmosphere" (Anderson 2009) that put the normative "fucking queers" discursive framework under pressure in tacit rather than verbalized ways. This enabled me to understand that homoerotic desire was often part of the complex emotional and economic transactions being operationalized through sex work. For instance, some interviewees felt like telling me they were worried about eventually "becoming queer" if they regularly engaged in sex with other men. Some went as far as admitting to themselves and to me that memories of sexual encounters with customers had become a regular part of their sexual fantasies. Others conceded that they were attracted to some of their customers and to me, although only a few actually claimed to be "homosexual" or "gay."

Although these private confessions contradict the reductive and normative terms set by the "fucking queers" and "economic necessity" discourses, these discourses remain the hegemonic selfrepresentations defining sexual relations between men at home and abroad. Young male migrants' mobile orientations and embedded experiences of agency can be better understood by exploring the contradictions emerging between their selfrepresented and observed lives. In the next three chapters, I analyze how young migrant men's ability to navigate these contradictions influences the forms of social, spatial, and psychological mobility they engage in and the degree of agency that characterizes their mobile orientations. In the remaining sections of this chapter, I explain how I came to understand that young people's engagement in migration and sex work was the consequence of a decision, and that this decision had been taken in relation to a macrohistorical event: the further "liquefaction" in late-modern times of the traditions, institutions, and authorities already fluidified by modernity, thanks to the neoliberal convergence of postindustrialism, commodification, and individualization (Bauman 2000).

Agencing Decisions

It all became clear to me one morning when I urgently needed to print a guideline questionnaire for semistructured interviews with Albanian migrants in Italy. I went into an Internet cafe in Trastevere and started talking to the young Moldovan man who was in charge. As we waited for the printer and computer to start up, he asked me what I was doing in Rome. I told him I was doing research on young migrant men selling sex, and that right now I was trying to understand how their involvement in the sex industry came about. I asked what he thought about the fact that many young men felt they had no option but to sell sex. This is what he said:

> They would say that, of course. But the reality is that they would rather do that than waking up every morning and wait to be picked up by a plumber or a builder for a day's wage. In the end, it's their decision. When I got to Rome, it became clear to me that I could not do that, nor steal. That's not the way I am. I would rather wait and work for a pittance as a builder. For me it would be impossible to do what they do; for them it is impossible to do what I did.

There it was. In my head I visualized again the different pick-up places I had encountered for different deskilled jobs in similarly irregularized sectors: the sex industry, agriculture, construction, care, hospitality. These interrelated pick-up places were marked historically by the needs, priorities, and mobilities framing precarious labor and employment. Faced with these different options, young migrant men made agencing decisions according to their own understanding and experience of the boundaries between labor, exploitation, advantage, and safety. Their decisions responded to the heterosexist, sex-gendered selfrepresentations they intersected by migrating and also to their understanding and experience of the hierarchies of "hegemonic masculinity" (Connell and Messerschmidt 2005, 849) emerging from the globalization of neoliberal values and associated lifestyles. These include roles such as the proficient and individualized consumer, which contradict the more traditional role of the dutiful son sacrificing his individual fulfillment for the survival of the family. The understandings of agency characterizing their mobile orientations and their embedded agencing decisions were shaped by individual understandings of such contradictions and by individual evaluations of the different degrees of exploitability, respectability, and advantage characterizing "straight" jobs and the sex industry.

The conversation I had had just a few days earlier with Fatjon was still at the forefront of my mind:

FATJON: I don't want to work as a builder for thirty-five euros a day. . . . Look at my hands. . . . They have to stay like this. . . . They are not builder's hands. . . . Here in Rome I have to spend €600 in rent every month. . . . What can I do? . . . Back at home I have already built the second floor . . . for myself, when I go back. . . . I need money also for my friends and neighbors. . . . You know, when I go home I pretend, . . . I mean, I tell my friends that I am a boss here. . . . They don't know anything; . . . they see I have money. . . . I have been living here since the age of thirteen; . . . got here with my cousins and started selling drugs on their behalf: . . . dope, . . . pills, coke . . . sometimes. . . . Then they were arrested and I had to run up here in Rome.

NICOLA: So how do you find the money now?

FATJON: Can't you see what I am wearing? It is all good stuff, Armani, look, look, Energie. . . . How the hell do I find the money for this, eh? Not working as a builder. . . . You know, when you live in the street, you have to make a bit of everything; . . . sometimes rich people come here and bring you home; . . . sometimes you do what they want, sometimes you go there and empty their apartment. What can you do? They have so much money, and we have nothing.

Fatjon's admission that he would rather sell sex than work as a builder put many other interviews in context. Except in a few cases, resorting to sex work was never presented as a choice, but justified and experienced as a *decision* amid a very restricted range of possibilities that were presented as more exploitative and less profitable. Florin, a twenty-one-year-old Romanian man who later also became an important informant, explained to me how selling sex becomes preferable to stealing when young migrants cease to be minors and hence are vulnerable to prosecution.

NICOLA: To be honest, it feels a bit strange when you say, "I do this because there is no work." I have interviewed hundreds of migrants, and they all work, . . . so there must be some "normal" work around, no?

FLORIN: Listen, it is about the money. Why do I have to work all day like a slave for fifty euros when I can get them in ten minutes by fucking a queer. . . . I can fuck all the men of Rome for money. . . . I used to steal when I was in France, for the money. It was better money than fucking queers, but I could only do it as I was a minor.

Florin's reference to "normal work" as slavery turns the neo-abolitionist conflation of prostitution with trafficking and "modern slavery" on its head. Many young men I interviewed explained to me very clearly along very similar lines that they would rather sell sex than take up underpaid and exploitative work opportunities in other sectors.

The decision to work in the sex industry rather than (or as well as) in construction or agriculture takes place at a very individual, yet socioeconomically framed, level. Young migrant men position themselves between the pick-up points that offer them access to various kinds of precarious and irregular labor produced and/or exacerbated by neoliberal policies and politics in the Global North, thus "entering the labour market at the lowest possible point in their effort to secure work" (Lewis, Dwyer, Hodkinson, et al. 2015, 592). Facing different kinds and degrees of exploitation and relative disadvantage within traditionally male sectors of deskilled migrant employment—which include the sex industry—they decide on a makeshift livelihood on the basis of what they find relatively acceptable or preferable in relation to the sex-gendered selfrepresentations that frame their mobile orientations. As we shall see in the next three chapters, the agentic salience (or not) of this decision is greatly influenced by the socioeconomic pressures they are under, as well as by the psychological resources they can mobilize to manage the complex, subjectifying scenario they are navigating abroad.

The concept of "decision" is central to the argument of this book. It needs to be contextualized within the social dynamics that define all late-modern societies, even if they are more prominent within postcommunist societies. Young migrants selling sex become subjects according to competing and contradictory regimes of subjectification that originate from their social and cultural contexts of origin, which in the last thirty years have been increasingly open to global media, development projects, and tourism. The encounter between these different narratives of subjectification fosters deep dynamics of social change, one of whose main manifestations is youth migration.

Within this general globalized scenario, postcommunist, late-modern societies have been exposed to specific phenomena. Because early cultural constructions of Western capitalism as an alternative to Communism drew on the selfrepresentations disseminated by Western media, participating in Western material culture became a way to gain access to alternative subjectivities and lifestyles (Mai 2001b). Many young people first experienced the West "virtually," through the lens of relatively deprived material cultures, conservative, sex-gendered mores, and sociopolitical authoritarianism. As a consequence, some young people constructed capitalist democracy as a utopia of individualized freedom and unrestricted consumption where it was possible to change one's personal and social identity overnight by "making money" abroad and "performing it" through commodified deeds—that is, through the possession and display of specific objects to strategic audiences. In the process, young people were also addressed as desiring and consuming subjects by the selfrepresentations disseminated by Western media. This led them to imagine their lives and agency in more individualized ways.

In order to account for the role of materiality and mobility in the emergence of migratory forms of subjectivity, I have reappraised the concept of the "migratory project" in the light of actor network theory (Latour 2005). The latter frames the subject as the result of an assemblage of heterogeneous material, including bodies, objects, and narratives. My resulting concept, "mobile orientations," describes how specific cultural objects, narratives, bodies, gender/sex roles, and mobility patterns become the space for action of specific subjectivities (Ahmed 2006). As already discussed, at the center of mobile orientations are *agencing decisions*: arrangements of objects, selfrepresentations and mobilities that provide mobile orientations with agency and a sense of direction, expressing migrants' capacity to act in relation to the constraints, needs, and priorities they experience.

The concept of mobile orientations enables a complex analysis of migrants' understandings and experiences of agency and exploitation by contextualizing them within deep onto-epistemological, and hence sociocultural, transformations. In order to explore this contextualization, I refer to Caroline Humphrey's (2008) anthropological reappraisal of Badiou's concept of "event" as a deep, onto-epistemological shift introducing a "rupture of intelligibility" around which new compositions of the self emerge through equally deep, subjectifying decisions taking place on the basis of both emotion and deliberation. The globalization of neoliberal late modernity and its individualized commodification of subjectivities, livelihoods, and hierarchies of values are the key onto-epistemological events framing the emergence of young migrants' mobile orientations and their embedded agencing decisions.

In this book I refer to the interlocking of social, economic, and cultural changes consistent with the rise of the "post-industrial society" (Bell 1976) in terms of "late" (Giddens 1991) modernity, rather than "postmodernity," in order to underline the elements of continuity between two different phases of the same historical formation (i.e., modernity). Following Bauman (2000, 7), I define late modernity as "liquid" to emphasize how, in late-modern times, the "melting of solids"—that is, the challenge by modern critical thinking to previously fixed and unchangeable premodern traditions, institutions, and moralities—is transferred from a macro, structural political level to a more privatized micro level, via the convergence of consumerism and individualization. Currently we are caught up in an "individualized, privatized version of modernity, with the burden of pattern weaving and the responsibility for failure falling primarily on the individual's shoulders" (Bauman 2000, 8). To this process of individualized liquefaction, we must add the impact of neoliberal market fundamentalism and of restrictive migration policies on the labor rights associated with established and new, precarious livelihoods, which have been dismembered and reordered according to the mantra of economic profitability.

The liquefaction of established modes of production, sex-gendered roles, authorities, moralities, and mobilities produced by neoliberal late modernity and its subjectifying promotion of globalized consumption produce the sets of opportunities and constraints in relation to which the agencing decisions of migrants working in the sex industry take place. On the one hand, the fluidification of moralities, mobilities, and lifestyles can be seen as providing prospective and actual migrants with new opportunities for individualized self-realization. On the other hand, the agencing decisions made by Fatjon and the other young migrant men "fucking queers" in Rome show how these opportunities for individual self-realization are curbed by the socioeconomic polarization, erosion of labor rights, and restrictive migration policies enforced by neoliberal politics and policies.

The difficulties of navigating these complex socioeconomic transformations are aggravated by the fact that global media and returning migrants disseminate contradictory, sex-gendered selfrepresentations and models of personhood, which exacerbate the burden of self-reflexivity and self-management for many minors and young adults worldwide (Elliott and Lemert 2006, 172–74). In the next chapter I show that making sense of these profound and contradictory transformations is essential if we are to understand the degree of agency characterizing young migrants' mobile orientations and embedded decisions. Not all orienting decisions to migrate and to work in the sex industry are equally agencing: migratory projects and experiences are often characterized by loss, marginalization, and exploitation. Drawing on the experiences of young migrant men selling sex in Seville, I argue that the ability to master the fluidification of sex-gendered selfrepresentations distinguishes mobile orientations characterized by agency from those marked by the loss of a sense of direction.

THREE

Selling *Comidas Rapidas* in Seville

I first went to Seville in July 2004, in the context of making a documentary funded by the Arte network about young men in situations of *errance*. "Errant mobility," a translation of the French term *errance*, became a prominent category of scientific analysis and social intervention in France in the late 1990s, a time characterized by the development of a securitizing, authoritarian, and policing attitude toward marginalized young people and the emergence of humanitarian paradigms of resistance (Pattegay 2001, 274). The concept of *errance* is inherently ambivalent: it encompasses a plurality of meanings, from romanticized understandings of nomadism and drifting, to pathologized notions of homelessness and vagrancy. In the world of social interventions in the late 1990s, *errance* was used in France to indicate minors and young people who had left their families, moving from city to city in situations of marginalization, homelessness, and lack of regular employment (Chobeaux 1996). However, by the early 2000s the term was mainly used in research and social intervention contexts alike to indicate the mobility and marginalization of young migrant men, and it became intertwined with the issue of unaccompanied minors.

By the early 2000s the "unaccompanied minor" category had also established itself as a powerful humanitarian biographical border. For groups of minors leaving "home" in search of a better future for themselves and economic survival for their families, appealing to the categories of "unaccompanied minor" and "separated children" (i.e., separated from their families) became the only way to gain social protection, legal status, and access to work. At the same time, child migration all but disappeared as a heuristic and policymaking category: the independent mobility of children became framed by the combined humanitarian, biographical borders of "child-trafficking" and "unaccompanied minor" (O'Connell Davidson

2005, 64–84). The problem is that research and social protection frameworks embedded in those humanitarian categories obfuscate the labor experiences of teenagers, and almost exclusively highlight their exploitation and lack of agency (Howard 2017), particularly when they are involved in sex work (Montgomery 2011). Academic and policymaking literature addressing child and youth migration emphasizes their potential vulnerability to sex trafficking and rarely addresses the complexity of their migratory projects or their specific experience of work in the sex industry, which is identified with the sexual exploitation of children *tout court* (Mai 2011). Furthermore, the focus on minors neglects the specific vulnerability of young adult migrants, who become even more vulnerable when they come of age because they are no longer entitled to protection and face the risk of deportation.

The majority of young migrants, including children,[1] leave home in pursuit of a complex migratory project encompassing a range of desires, priorities, and necessities, such as the aspiration to create a better life for themselves, the desire to contribute to the economic improvement and well-being of their families, and the need to escape brutality and oppression, whether the latter are experienced in the family or in wider social contexts. Thus minors and young people make agencing decisions to migrate and work in the sex industry in the context of specific opportunities and constraints. Those opportunities and constraints are firmly rooted in the liquefaction of established livelihoods—and of associated sex-gendered roles and authorities—by the globalization of the neoliberal, late-modern onto-epistemology, which promotes individualized consumption as a strategic arena of subjectification while eroding labor rights.

These macroscopic transformations encompass all global societies. But at the geopolitical and socioeconomic peripheries of the Global North—which include marginalized communities *within* the Global North—they also coincide with what Mercedes Jiménez (2004) calls the "minorization of poverty." As a result, more and more minors and young adults are becoming responsible for the economic viability of their households, and are subject to a process of early adultization and responsibilization that exerts formidable pressure on established authorities and their ethical, social, and economic anchoring. The economic unsustainability of established authorities such as the state, formal education, and the family ushers in the hegemony of neoliberal hierarchies of value, devaluing established artisanal, industrial, and agricultural livelihoods and associated models of personhood (Herzfeld 2004). At the same time, the onset of neoliberal social ontology subjectifies the individual as an entrepreneur according to a "social rationality of success, not identity" (Winnubst 2012, 86). This means that young migrants' subjectivities are validated by peers and other relevant audiences (their family, neighbors and wider communities) through the successful embodiment and performance of individualized lifestyles marked by "objectualization"—that is, the social investment of strategic objects with subjectifying qualities (Knorr Cetina 1997, 9).

These aspects are often all present and tightly interwoven in minors' and young people's mobile orientations, and need to be addressed in their entirety if we want to grasp their understandings and experiences of agency and exploitation. Migrant minors' complex system of needs and priorities is addressed univocally through the humanitarian biographical borders enforced by social intervention initiatives, according to the political and legal regimes of social protection in force within each country. This highlights the North-centrism embedded in current categories of social interventions that target migrant youth. Many migrant children and adolescents who are framed as "unaccompanied" or "separated" are already subjectified as young adults who have to provide for themselves as well as their families at home. Whereas adolescents are primarily conceived of in the Global North as bearers of rights, in many other contexts (including the poor strata of societies in the Global North), they are seen primarily as bearers of duties (Whitehead 2007). Consequently, they feel controlled and impeded by the very instruments of protection that prevent them from working in the name of avoiding child exploitation. For instance, when asked why they would not want to stay at a residential project for unaccompanied minors, most male minors selling sex in Rome replied that they had no time to waste: they felt like "grown-up men," and as such they needed to "make money" to help their families (Mai 2008; 2010). These priorities are not at all uncommon among migrant children and young people across the European Union. As a result, many leave the institutions and programs targeting them and decide to work in the informal employment sectors available to undocumented migrants, including the sex industry.

As I explain in the remainder of this chapter, precarious and criminalized livelihoods are often preferred to humanitarian protection because they allow migrant minors to meet their contradictory aspirations to a late-modern, individualized, and objectualized lifestyle associated with freedom and the necessity to provide for their families at home by "making money." Even more paradoxically, but hardly surprisingly, children who disappear from shelters are seen by the social protection initiatives targeting them as retrafficked by default (e.g., ECPAT 2016; Sigona and Allsopp 2016). This is because the (sexual) humanitarian epistemologies and funding priorities of organizations and institutions that "control and protect" them cannot comprehend the possibility that minors might decide for themselves that they would rather make money than be taken care of as the kind of children they have never been and do not want to be (Musto 2016, 12–15).

My interest in errant mobility was fueled by the absence of any specific study that used the concept to explore young migrant men's experiences of selling sex, other than in terms of their assumed involvement in sexual exploitation and trafficking (Oude Breuil 2008). This research interest was also fueled by the stark difference I noticed between the plurality of experiences of agency I had come across during my research on young migrant sex workers in Rome and Athens and the monotonous reduction of this complex plurality through the victimizing tropes and stereotypes of sexual-humanitarian biographical borders. My heuristic curiosity and scholarly dissatisfaction prompted me to look further. Luckily, I was not the only one who wanted to explore young migrant men's experiences of prostitution. When I mentioned my research topic to the director of the Marseille-based Jeunes Errants (Young Errants) association, she immediately put me in contact with the documentary film director Bruno Ulmer. This is how I became involved in the research, development, and shooting of a documentary initially called *Le Fil Rouge*,[2] following male sex work as a "red thread" through experiences of *errance* across the European Union. The production team needed the assistance of an anthropologist, and I jumped at the opportunity. I did so in order to pursue my research aim of identifying elements of complexity and agency within a pathologizing social intervention framework. My role was to assist the director in eliciting the ethnographic material on which to base the documentary. This proved a productive experience in many ways. I had the opportunity to undertake multisited research in a range of settings to which I would not otherwise have had access. By studying recurring mobility patterns and livelihood dynamics across the multiple locations of the film, I was able to understand the different mobile orientations that had been subsumed under the pathologizing, sexual-humanitarian concept of *errance*. In the process, I considered young migrant men's engagement in sex work as a strategic prism through which to explore the psychological and social dynamics underpinning differently agentic (and non-agentic) forms of mobility. During the making of the film, I also had the chance to engage firsthand with professional documentary filmmaking.

The first location of the filmmaking research was Seville, a strategic crossroads for the mobile orientations of young Moroccans and Romanians gravitating toward the heart of Europe while officially picking strawberries (and more often selling sex) in Andalusia. Seville is also where I first started using filmmaking for the gathering, analysis, and dissemination of research data emerging from intersubjective and affective social interactions. But that agencing decision only happened when Tarek took my camera and started pretending he was me.

Seville

Andalusia is Spain's southernmost region, separated from Morocco by just 14.3 kilometers across the Strait of Gibraltar. Seville is Andalusia's capital. The city embodies the region's contradictory positioning at the center of a national and globalized imaginary of Spanishness, marked by corridas, flamenco, and sherry. At the same time, Seville is the hub of a transnational space historically marked by communications, exchanges, and conflicts with Morocco (Stallaert 1998), the "constitutive other" against which Andalusia selfrepresents as quintessentially Spanish (Hall 1996).

I first stayed at a small pension in the city center, just a few hundred meters from the famous cathedral. From preliminary contacts with people working for social services and NGOs in Seville, I understood that the police restricted recent young arrivals from Morocco and Romania to the Plaza de Armas bus station. They were tolerated in this marginalized part of Seville on condition that they never attempted to leave it and mix with the thousands of tourists sightseeing in the city center. "Tourists (and most importantly tourism) must not be disturbed" seemed to be the implicit maxim regulating marginalized groups' access to the center.

The bus station is surrounded by empty surfaces and underpasses that offer many informal opportunities for accommodation and recreation, as do the bridge and adjacent riverbank. The contrast between the lush, tourism-intensive city center, less than one kilometer away, and the marginalized feel of the bus station was very sharp. I decided to start by sitting on the street corner opposite the station, where there was an informal seating area in front of a local bar and a shop selling cheap beer to a group of locals and young migrants.

La Esquina, the corner in front of the Plaza de Armas bus station, is the hangout place for many young Moroccan migrant men and their local girlfriends, most of whom are Spaniards of Roma background. They spend their evenings drinking 1.5-litre bottles of cheap beer from the all-night shop. La Esquina ("corner" in Spanish) is the encounter place for other kinds of marginalized and liminal groups too, including young Spaniards

1. One of the many informal social spaces surrounding the Plaza de Armas bus station in Seville.

buying dope, and homeless people. It is at the center of a "moral region" (Park and Burgess 1967, 43) hosting several hustler bars where young migrant men sell sex, mostly to older Spanish homosexual men, the *maricónes* ("queers" in Spanish). The most popular of these venues, the 69, has a couple of rooms behind the bar area where sex can be sold on the premises. While they hang around the bus station, young Moroccan and Romanian men mix with people coming from and going to neighboring villages, other cities in Spain, and distant foreign destinations. They usually sit in groups at the top corner of the steps and in the cafeteria, catching the attention of local *maricónes*. The two groups of young migrants do not mix. Nor do *maricónes* mix with the young men they buy sex from—not publicly.

I started my fieldwork by sitting on the bus station steps in the evening. On my second evening, I began talking with a young Moroccan man who was looking for an opportunity to make some money. Paco was nineteen years old, smartly dressed, and really wanted a drink. He invited me to La Esquina and suggested we share a bottle of beer. Soon enough I was sitting with a group of friends who knew each other well and spent most evenings hanging out at La Esquina and in the rest of Seville's moral region. Little by little, the group accepted my presence, which I explained in terms of writing a book on migration and helping the film director find interesting stories for the documentary. All true. Sitting down at La Esquina meant witnessing illegal activities such as the sale of dope to Spanish youngsters or the trade in stolen goods (usually mobiles), as well as getting information about other income possibilities. It also meant entering a social space where conviviality involved picking fights and looking for trouble (*"buscar problemas"*) as a way to spend time and have fun. It was a sad kind of fun most of the time, but fun nevertheless.

Pursuing the European Magic Island

During the summer or on days with good weather, the Esquina group would descend to the riverside park and cross the river. The road linking the river bridge to the *Isla Magica* (Magic Island) theme park, which occupies the original Expo 1992 site, is a huge avenue where different youth groups would meet at night before going to the nearby discos. The Esquina boys and girls entertained themselves by chatting up passers-by going to and from the discos. They picked up their cigarette butts, exchanged jokes, laughed with them. Most importantly, they helped them park their cars, an important source of income for most of the men at La Esquina besides sex work, small-scale drug dealing, and fruit-picking during the summer. As we watched people go by, the game became to try to guess who was a queer (*maricón*) and who was a whore (*puta*). We laughed like crazy. *Maricón! Puta! Maricón! Puta!* It was exhilarating at first, but then we got bored. And a bit sad. I could not help thinking that we all realized after all that many of us were closeted *maricónes* and *putas* ourselves, shouting out our internalized stigma at other people.

As the *maricón/puta* game wound down, we fell silent. Suddenly, the female leader of the group, a very domineering young Spanish Roma woman, asked me if I had ever been to the 69. I replied affirmatively.

"Have you ever seen Momo [her boyfriend] there?" she asked.

"In Italy," I said, "we name the sin, but never the sinner."

It was an instinctive response; the last thing I wanted was to be (or be seen as) a snitch, either in research settings or more generally. A bitter smile of appreciation and disappointment lit up her face. There were looks of tacit and satisfied approval in the group. It was the right answer. *"Tu eres buena gente,"* she proclaimed. I was in; I was "a good person." I could keep my mouth shut. She dropped the conversation. It was then that Tarek, a twenty-one-year-old man from Morocco, asked me what it meant to be a *maricón*.

"And why are you asking me in particular, how would I know?" I said, jokingly and a bit campily. We started laughing, but I sensed that he really needed to know.

A few hours later, as we headed back into town, Tarek pointed to the Chalet (*villa* in Spanish), the little wooden shelter where he lived under the Cristo de la Expiration bridge on the Guadalquivir river, right next to the station. "This is life, you go that way, and we go that way," he said with a sad and cheeky look on his face. I think he was referring to the inequalities separating us. And of course he was flirting.

I felt the same unease. After all the fun we had shared, I was still going back to a comfortable hotel room in the tourist-ridden center, and he still lived under a bridge with the other Esquina boys. "I know . . . But at least we had a good time all together tonight, right?" I said. I felt stupid, but what else could I say? Maybe nothing, as he did. We nodded and parted.

On my way back to the hotel, I stopped at the 69, where I found quite a few Esquina guys chatting to local *maricónes*. They greeted me embarrassedly, so I smiled, winked, and quickly looked away to signal complicity and give them some space. Unexpectedly, this time the owner warned me against Tarek, as if he knew about our impending brotherhood. "Be careful not to mix with the one with the baby face; he is very dangerous, . . . although he does not look like it," he said. Apparently he had tried to set fire to the 69 on more than one occasion and was no longer permitted on the premises. He had also allegedly threatened to kill the owner and terrorized him several times on the street. I both registered and ignored the warning: I already felt Tarek was the person with whom knowledge would happen in Seville.

Back at the hotel, I could not sleep. I kept thinking about what I had just witnessed on the way to the *Isla Magica*. I reflected on the Esquina boys and girls, on how they lived on the margins of the objectualized terms of subjectivity set by the youth culture disseminated from the Global North. I also started thinking about the strong link between sexual identities and processes of commodification under neoliberalism (Bell and Binnie 2000), and specifically about how the capillary commodification of sex-gendered lifestyles and subjectivities is key to the development of young migrants' mobile orientations. Reviewing the events of the evening, I was struck by the ways the young Moroccan men and their Roma Spanish girlfriends assembled the garments and objects that constituted their Spanish peers, those who were able to enter the disco. My indirect reference to the concept of mimicry here is obviously not meant to institute a North-centric, neocolonial hierarchy of sociocultural competence (Bhabha 1994). It refers rather to mimesis as a sensuous capacity to imitate, know, and understand the world—in Taussig's words, "the faculty to copy, imitate, make models, explore difference, yield into and become Other" (1993, 233). Taussig's analysis of how Western images, goods, and symbols enter the cosmology of previously separate cultures in times of colonialism and globalization is useful for understanding how, by participating in Western, commodified youth culture, young migrants attempt to "become others"—or to become versions of themselves that are endowed with new powers and ways of being.

Deleuze and Guattari's (1986) notion of "becoming" offers opportunities to address the affective and material dimensions through which young migrants' sex-gendered subjectivities and mobile orientations emerge through the embodiment and arrangement of objects invested with subjectifying qualities. By wearing Adidas vests and Nike trainers, my Moroccan friends and their Spanish Roma girlfriends were not simply trying to fit in. They were performing their selfrepresentations of being young, for themselves and for their relevant audiences: they were actually "becoming young" according to new, commodified, and globalized canons of youth. At the same time, their becoming was interrupted by existing social hierarchies and exclusions. The Esquina boys and girls arranged the material objects and practices that constituted their Spanish peers. They helped them park their cars, they smoked their cigarette butts, they stole their mobiles, and sold them dope. They flirted with them as they entered the disco; they fucked them too sometimes, but overall they remained outside the gates of the European magic island—that night and every night.

Selling *Comidas Rapidas*

It was Tarek who gave me the idea of how to make my first film, by taking my camera and interviewing fellow male sex workers while pretending to be me. It was hilarious. The 69 was not the only place where sex work occurred within the perimeter of Seville's moral region. The bus station cafeteria *Comidas Rapidas*, as well as the station waiting room, toilets, outdoor balcony, and main steps, were the sites of a tearoom trade that remained hidden in plain sight. I was oblivious of it at first, just like all the other passers-by. But once I understood what was going on, it was all I could see.

It was in the context of this observation that filmmaking (and the knowledge that emerged in the process) happened between me, Tarek, and the other young men I hung around with while doing research in Seville. And it was within our joking and hanging out around the spaces and practices of male sex work in Seville's moral region that the expression *"comidas rapidas,"* meaning "fast food" in Spanish, became code for talking about selling sex without actually naming it. The day this happened was also the day filmmaking began, at the tables of a kiosk outside the station that acted as a sex work "contact zone" (Pratt 1991) between young migrant men and their Spanish and older clients, just like the indoor cafeteria. As I was drinking with Tarek and Samir, a twenty-year-old Moroccan man also living and selling sex in Seville, we were joined by a couple of Romanian peers who had heard I was looking for people to interview.[3] Unexpectedly, Tarek started pretending to be me and went through all the motions. He asked them to sit down, took my clipboard, flicked through my interview guideline questionnaire, started explaining to the interviewees that the interviews were confidential and anonymous, and got the interview started. All I had to do was film, which I did. I was amazed and excited. Tarek asked all the right questions, while mocking both them and me.

In the days that followed, Tarek and I conducted several filmed interviews together, exchanging the roles of interviewer and cameraperson. We also went around the bus station and filmed outdoors and in the cafeteria before the owner decided we were attracting too much attention and asked us to leave. The expression *"comidas rapidas"* proved to be very effective in allowing people to talk about different aspects of their involvement in male sex work without naming it. Samir, who had witnessed our filmmaking project's opening scene, was one of our first research subjects and one of the most candid. "*Comidas rapidas* is. . . . Well, you go to a club and have a good time with guys. Young guys, because I don't go with older men. . . . I go with young guys, because I like it." It was a great beginning. Samir continued to answer our questions:

> What happens is that there are lots of older men looking for young guys to suck their dick . . . for money, but to tell you the truth sometimes also not for the money, because some people like it. The way it works is that the guy [doing it] thinks he gets a good deal, he has fun for half an hour and he gets paid for it.

Later, at the Comidas Rapidas bar, Samir talked to us about another, less agentic aspect of his involvement in sex work. He showed us his temporary permit to stay, which he had gained previously as an unaccompanied minor. It clearly stated that he was not authorized to work. "Look at this,"

2. *Comidas Rapidas*: Samir talking about *comidas rapidas*.

Samir said, "they don't want to give us a work permit; that's why we are looking for *comidas rapidas* here." I registered this, as well as the other sides of his story.

Right before we were asked to leave, Abdel, a twenty-three-year-old Moroccan man, joined us. Tarek quickly started interviewing him, as they were friends. "Why did you come here?" he promptly asked.

"To try and get some life (*buscando vida*)."

According to Spanish anthropologist Mercedes Jimenez (2003), the expression *buscando vida* frames the complex migratory projects of young Moroccan men, expressing both the economic need to support their families and the yearning for a more individualized life in the West. Aware of the wider resonance of this term, I was satisfied with this answer, but Tarek was not. To him, it was a cliché. I think he wanted to dig deeper into what he perceived as a standard reply to the question about reasons for migrating. The fact that he shared Abdel's mobile orientation, livelihood, and lifestyle meant that he knew there was more to be uncovered. What follows is an excerpt from the exchange that ensued, during which Abdel succinctly and effectively explained to us the relation between migration, selling sex, and "fucking queers."

TAREK: Always the same reply. . . . Why did you come here from Morocco?!
ABDEL: To work.
TAREK: And what did you do?
ABDEL: I did not find any.
TAREK: So what do you eat?
ABDEL: *Comidas rapidas.*
TAREK: What's in it?
ABDEL: Fucking queers!

As Abdel said this, we all started laughing. The double entendre was funny, but I think we laughed to discharge the unease and excitement provoked by Abdel's witty and honest responses. The ironic sensibility generated and shared through jokes and wordplay had created an interstice between preferred selfrepresentations and lived experiences, through which knowledge emerged between us. It was at that moment that the manager of the bar asked us to leave. The discourses, practices, and affects framing the tearoom trade had become too audible and visible for business to continue as usual.

In the months and years that followed, I struggled to find a way to edit the filmed material and knowledge that had happened between us back then. Anonymity was an important concern. Although most of the young men had given me verbal consent to show their faces, I did not think it would be ethical to do so, given that they would potentially be exposing themselves to homophobia, the racist stigmatization of irregular migrants, and whore stigma. But anonymity was not the only concern. I also wanted to find a visual and aesthetic format that could embody the regime of invisibilization and the sensuous environment through which sex work and knowledge happened in the moral zone encompassing the bus station.

In London, five years later, as I edited the visual material I had gathered in Seville in 2005, I decided to use chromatic filters and editing. By superimposing blurred silhouettes of young male sex workers, clients, and people transiting through the bus station, I wanted to visualize the paradoxical invisibility in full sight of the practice of male sex work within the normative spaces and mobilities surrounding the bus station. At the same time, I wanted to provide viewers with the rhythm and sensuous sonorities framing these dynamics. I decided to do so by alternating interviews with excerpts from a Seville song, "*El Adiós*," which clients had been singing next to us while we were sitting around the outdoor kiosk table where the filmmaking first took place. It had all happened at the same time: the filming, the knowing, the singing. There was definitely something in the air that

3. *Comidas Rapidas*: Young men selling sex and sharing knowledge in the Comidas Rapidas cafeteria.

day, an intersubjective and ironic "affective atmosphere" (Anderson 2009) that allowed a complex and nuanced kind of knowledge to emerge.

The Chalet under the Bridge over the River

I had been asking Tarek for a proper interview since the very beginning of our friendship, but I never insisted, thinking that the time was not yet ready. As my departure from Seville approached, I asked him again, and he suggested we meet at the Chalet. I was delighted. The Chalet (*villa* in Spanish) was a wooden platform tucked away between the arch of the bridge and the road surface above. Huge totemic penises on one side and men in ties on the other welcomed you as you approached, as if to indicate the association between young migrant men's involvement in sex work and their mobile orientations towards hegemonic neoliberal masculinities. They were graffitied onto the bridge pillars that ushered you into the Chalet. A set of white sheets, constantly moved by the river breeze, demarcated a square central area. Although at first one could only see a worn-out mattress in the middle of the central space, within the huge metal arches on

4. El Jefe, Tarek, and Abdel at the entrance of the Chalet, under the arch on the right.

the sides of the bridge were dwellings, which folded up and disappeared into the bridge structure during the day. Every single interstice was used as storage space. The most valuable things were hidden in the vertical side walls for safety reasons, because they were not visible. To reach them one had to lean right out of the bridge and hang suspended above the water.

We finally got to the Chalet after a long night, one of my last evenings in Seville in 2005. I was excited to finally get to the Chalet and interview Tarek in his own place. As we were walking toward the bridge, he asked Mouad to join us, which I interpreted as an act of preemptive closure. I was very disappointed. I had wanted to be alone with him and talk about personal matters—both his and mine. I wanted to answer his original question about what it meant to be a *maricón* more fully and not publicly. But I was given no choice. Mouad's nickname was El Jefe—the Boss. He was the oldest of the Esquina guys and a respected authority, especially by the youngest members. Inviting him to join us was an act of boundary-making. I knew Tarek was not going to be able to open up in front of him.

"Tarek, so why don't you go to the 69 any more?" I asked him as we lay on the mattress in the central space at the Chalet. I said it a little aggressively, provoked by my frustration at the presence of El Jefe, who sat smoking dope on the bridge arch a few meters away. The river ran placidly beneath us, and disco boats blasted every twenty minutes. The spare noise of passing cars alerted us to the proximity of the road just a few meters above us, but the rest of the time we were immersed in a timeless and silent atmosphere. We were suspended under the arches of the bridge, right on the river. I guess that was why I felt I could ask him the unaskable question. I could feel he was tense; that he did not want me to talk about him and the 69, not in front of El Jefe. But then he did.

TAREK: I was there once. I had been smoking joints and started laughing about the *maricónes*. . . . That was it. . . . The way they move their hands, their face, . . . it made me laugh . . . that was it. . . . Then I had an argument with the *dueño*, . . . and now I cannot go there any more. . . . I can't go and I don't want to go, two things . . .

NICOLA: And this thing of the fire? You told me that . . .

TAREK: Yes, I tried to set fire to the 69. . . . Isham actually did it, but I was with him.

NICOLA: Because the owner told me to be careful not to get in touch with you.

TAREK: *Claro claro, . . . son maricónes*. . . . They want to fuck, but I don't want, I don't like it, . . . I don't like it. . . . He tried to have sex with me in the back rooms, but I refused.

NICOLA: Have you ever fucked a *maricón*?

TAREK: I told you, I do not like it.

NICOLA: That you like it or not is not really my question, what I want to know is if you have ever fucked one.

TAREK: I told you, . . . right now I don't go with *maricónes*.

NICOLA: Right now you don't, . . . but before?

TAREK: I have been just with one, . . . as I told you before.

NICOLA: Only once?

TAREK: Only once. . . . I fucked him for thirty euros. . . . I bought the bus ticket . . . from Almeria to Seville. . . . Right now I steal money; . . . better than fucking *maricónes*. . . . I'd rather steal money and then spend it to fuck women.

NICOLA: And you fucked a *maricón* only once? . . . All of these years in the street and you did it only once? . . . Come on, Tarek, it is a bit difficult to believe this. . . . I mean, right now we are the only ones who are not at the 69, . . . you, me, and El Jefe. . . . All others are there *buscandose la vida*?

TAREK: Listen, . . . you like men, no?

NICOLA: Yes.

TAREK: And I like women; . . . *hombre*, are you crazy or what? . . . A woman . . .

> when she is naked, . . . she has got tits; . . . they are soft and hairless; . . . they have a good body. . . . I could eat them from the pussy to the head.

Tarek went on celebrating how much he liked eating pussy for another minute or so. It was the only selfrepresentation he could perform in front of El Jefe, I thought. But I knew more.

Throughout his heterosexual selfrepresentation under the bridge that night, I remembered when we went to the beach in Matalascañas and the way he looked at me when I was swimming and sunbathing. I remembered how he looked at me when we parted at the Isla Magica; how he looked at me most of the time. I also remembered when he told me that he had been with men several times, and that he felt let down by them each time. How they had promised to help him with jobs and papers before having sex, but never followed through afterward. But this time, while we were floating on the bed under the bridge over the river, with El Jefe smoking silently next to us, Tarek told me that he used to have a girlfriend, and that he lost her because of her parents. He showed me her picture. Another imaginary girlfriend from another closeted young man, I thought. By then I had seen so many of these heterosexual wallet icons that I was skeptical. But what if these possibilities were real? After all, having a *rubia*, a blond woman from the West, was the ultimate sanction of one's status as a successful man, as having "made it"; it was part and parcel of a successful mobile orientation.

According to Tarek, this alleged *rubia* girlfriend gave up on him because he was a *moro*, a derogatory name in Spain for migrants from North Africa. Prompted by this painful memory of rejection, Tarek started speaking like the river above which we were floating together. El Jefe was still smoking and sitting a few meters away; he was still there, but he remained in the background. As one memory elicited another, Tarek told me how he had been attacked several times by Spanish youth for being a *moro* while working in the countryside. He showed me the scars on his head and arm. I felt angry and saddened at the humiliations he had had to endure. I also felt moved by how intimate we had become, honored to have been chosen as the privileged recipient of this intimacy, and ashamed for having felt disappointed earlier, as well as for the aggressive affect with which I had asked my first question that night.

But our intimate, intersubjective exchange was not over yet—far from it. While he was selfrepresenting his (frustrated) heterosexuality to El Jefe and me, I could still note the mix of seductive campiness and macho aggressiveness characterizing his gestures. It was right then that El Jefe asked:

"Why don't you take him with you to London?" He was obviously much more streetwise and shrewd than I thought.

NICOLA: [To Tarek.] And what do we do in London, . . . me and you?

TAREK: I don't know. But I know what I would do in Amsterdam. . . . I was twice, last spring and when I was fifteen. I only got back because I did not have anywhere to stay, and it was cold. Plus, I have a family. I had to go back. I went there because I was tired . . . of this fucking country. . . . If I had a house where to stay I would not return, I swear, . . . I would not return here. . . . *Hombre*, if I had papers I would go and live there. . . . I liked shops there, . . . what you can buy. . . . If I had the money, I would buy these things in Holland: . . . a Mercedes, . . . a beautiful home, . . . a blond girlfriend, . . . and fuck the rest. . . . If I can have just one week like that, . . . then people can kill me, . . . I don't care; . . . a beautiful blond . . . with nice little tits, . . . I swear, . . . that makes me hot. . . . And now we are at the bridge; . . . there is no house, no blond, nothing. . . . But it must happen., . . . if Spain does not give me any money . . . I will send somebody to the cemetery.

NICOLA: You are very aggressive, Tarek . . . why are you so angry?

TAREK: What the fuck am I going to do . . . return home empty-handed? I can't . . .

NICOLA: Why can't you go back . . .

TAREK: *Tengo mi cara, . . . hombre*, I have my pride. . . . It's five years since I left, . . . for nothing.

NICOLA: Why, what do you have to do? What do you care about what people think? Do you have to have a Mercedes to go back?

TAREK: This is the problem, this explains everything. . . . I don't care about people. . . . I am talking about my family. . . . I return there after I have not called or anything. . . . "Where have you been?" "I have been to Spain . . . mama . . ." "And why did not you stay at home with us? Why did you go to Spain?" What will I say, eh? With nothing in my hands to come back with . . .

The impossibility of going home "empty-handed," again. The existential necessity of possessing the subjectifying goods that enable the embodiment of the "successful migrant" mobile orientation: the clothes, the blond woman, the car, the papers. Under the bridge over the river, Tarek presented his life history as the failed attempt to arrange the material terms of his mobile orientation, which were also the terms of his agency.

Right then he stopped talking and asked me a river of questions. About how and when I discovered I was gay, what it meant to me and my parents, about my boyfriends. I answered succinctly but exhaustively. Tarek listened very attentively. He had been waiting for this opportunity for a long time. Our relationship of friendship, safe flirting, and trust enabled him to finally break out of the selfrepresentations and discursive limitations regulating conversations with *maricónes* and ask me (and himself) the questions he had always wanted to ask. He was very impressed by the fact that I loved my boyfriends. He laughed in amazement, not scorn. He then went on asking me everything about my sexual experiences. Everything. I answered without reticence or hesitation. "It is only fair," I thought, "after all the many questions he has had to put up with."

He then asked if I wanted children. When I replied that I was considering adoption in the future, he said, "You find me a woman, for the papers, I make a child in order to get them, and then I leave her and give the child to you." I did not even have time to think about this crazy suggestion when he took my hand and said, "Hey, Nicola, we are brothers, aren't we?"

I closed my eyes, then looked at the river flowing silently beneath us. A cool, sobering breeze blew on our faces. I focused on the reflections on the river and wished I could hug him and tell him that everything would be all right, that he would be able to become a man, the man he had wanted to be all his life, the embodiment of his own successful, migrant mobile orientation. In that moment I wished we *were* brothers, because he would have had a much easier life. He would have had a chance to become who he wanted to be. I had it infinitely better in life. I had been given a chance to be myself. But I also came from the right social class and had the right papers, education, race, and gender to have the opportunity to get ahead in life. He did not. As Samira, the Algerian "transsexual" I discussed in the introduction, would have put it, I was "French" after all: a privileged, white male from the Global North.

"Of course we are brothers," I said. I squeezed his hand between both of mine.

He did the same, and then said, "So you are going to call me sometimes, OK? To find out what's going on."

"Of course I am going to call you, brother; of course," I said, looking at him, then looking away. It was both an act of closure and a goodbye. I was about to leave in a few days. We lay in silence on the Chalet's main bed.

El Jefe had been completely silent for the last thirty minutes. The breeze was now getting cold. After a long pause, we resumed chatting as usual about everyday life at La Esquina. Those last images of me, El Jefe, and Tarek talking away in the Chalet, the boats passing beneath, the cars passing above, gorgeous, tourist-ridden Seville shining afar, and the river flowing beneath, reflecting the city, will stay with me forever.

This Is Not Europe: Introducing Errant Mobility

In the two weeks following the night at the Chalet, I felt I had come to better understand some of the main determinants of errant mobility. My conversation with Tarek was a catalyst for the elaboration of my own theorizations, which were to draw on scholarly work, previous and subsequent ethnographic observations, and interviews with the young migrant men I would meet in various countries of origin and destination. I discuss these theorizations in more detail in the next chapter.

Tarek had left Marrakesh at the age of fourteen and lived in Tangiers for three months while waiting to go to Spain. He tried to leave Morocco twelve times, most spectacularly by hiding in the mudguard of a large bus. He tensed his body in an arch right over the wheels while the bus was crossing the port gates in Morocco and Spain, dirt spraying on him. "Making it" in Amsterdam, the cusp of a cultural construction of Europeanness in terms of individualized "freedom," and the dream of "having" a *rubia* in their lives were shared aspects of the mobile orientations of many young migrants trying to become men by going to Europe. Tarek's determination to pursue his dream of becoming a "free" man in Europe was particularly entrenched in his mobile orientation. "There are people who came for the money, people who came for freedom, and people who came for both. I came for freedom," he often claimed.

Tarek had not been able to own the material, psychological, and social terms of his mobile orientation. Living on the leftovers of Spanish material culture and being excluded from Spanish society did not allow him to arrange and embody his existential aspiration to become a successful migrant in Europe. He had no *rubia*, no papers, no car with which to perform his success for his peers and family. He also had no introspective relationship with himself that might have enabled him to accept the complexity of his sexuality, which was larger than heterosexuality. These limitations did not allow him to fully adopt new subjectivities in the name of the freedom for which he had left home.

As the film-production team was about to leave Seville, Tarek agreed to return to Morocco with the director and attempt to get the papers to migrate legally. I was skeptical about the feasibility of this operation and about Tarek's ability to endure his return to Morocco "empty-handed." The plan was to insert him from the Moroccan side into a bilateral agreement for seasonal migration and to take it from there once he was legally present on Spanish soil. But Tarek felt that he had been waiting long enough to become the man he wanted to be, and he could wait no longer. By then he must have lost all trust in Spanish and EU authorities and promises. He abandoned this opportunity just a few weeks into the procedure. The last I heard of him was that he had been arrested for theft and was in jail in Morocco. Nemesis could not have found a harsher punishment for Tarek's hubris: a Moroccan jail, for someone who had been looking for freedom in Europe all his young life.

By focusing on Tarek's trajectory in this chapter, I have outlined in detail the main features of *errant mobility,"* a term referring to psychological dynamics and mobility patterns characterized by a loss of agency and orientation. As I explain in the next chapter, errant mobility is characterized by experiences of extreme marginalization and psychological dynamics that are often related to an unresolved detachment from parents and a lack of acceptance of one's sexuality. This interplay produces utopian migratory projects, whose unavoidable failure is repeated at each new destination of itinerant mobilities across Europe, which is constructed in the process as an idealized space for subjectification.

Although Tarek's determination to strive for freedom was unique, the persistence of his utopian dream of becoming a successful man in Europe, and the way it collided with marginalization and stigmatization, were not. His multiple displacements across several EU countries in the name of an idealized image of Europe were a significant and shared aspect of the life histories of many young migrants whose mobile orientations were marked by loss and marginalization. Most of those living in the moral zone surrounding the Seville bus station were equally "looking for Europe." They were trying to "become men" by arranging the material objects that constituted successful male migrants at the very margins of youth culture in the Global North. For many, Europe was a superior material world of access and entitlement that would make them men according to their mobile orientations and their embedded and preferred selfrepresentations. Outright. It was also a space of unmediated freedom and opportunity: an existential chance to escape the many economic, social, and cultural limitations that their desire to become successful men encountered at home.

By the time I got to Seville, *"recogiendo fresas"* (picking strawberries) had become a tongue-in-cheek expression used to designate selling sex among people at La Esquina. In the previous couple of years, many Moroccan migrants had been made redundant by the arrival of *rubias* from Eastern Europe, who were recruited as genuine fruit pickers through agencies, and who were preferred to *moros* because they were female and Christian. The process of symbolic and material emasculation could not have been more complete. Not only could young Moroccan young men not include a *rubia* in the arrangement of their mobile orientations toward becoming successful men; in their eyes, the *rubias* also took "their" fruit-picking jobs, and marginalized them further by restricting their livelihood options.

In response to the frustrations they met in Seville in relation to the dream of "making it" in Europe, many young migrants reoriented their utopian expectations toward the North, according to a symbolic and North-centric hierarchy of Europeanness they had both internalized and reproduced. Within this cultural construction, Seville, Rome, and Athens—usually the first entry points into Europe from Morocco or Romania—are "as bad as" their country of origin. A recurrent discourse among young migrant men in southern Europe was that "this is not really Europe. England is Europe. Holland is Europe." Amsterdam is where many, like Tarek, went to try their luck at becoming men, according to utopian selfrepresentations of what a "successful" migrant looked like. It is also where we follow them now, to observe the unfolding of their mobile orientations between "errant" and more agentic forms of mobility.

FOUR

Boditarian Inscriptions

In the two years following my first arrival in Seville in 2004, I followed and supported the *Le Fil Rouge* production team in a range of migrant countries of destination and origin. I complemented this with independent fieldwork funded by the London School of Economics, where I had started to work as a Morris Ginsberg Research Fellow in the Department of Sociology in 2003. This research on errant mobility was undertaken over a period of twenty months, from spring 2004 to the end of 2005, in eighteen cities across ten EU and non-EU countries: Albania, Belgium, France, Germany, Greece, Italy, Morocco, the Netherlands, Romania, and Spain. During this period I gathered most of a total of eighty-two semistructured interviews with minors and young migrants from Albania, Algeria, Morocco, Romania, Tunisia, and Turkey.[1] Drawing on this ethnographic and interview material, I addressed the independent migration of minors and young people as a "rite of passage" (Monsutti 2007), a liminal and ritual practice through which "becoming a man," the passage to adulthood, is negotiated socially and individually at a time of heightened social change. More specifically, I contextualized the mobile orientations of migrant young men within the emergence of new, globalized rituals of passage toward models of adulthood and manhood that are rapidly transforming under the pressure of the combined, neoliberal forces of individualization and commodification. One of the most significant destinations for my analysis of mobile orientations was the place young migrants perceived as the apex of the European hierarchy: Amsterdam. It was here that many felt they would either "make it" or "break it."

Making It and Breaking It in Amsterdam

"This is a place for people who don't know what they want," Lucy told me as we were drinking and observing at the Palace, a late-night club where people would converge after the hustler bars around Rembrandtplein had closed. Lucy was my main informant in Amsterdam. She was a twenty-eight-year-old, pre-op, trans woman from Curaçao, one of the island territories of the former Netherlands Antilles. She was selling sex while waiting for (and partly in order to pay for) her sex-change operation. We met at the Palace one night when I was hanging out with young men selling sex, and we started talking. The Palace really did feel like a place for people who did not know what they wanted, or rather for people who were trying to find out. "If you want a man, you go to a gay bar; if you want a woman, you go to a straight bar; if you don't know what you want, you come here," Lucy told me the night I first met her. I could not agree more. I was in the right kind of place for my research. On the dance floor there was a heterogeneous crowd of young Romanian and Moroccan men and trans women from Latin America, as well as people who had come from straight or gay discos and clubs, all mixed together for a few hours, looking for work, fun, and money. It was easy to join in.

The Palace was part of the circuit of discos and bars that punctuated the moral zone encompassing Rembrandtplein. Another was the Nightlife, a hustler bar where older Dutch men bought sex from young migrant men. The Nightlife quickly became my main ethnographic site in Amsterdam, as it was the place where most young Romanian men hung around to sell sex and socialize. It was also where Ciprian, a twenty-one-year-old Romanian man living and selling sex in Amsterdam, finally showed me his very special tattoo. He had mentioned the very first time we met that he had the word *LUX*—"luxury" in Romanian—tattooed on his penis, after I had explained the topic of my study to him. Although he offered to show it to me again later in our relationship, I felt awkward about accepting the offer until we had become close enough for me to feel sure it was not an attempt to sell me sex. In the meantime, I had been thinking about the significance of this inscription: an embodiment of his aspiration to join a world of luxury and privileged material entitlement. In my imagination, the tattoo was very professionally done, with imposing Latin capital letters. In reality, as I was to discover at the end of my last night with him in Amsterdam, it was a rather poorly done self-tattoo. He had done it with a ballpoint pen a few years earlier in Romania, when he was reappraising his migration and work plans while between two Amsterdam trips.

Ciprian was part of a group of young Romanian men who became my main reference point for ethnographic observation in Amsterdam. Besides his tattoo, he also had a deep scar on his belly, given to him by a Dutch trans woman he had lived with when he first came to the Netherlands. She had apparently stabbed him to prevent him from leaving her. As a result, he had lost a lot of blood; he had also lost a lot of confidence. He almost died, and had only started to recover a few months before I met him. Ciprian was not the only young Romanian man who had lived with a "tram" (*tramvai* in Romanian), a slang word echoing the word *trans* that his peer group used to indicate transgender sex workers. Florin, a twenty-three-year-old Romanian also selling sex at the Nightlife, used to live with a tram in Amsterdam too, but then he had to leave because he felt "controlled" by her. They all did, eventually. I discuss these relationships between young Romanian men and trans women later in this chapter.

Florin became another important informant in Amsterdam. He was one of the most successful and best-looking young men in the group. He still had not given up his intention to study informatics back in Romania. Florin had lost his mother a few years earlier and also had to support a retired father, who—like Ciprian's father—only received a pension of a hundred euros a month. A pittance. Ciprian and Florin's combined life histories express the most significant features of the mobile orientations of their peer group. In this chapter I focus on specific aspects of these two young men's migration trajectories as a way to talk about more general circumstances and situations.

Ciprian had first left home to work in Turkey at the age of eighteen. He was the oldest son of two retired parents who needed help to make ends meet. Like most of his peer group, he had arrived in Amsterdam after multiple displacements between Italy, southern France, Spain, and Belgium. Florin, too, was in a difficult economic situation following his mother's death. He had decided to come to Amsterdam to sell sex to other men, an opportunity for "making money" that he had become aware of while in Romania. However, he took a long detour through Italy, southern France, and Spain, including Seville, before amassing enough money to reach Amsterdam. In each of these settings, Ciprian and Florin were confronted with the decision between selling sex to men, stealing, begging, and working in irregular and underpaid jobs in agriculture and construction. They both resorted to a combination of stealing and selling sex, a decision they justified as less risky (in terms of being visible and potentially deported)[2] and more economically rewarding than any other option. Florin's experience in Seville matched the marginalization and poverty I had witnessed during fieldwork, which had also been related to me by Tarek and the other young Esquina men.

NICOLA: In Seville, where did you stay? Around the bus station?

FLORIN: Yeah, full of Romanians, Moroccans, and Albanians for a little, we think different than the rest of European. We live very hard, and there are situations we don't have money for food. But in Italy, . . . I don't think there are people in Italy with no money for food. They don't know hard life. We had to help ourselves. We know how to survive. We steal. For that we steal.

In expressing his perception that (Western) Europeans do not "know hard life," Florin seems to be underlining the disadvantaged socioeconomic conditions that frame young migrant men's agencing decisions to resort to criminalized and stigmatized livelihoods. In the accounts of the displacements of young migrants who sell sex, a recurrent emphasis on the need to help impoverished parents, and on poverty more generally, often felt like a discursive justification for their resort to irregular, stigmatized, or illegal activities. As discussed in chapter 2, these "survivalist" discursive strategies, whether they reflected reality or not, were often mobilized to morally legitimize the aspiration to and enjoyment of the freedom associated with migrants' adventurous wanderings—a sense not primarily motivated by "economic necessity." More often than not, young migrants' accounts of travel and survival in Europe resonated strongly with normative backpacking experiences of youth travel and experimentation (Schapendonk, Liempt, and Spierings 2014), albeit from a much less entitled perspective.

In many respects, young migrants' mobility can be understood as an underprivileged gap year, interweaving survival, need, and hardship with adventure, experimentation, and curiosity. For instance, Claudiu, a twenty-one-year-old Romanian man and one of the most self-reflexive members of the Amsterdam group, once described himself as a "*voyou voyageur*." This French term can be translated as "traveling drifter," and it evokes a quest for new adventures beyond moral and geographical boundaries, and beyond survivalist discourses and realities. Claudiu explains in his own words:

> I have already spent quite a few years in the street, and I know quite a few things. . . . There are people much older than me who don't know half of what I know. . . . Now I am in Amsterdam, but I want to know other countries, other capital cities, other places too. I am a traveling drifter. . . . I mean, . . . I don't know, a drifter is . . . I can't explain it really. . . . It's a vagabond. . . . A thief. . . . I don't know how to explain. But I guess it is a guy who

> cannot stay in the same place all the time; he wants to move all the time, to see everything and to have everything, to see and have absolutely everything that goes on in the street.

The notion of "traveling drifter" expresses how a desire to explore different social settings, an aspiration to greater freedom, and economic necessity are intertwined in the adventurous trajectories and mobile orientations of many young migrant men through Europe. Ciprian's account of his *rocambolesque* journey to Amsterdam, which he describes and experiences as a paradise in comparison with his meager circumstances in the rest of Europe, summarizes the agencing decisions made by many young migrant men in similar situations.

> I really liked Monaco. It's beautiful, because only rich people live there. I thought I could make money there, but it's not possible. I went away because you cannot steal; they don't let me go in the shops because I'm poor. I sleep in the street and in the park near the castle. After I go to Nice, then Marseille, then Paris. Because Paris is the capital, so you can do many things. I still had no money. I went to the Gare du Nord and joined the other Romanians waiting for queers there. I stayed with queers, and in the night I steal from cars: baggage, clothes, laptop, cameras. Then from Paris, I go to Antwerp. I was thinking it's close to Holland. I learnt about queers in France. And I thought that since Holland is the country for gay people, I could make more money. In Antwerp I don't see any Romanian to tell something about the city. So I go to steal cell phone on the street at the traffic lights. I stayed there one month, in an abandoned house. When I arrived in Amsterdam, it was nine in the evening. I get to the bar. We were new, and every queer set eyes on us. They give me a drink, and I say, this is paradise. Because no one gave me drinks like this in a bar, . . . no one! But here it was something else. They asked me, "Do you have a place to sleep? Come with me tonight, I take you in my house, I give you some money." In Italy or France, they never told me this. No one. From the first night I came here, I started making easy money. I wash my clothes, I send money to Romania, to my family, and after I rent a place. My place.

I will complement Ciprian's Amsterdam-bound itinerary with Florin's outbound trip from Amsterdam to Ibiza. When I interviewed Florin and asked him what identity or term he found most useful to describe himself, he responded that he was a clubber. His trip to Ibiza exemplifies the mix of survival, hedonism, and adventure that constitutes many young migrant male sex workers' journeys through Europe.

> I was here in the train station with three euros in my pocket, and I asked myself what to do here. It was summer, many people out. And I ask where things are, and I went there, and it was full of Romanians, and they help me with place to sleep. They taught me how to sit in a bar and what to do if you see that a man wants you. How to talk to him and fix the price. In the beginning I was new, and they all like me; they offered me €500! It impressed me. It was nice, OK. I was with three men in the night. Making a lot of money. And after that friends called me to go with them to Paris. We stay four days. There I make two queers at the Gare du Nord and in a wood. Then I went to Marseille; after that I go to Valencia, because I wanted to go to Ibiza, but I didn't have money to go there by ferry. So I go to Seville for one day, because it was on the way. We didn't have money. So we go in supermarket and buy salami and bread. In Seville I ate the last day. Then it was very bad. I go by train back to Marseille. After we go to Saint Tropez, Cannes, Nice. We didn't eat for two and a half days. When we arrived in Saint Tropez at night, everything was closed. We found food in the garbage, and we ate it. Two days later I go back to Cannes and meet a few girls. . . . We were wearing very good clothes and got into a free party. We went back to the room with two Russian girls to fuck. We stole their cameras, money, mobiles, jewelry, everything. I stole €400, and we sold the rest to other Romanians, because it's a network. With the money we went to Ibiza.

The complex interweaving of marginalization, hedonism, and experimentation that characterizes young men's accounts and experiences of mobility mirrors the complex ways they selfrepresented and experienced their sexual selves. This is another facet of the interconnection between neoliberal, hegemonic masculinities, mobility, and selling sex discussed in chapter 2. After emigration, young migrant men reposition their heterosexual, sex-gendered selfrepresentations and identities within a new social, cultural, and economic environment. On the one hand, migrants' practice of sex work abroad is consistent with the hegemonic negotiation of the relationship between masculinities and sexual conduct in their home countries: hence "fucking queers." On the other hand, engaging in sex work in Europe often means experimenting with relationships, lifestyles, and desires that have the potential to destabilize preexisting sex-gendered selfrepresentations and experiences. As I argue in the remainder of this chapter, it is the psychological ability to navigate this complex, subjectifying scenario that distinguishes *errance* from more agentic mobility patterns. Before I get to that, however, in the next section I introduce the geometrical concept of the fractal to explain how migrants working in the sex industry experience and manage contradictory sex-gendered representations and roles across intersecting transnational social fields and migration spaces.

Between Errant and Minor Mobility

In *Entry Denied,* Eithne Luibhéid (2002) suggests that the state monitors migrants' movements through the inscription of racialized, class-based, and sex-gendered narratives onto the migrant body, as well as through legal, political, and economic restrictions. The majority of the migrant minors and young adults I interviewed for my research were challenging these restrictions through discourses and practices that remained "tacit" (Decena 2011)—that is, not explicitly verbalized—in relation to LGBT criteria of sexual orientation and identification disseminated from the Global North. These tacit discursive and embodied practices framed young men's involvement in migration and sex work as only (or predominantly) related to survival, and selfrepresented them as straight men "fucking queers." Such practices allowed these young men to remain connected to their peer groups and wider ethnic communities, both abroad and at home. At the same time, by mobilizing tacit discourses and engaging in embodied practices such as migration and sex work, they could have sex with other men without having to internalize undesirable and stigmatized sex-gendered orientations and identities. They could also challenge class-related, ethnicized, and sex-gendered restrictions on social and international mobility.

To underline the intersectional relevance of class in the adoption of these tacit discourses and embodied practices, I introduce the concept of "boditarian cosmopolitanism." The term *boditarian* emphasizes the prevalence of bodily over self-reflexive and verbalized dimensions in young migrant men's mobile orientations. Migrant male minors and young adults selling sex can be seen as "boditarian cosmopolitans" because they challenge the heteronormative, class- and age-based exclusions from social mobility in force "at home," by displacing and using their bodies—the only means of production they own (Mai 2015). The notion of boditarian cosmopolitanism draws on studies of "vernacular" (Werbner 2006) and "subaltern" (Bonaventura de Sousa 2005) forms of "cosmopolitanism from below." These forms coincide with the formation of new, transnational practices and identities (Tarrius 2000), and express the participation of marginalized social groups in lifestyles and socioeconomic practices previously reserved for elites. By evoking the notion of the underprivileged proletarian together with that of embodiment, the concept of boditarian cosmopolitanism emphasizes the class-based salience of the embodied (rather than verbalized) aspiration to transcend the racialized and sex-gendered normative limits that restrict people's entitlements to socioeconomic and spatial mobility.

The boditarian prevalence of embodied and tacit practices that challenge restrictions on mobility and forms of normativity also highlights the "fractal" quality of the mobile orientations of migrant minors and young adults. The geometrical concept of the fractal refers to fragmented and irregular shapes whose scalar repetition creates forms of regularity (Mandelbrot 1982).

The concept of the fractal highlights the contradictory relation that connects irregularity to regularity through recurrence. It is therefore particularly useful for understanding the sex industry as an oxymoronic space of normative transgression in relation to the globalization of new and old sex-gendered normativities. This oxymoronic role reflects how prostitution has historically complemented heteronormative institutions by offering itself as a space where transgressive and stigmatized desires can be satisfied (Pheterson 1996). In social theory, the metaphor of the fractal has been

5. Romanesco broccoli is often used as an example of a naturally occurring fractal.

used to refer to the proliferation of "irregular" and marginalized spaces coinciding with neoliberal postindustrialism (Soja 2000). More recently, and most importantly for my argument, the concept has been used to frame the emergence of new, sex-gendered subjectivities through the creative challenging and reproduction of the division between public and private in postcommunist times (Roman 2007, 128–29).

By creating an international platform for sex work, the sex industry offers young migrants a fractal space in which they can afford, both economically and morally, to challenge established, heteronormative life trajectories and patriarchal gender/sexual roles "abroad," without taking full public responsibility for their actions "at home" (Mai 2012). These dynamics have a direct impact on the degree of agency characterizing the mobile orientations of migrant minors and young adults. Selling sex abroad enables many migrant minors and young adults to tacitly negotiate their mobile orientations in fractal terms. For instance, by working in the sex industry abroad, many young men and women are able to engage privately in transgressive sexual practices, while publicly embodying and performing heteronormative subjectivities in ways that allow them to fully participate in their ethnic socialities. Against this emancipatory and empowering perspective, it is important to emphasize that young migrants, particularly minors, often find it difficult to sustain the moral and psychological contradictions that emerge from their fractal involvement in sex work, and this in turn can lead them to become implicated in "errant" mobility patterns.

On the basis of people's ownership of the material and psychological terms of their own mobile orientations and subjectivities, I identify two separate but interlinked mobility patterns: minor and errant mobility (Mai 2009a). The concept of "minor mobility" aims to capture the agentic potential informing migration. It draws on Deleuze and Guattari's (1986) concept of "minor literature" to draw a parallel with the way a majority literary language can be politically deterritorialized and "owned" from a marginalized or minority position. The parallel lies in the way migrant minors and young adults reinterpret globalized and commodified youth culture according to their own boditarian and fractal experiences of subjectification. Against this empowering potential, I identify "errant mobility" as an unresolved liminality. Errant mobility is characterized by the inability to deterritorialize socially and psychologically from "home" and reterritorialize elsewhere.

As mentioned in the previous chapter, the French term *errance* emerged in the early 1990s as a social intervention framework that resisted the securitizing approaches to migration that were prominent under the right-wing Sarkozy government of the time. The term instituted a field of social research that was able to identify specific aspects of psychosocial vulnerability. Within this field, the work of the psychoanalyst Philip Gutton is particularly significant, because it investigates the relationship between errant mobility and psychological dynamics, notably in papers published in the journal *Adolescence* (Gutton and Slama 1994). According to Gutton, adolescents involved in errant mobility experience a "rupture of intergenerational filiation"—an interruption of their history of attachment to and detachment from parents—which leads to a failed separation between internal and external space. In the process, mobility acquires a fetishistic connotation, and becomes a spatialized attempt to restage the structurally incestuous scene of failed separation from the primary idealized object, the (phallic) mother. This takes place through (male) adolescents' search for possible "idealised objects of completeness" in "real space": "heterosexual" objects embodying the child's fantasy of omnipotent union with the phallic mother, and "homosexual" objects embodying the child's ambivalence between idealization of and disappointment with the father (Gutton and Slama 1994, 66–67). As "real" union with these figures of projection is psychologically unsustainable, young men engaging in errant mobility can be seen as constantly replaying the same scene of interrupted individualization in different locations.

As I reflected on this psychoanalytic conceptualization of errant mobility, my thoughts often went to young men's narrations of their relationships with trams (to use their own emic terminology). Although young migrant men often presented living with trans female sex workers as an inevitable "economic necessity," there were many aspects of their relationships that echoed Gutton's failed Oedipal script of separation. Trans women might be seen as embodying the combined unconscious fantasies of the omnipotent phallic mother and the disappointing/idealized father. In the context of young migrant men's sex-gendered selfrepresentations, which are shaped by a clear-cut dichotomy between masculine and feminine, the figure of the tram represents a form of mediation and reconciliation on different levels. First, since selected aspects of the behavior and appearance of trams are perceived as female, young men can afford to have sexual and emotional relationships with them without feeling exposed to homophobia, including their own. Secondly, trams' generally superior economic position usually allows them to act as "sugar mamas/daddies," providing young men with the preferred selfrepresentation of "only doing it for the money," which further soothes their own homophobia. Thirdly, as most trams are more experienced than the young men, both in selling sex and in life in general, they also become sources of protection, guidance, and emotional support. In the following excerpt, Claudiu openly explains that one of the advantages of having a relationship with a tram is the opportunity to be taken care of in a pseudo-parental fashion. In particular, Claudiu contrasts the parental relationship offered by trams with the more "adult" role required by a relationship with a woman, which needs to be economically sustainable.

> You have to stay with trams, so that you have no problem. You form a couple with them and stay at their place. You can eat at their place, shower. . . . They can also help you, every now and then, with pocket money. . . . It's not like with a girl. . . . With a girl, you need money all the time. If you go out with her, you need to be able to buy her a drink, a bite to eat, . . . flowers. . . . And then . . . the tram controls you all the time, and he takes care of you as well. . . . He comes with you, buys you new clothes, . . . all things girls can't afford. He helps you with the money to send home. . . . The trans is like a father . . . and a mother at the same time. He cares about you, gives you advice, gives you a good example, so that you don't get in trouble. Because, when you need money, you must ask him. . . . When you are in trouble, you must call him; the same with your parents.

At the same time, protection comes at the cost of dependency and infantilization. The following excerpt from interviews with Florin reveals the intricate combination of protection, control, and sexual attraction that characterizes relationships between young migrant men and their tram partners.

> I lived with one of them. I was shocked because she was so beautiful. I was trying to look and see a man, and I couldn't. So perfect. [. . .] She was giving me money, . . . food, yeah. . . . It was the first man I fucked. But it was nice because I didn't feel his dick. [. . .] I broke up because I don't want to stay any more. When you are with somebody, you can't do what you want, and I'm a free spirit. . . . I want to go meet with girls and boys, do business. . . . She didn't give me enough money. Two to three euros to drink, no big money to have. And that was the reason why I said, "OK, I go," and she was OK with that. When I broke up with her, I made business with men.

These two excerpts show us clearly that, for many young men, engaging in sex work means getting involved in different kinds of relationships that offer different degrees of support, dependence, and autonomy, in both psychological and economic terms. The degree of agency characterizing their mobile orientations depends on whether they are able to make sense of their emotional lives and migration trajectories with the material, discursive, and psychological resources available to them.

For example, Tarek's story in the previous chapter shows that having a relationship with a young woman offers young migrants the chance to become men according to hegemonic and heteronormative sex-gendered selfrepresentations. But are these selfrepresentations socially, economically, and psychologically sustainable? Claudiu's experience in this chapter suggests that having a *rubia* girlfriend often prevents young men from accumulating the money they need to "become men" by arranging the objectualized deeds and material goods that form their desired mobile orientations. It also potentially prevents them from having sex with other men (if they want to) and from accessing transactional sexual relationships in which they are parented and cared for. Young migrant men often considered a relationship with a transgender sex worker to be a better response to the complexity of their needs, as trams provided them with money, sex, care, and advice. However, Claudiu's and Florin's words in the two extracts above also illustrate how the superimposition of the roles of parent and sexual partner, along with economic dependency, could have an infantilizing quality from which young men would tend to run away in the long term.

These dynamics are key to the agentic salience of the mobile orientations of migrant young men, some of whom can experience Europe as an idealized space charged with Oedipal characteristics. The psychological difference between errant and minor mobility lies in the subject's ability to separate from parents and transform the utopian quality of the initial narcissistic configuration into a more realistic one by achieving "the paradoxical balance between recognition of the other and assertion of self" (Benjamin 1988, 46). As far as sex-gendered identities are concerned, this post-Oedipal realistic shift corresponds to the subject's ability to manage the inherent ambivalence and instability of masculinity and femininity, in itself and in others (Benjamin 1998, 79). The questioning of heterosexual identification produced by male sex work was problematic for most of the young men I met through my multiple research projects, as it sat at odds with the hegemonic and heterosexual sex-gendered selfrepresentations that would allow them to become successful men.

It is the ability to reconcile contradictory sex-gendered selfrepresentations and experiences that distinguishes different levels of agency within young migrants' mobile orientations. The lack of post-Oedipal ownership of their own desire often prevents young migrants from either deterritorializing morally, socially, and psychologically from home or reterritorializing in the context of emigration. Consequently, whenever the reality they meet in Europe fails to meet their idealized fantasy of (phallic) Mother Europe, this fantasy is reprojected northward, according to an internalized hierarchy of Europeanness that leads from Seville and Athens to Amsterdam and London. As reflected in Tarek's wanderings (analyzed in chapter 3), errant mobility, in terms of its spatial mobility patterns, is characterized by the repeated clash between the utopian expectation of a linear and "easy" upward mobility in Europe and the reality of social marginality at every step. This repeated clash can be observed on two interconnected spatial and social levels. On a macro level, once a young migrant's utopian migratory project has failed in their first country of entry into the European Union, it is reproduced across other countries, ranked according to an upward trajectory of perceived Europeanness: first Italy, Greece, and Spain; then France and Germany; then the United Kingdom and the Netherlands at the top. On a micro level, having been excluded from the work, social, and recreational opportunities available to the citizens of the destination country, many young migrants settle on livelihoods that allow them to perceive themselves as successful through the eyes of their peer group and according to their sociocultural interpretation of hegemonic selfrepresentations of masculinity.

As previously described, all of the young migrants who participated in my research had tried working in the "straight," informal productive sectors traditionally available to young male migrants (notably construction and agriculture). Most had rejected those occupations, which they perceived as exploitative, and decided to work in the sex industry instead. Thus "owning one's own desire" is only one of the strategic aspects distinguishing minor from errant mobility. The ability to negotiate a post-Oedipal subjectivity is rooted in the psychological circumstances of each migrant minor and young adult, and is a key factor framing the agentic salience of mobile orientations. However, individual psychological circumstances also need to be measured against the brutal dynamics of social exclusion that young migrants face, both at home and during the migration process. Most of the young migrants I interviewed had been subject to similar social, economic, and cultural transformations in their countries of origin, which in chapter 3 I defined as engendering the "minorization of poverty" (cf. Jiménez 2004). They were also exposed to the harsh dynamics of social exclusion and stigmatization in the context of immigration. In this respect, "serial" migration (Ossman 2013), socioeconomic marginality, and criminalized and stigmatized livelihoods can be seen as aspects common to both minor and errant mobility.

Often, after multiple experiences of socioeconomic marginality, young migrants close their migratory journeys by returning to the country through which they first entered Europe. This country can be seen as a morally safer third space between home and the potentially destabilizing experiences of Western modernity. The fear of "losing themselves" morally after having engaged in stigmatized and criminalized practices attracts them to places whose moral and social worlds they perceive as more culturally "intimate" with their country of origin (Herzfeld 2005). This is usually Italy for Romanians, Greece for Kurds, either Italy or Greece for Albanians, and Spain for Moroccans. These "return" places are the result of a mediation between the (ambivalent) desire to return to the country of origin and the impossibility of doing so "empty-handed"—that is, without a history of successfully becoming adult that can be proved with commodified deeds and possessions such as expensive clothes, visible plans to improve the household, cars, and gadgets (mobile phones, etc.). In the excerpt that follows, Alexander, a twenty-one-year-old Romanian man living in Amsterdam, frames his return to Italy as an idealized return to a (hetero)normative mobile orientation that is different from the one he is inhabiting—one that probably never existed in the first place and that he reconstructs retrospectively.

ALEXANDER: I would like to go back to Italy, . . . maybe because it is more similar to Romania. . . . I don't know, I think it's the single country in which I could settle down. . . . I want to go in two months and work legally. Because I want to have a regular job, my house, to own things. I want to give. I want to go to Italy, meet a girl, have a family. It's time. It's everybody's dream.

NICOLA: And what about the life that you live here?

ALEXANDER: I close it like a book.

The migratory project of most young, migrant sex workers involved in errant mobility encompasses a strategic myth of return (Zetter 1999) to a regime of normality and discipline. This is an imagined and complete reterritorialization into hegemonic canons of successful and heterosexual masculine adulthood, as shown by the following excerpt from an interview with Ovidiu, a twenty-year-old Romanian man living in Amsterdam.

> I am saving money, you know. I have an account in Romania, and I am saving money to buy a house, . . . a car, . . . to have a better life. . . . I am not planning to go right now, but in ten years, when things will have developed

> there. . . . I need to get together enough money to start a business. . . . You know what I want to do? I want to enroll in the Foreign Legion, for five years, and when I finish, I go straight to Romania and never get out again. . . . I want to close this life forever.

These Augustinian accounts of redemption into heterosexual normativity after the excesses of youth show young migrants' difficulty in "owning their own desires." They find it difficult to integrate the new experiences they have gathered during a liminal phase of exploration in an adult third space where all the heterogeneous components of their subjectivity can coexist (Mai 2007). Paradoxically, by relegating undesirable aspects of themselves to a past to be left behind, errant young people confine themselves to a world of unresolved psychological, moral, and geographical liminality within which they struggle to arrange their mobile orientations around the complexity of their actual desires, hopes, and needs.

Owning the Terms of Subjectivity

I did not manage to see Ciprian again after he showed me his tattoo. It had happened at the end of my stay in Amsterdam, after a drunken evening. I had thought the tattoo, with its fading and irregular lettering, was a rather brave and poetic gesture. I was amazed that he had done it himself. He had engraved the three letters LUX on the beginning of the shaft. He told me he had done it back in Romania, while he was preparing to go back to Amsterdam. He had inscribed his mobile orientation toward a utopian life of luxury on the only means of production he had ever owned. I could not have found a clearer example of boditarianism if I had invented it.

Ciprian's mobile orientation was characterized by the prevalence of an errant sensibility. I do not think he owned the material or psychological terms of his moral orientation. This was exemplified by his understanding of his own future as an Augustinian redemption into the neoliberal, commodified, and heteronormative canons of "normal life" after the excesses of the past. A few months before he showed me his boditarian engraving, Ciprian had told me that he wanted to go to Spain, in order to "leave it all behind" and "live normal." "I want to find one job. One wife, my house, my car, some money, I can have one, two children. This is my dream," he told me. But I doubt whether he ever went to Spain. I do know that he had a substance abuse problem and that it was getting out of control. People in bars started to avoid him because he kept asking them for money. I don't know what happened to him. A couple of nights before I left Amsterdam, he started flirting with me as if I were a potential client. I was disappointed at first, as we had become quite close, and we had always agreed on the nature of our relationship. But I could see he was high and thought nothing of it. The next day he could not even remember it.

As for Florin, his mobile orientation was characterized by the prevalence of a minor sensibility, which translated into a more definite and realistic mobile orientation. From the moment I met him, Florin was adamant that he wanted to continue his studies, and that "this" was only a transitional phase in his life. The last time I saw him, we bumped into each other in the street a few days before I left Amsterdam. He was a bit high and very excited. He invited me to go with him and a young woman to her flat to take drugs and have a threesome. We laughed, but I declined as politely as I could. I was glad of the invitation, as it was an indication that he could own and voice his desire; that, albeit tacitly and fractally, he did own some of the terms of his mobile orientation. Just a few days earlier, during an interview, Florin had told me that he also wanted to have "two kids, a beautiful wife, a nice car, money, a nice job, to have a life, not like this." However, when asked what he liked about "this life," he did not say "only the money" as everybody else did. He hesitated a little and then said, "Well, you know, I'm a clubber. All my life I've been a clubber. Everywhere, starting from Romania. Clubs, girls, party . . ." I guess he was able to be honest with himself and with me about most of his priorities and desires. The last time we were in touch, four years after we had last seen each other, he replied to an e-mail I had sent to wish him a happy Easter. He said that he was fine, and that he was looking forward to working in Ibiza in the summer and hoped to meet me there. A few years ago I checked his Facebook profile. He had finished university back in Romania, and his life consisted of clubbing, work, family, and friends. He was able to pull his mobile orientation together.

In this chapter I have focused on the tacit and fractal ways in which male minors and young migrants challenge and reproduce the sex-gendered, class-based, and racialized restrictions on social and spatial mobility that they encounter at home and abroad. I have also analyzed the implications of these dynamics for the degree of agency characterizing their mobile orientations and embedded agencing decisions. By distinguishing the more emancipatory minor mobility from errance, my analysis walks a difficult line: on the one hand, avoiding the generalized pathologization and victimization that characterize hegemonic analyses of child and youth migration; on the other, acknowledging the potential and specific elements of vulnerability that can emerge. In the next chapter, I extend this analysis to the experiences of young men "performing love" in order to "parlay their access to foreign tourists into marriage proposals and visa sponsorship" in Tunisia (Brennan 2004, 91–100). These young men's mobile orientations are characterized by similar dynamics of idealization, agency, and loss in relation to the possibility of "becoming men" in Europe.

FIVE

Burning for (Mother) Europe

"In my life I have two things. The first thing is my mother. The second is Europe. If this year I am not going to Europe, I'll kill myself. Because I don't like it here. I don't like this country. Europe . . . or finish. Finish everything."

That is how the interview with Ahmed began. I was surprised by this start to the interview; he had not given me the impression of being so desperate. He was one of the two leaders of a group of young men, to whom I refer as the Tourist Shop Boys, working for commission at a tourist shop at the entrance to the Medina of Sousse. Our friendship and the context of the filmed interview provided Ahmed with the opportunity to show a different and less agentic side of himself.

The situation in which I was interviewing him was awkward. We were only a few meters away from Ivana, the thirty-year-old female tourist from Poland he was (working) with at the time. She was talking to her friend on the large rooftop terrace of the apartment Ahmed had rented for her holiday. Her five-year-old daughter was playing around us. It helped that they did not speak much English and that the terrace was huge. However, we felt it better to be safe than sorry, and we sat at the other end, Ahmed facing the sun, and me sitting in front of him, the camera between us.

My participant observation of Ahmed's everyday life and my reflection on the encounters and relationships that occurred during the fieldwork are the red threads running through this chapter, which presents an intimate, autoethnographic account of young men working as "professional fiancés" with female tourists in Sousse, on Tunisia's Mediterranean coast. The term *professional fiancé* draws from Heidi Hoefinger's work (2011) on the sentimental and economic relations through which "professional girlfriends" working in the tourist sex industry in Cambodia negotiate lives connected to the mobilities, lifestyles, responsibilities, and selfrepresentations engendered by globalized neoliberalism (Zelizer 2005, 37). Building on Hoefinger's work, I introduce the term *professional fiancé* to highlight that the Tourist Shop Boys performed love primarily to obtain access to international mobility through marriage visas. This chapter analyzes the affective, intersubjective, and embodied practices that characterize the forms of "intimate labor" involved, including sex (Boris and Parreñas 2011). The chapter also analyzes the process by which *Mother Europe*, the second film in my *Sex Work Trilogy*, was shot in Sousse and later reedited. It describes how postproduction stylistic and editing choices evolved in relation to post-fieldwork reflections on the politics and ethics of the representation of a very stigmatized group of people: young men selling sex and performing love to female tourists.

Burning Businessmen

"Our job? I guess we are businessmen, small businessmen," said Bilal, a nineteen-year-old friend of Ahmed. They were sitting side by side on the balcony of the villa where I was staying, on the beachside outskirts of Sousse. I had invited them for a joint video interview about their job for the documentary I ended up making in Tunisia. Although the documentary and the research informing it were not my original reason for being in Tunisia, I had decided to look more closely into the intimate economy around me while I was there on holiday. The first time I went to Tunisia, in August 2003, I was not planning to undertake any research. In my mind this was a relaxing family holiday. I was going to be sharing accommodation and time with my mother and a large group of family friends. I had not expected to be participating in Sousse's intimate economy—"the ongoing and dynamic interaction between market economies and intimate realms of life" (Wilson 2004, 189)—just by being there.

"Businessmen? What's all this nonsense of business? . . . We are sellers! We work in tourist shops during the summer, and then live off the savings for the rest of the year!" Ahmed responded quickly. By refusing to describe himself as a businessman, Ahmed was trying to avoid the stigma associated with the practice of *bezness*. The Tunisian term *bezness*—an amalgam of *baiser* (French for "fucking") and *business*—is currently used to stigmatize young men who sleep with female tourists from the Global North for financial and other gain.[1] According to *Tunisian Love Rats*, a website alerting female tourists to the dangers of so-called love rats in Tunisia, the term generally refers to "the pretention of love feelings toward women with the sole objective of gaining financial or material benefits or a residence permit in a Western country, preferably in Europe."

By framing themselves as economic entrepreneurs, Ahmed and the other young men working at the shop were selfrepresenting according to hegemonic neoliberal canons of masculinity, which is supposed to be informed by agency and rational risk-taking (Marques 2010; Freise 2013). However, their determination to leave Tunisia at any cost, including their own lives, can be seen as undercutting the rationality and agency of their decision to migrate: "I have got to get out of here. I can't stand this place any more. Europe . . . or finish. Finish everything." Ahmed framed his migration to Europe as an existential necessity that was embedded in his mobile orientation, in the meaning and experience of becoming the kind of man he was subjectified to be.

The other Tourist Shop Boys shared Ahmed's mobile orientation. Most of them had attempted to reach Italy several times, and they considered themselves *harragas*, just as the young Moroccan men selling sex in Seville's moral region had done. The term *harraga* comes from the Arabic verb *harga*, meaning "to burn"; it refers to young men burning their papers and, more generally, "burning" (i.e., yearning) for Europe. Prevailing media and policymaking representations of *harragas* obfuscate the rationalities and agencies involved in their decision to migrate by focusing on images of the numerous deaths caused by the ruthless enforcement of EU borders on the Mediterranean (Nair 2007). However, Ahmed and the other Tourist Shop Boys saw themselves as both rational risk-takers and brave entrepreneurs. For them and many other *harragas*, staying at home would be tantamount to social suicide in the face of the impossibility of following their mobile orientations and of "belong[ing] in what is experienced and described as an unjust social order" (Pandolfo 2007, 333). "Europe or nothing," in Ahmed's words.

The first time I saw Ahmed, he was trying to send tourists the correct "hooking code"—the self-advertising courting routines he used to attract potential tourist girlfriends—as they passed by the front of the shop. The hooking had to happen fast, as the flocks of tourists only stayed in the shop's visual and acoustic catchment area for about a minute. It took place in the "affective atmosphere" (Anderson 2009) of the Medina, which is characterized by transactions, connectedness, and transience. "Sweet boy, good boy, one hundred percent American style!" was one of his favorite hooking leitmotifs. It produced the desired effect, or rather the desiring affect required: female tourists started to smile and stopped walking. Like the Brazilian "*garotos de programa*" studied by Gregory Mitchell (2016), Ahmed knew exactly how to mobilize and perform the racialized and sexualized canons of masculinity affecting the intimate economy he was working in. By strategically performing his looks to attract tourists, he was working the geopolitical, racialized, and sexualized terms of colonial and postcolonial desire that encompass the Tunisian tourist industry (Young 1995).

Within the affective practice of "hooking up," the main issue was to connect with the transiting tourists by looking at them, guessing their country of origin, and saying something funny and specific in their language: a codified and commodified signal to elicit attention for goods and seller alike. In order to make people stop and listen, the Tourist Shop Boys had developed a repertoire of regional and vernacular expressions that transcended the merely national. Ahmed and his colleagues could make jokes in Russian, Italian, French, and Spanish (and many more languages) with reference to popular films, television programs, news items, and so forth. Their affecting skills were impressive.

The shop was just beyond one of the main entrances to the central souk, next to a tearoom popular with market traders and Tunisian families. The group of Italians I was traveling with was an easy target. Tunisians are particularly familiar with Italian popular culture, to which they have been exposed mainly through Italian television, whose signal can be picked up thanks to the two countries' geographical proximity. After a few funny jokes, we were willing to go along for the ride, and we all bought something we could pretend we needed in order to reward the Tourist Shop Boys' efforts and be able to leave. One of them, aptly nicknamed Sexy Boy, looked me in the eye for that special extra moment that made me wonder whether more was on offer than was officially displayed. I felt that it was, and I decided to go back the next day to have a closer look.

That's how my fieldwork began. I started going to the shop and drinking tea at the adjacent café almost every day after the beach, and I rapidly became acquainted with Fouad—Sexy Boy's real name—and later with most of the group. Their selling techniques were fascinating, and I was intrigued by their assemblage of fashionable sportswear, which I interpreted as a form of "conspicuous consumption" (Veblen 1899) enabling them to participate in globalized and commodified youth culture. Right at the beginning of my Tunisian fieldwork, I became a business prospect for Sexy Boy; I later understood that he had told the others to stay away from me. I liked Fouad, but not for the reasons he wanted. I thought he was interesting, hard-working, and daring. At first he tried hard to get into my pants and my wallet, and I tried hard to let him know that I knew exactly what he was doing, without offending him. "Later we talk about everything," was his silencing leitmotif, his discursive escape route whenever I asked direct questions that pointed at what was "really" going on. But this tension was not all there was between us. I think he appreciated my sexually uninterested curiosity about his life, as well as my company. So after a while he relaxed and allowed me to come closer to him as a friend.

This all became clear to me one night when Fouad invited me home for tea with his parents. I was surprised by this sudden invitation, which marked a transformation in our relationship toward greater mutual understanding. It was a very informative visit. I discovered that Fouad and most of the Tourist Shop Boys lived in the same semiperipheral neighborhood, which was inhabited by second- or third-generation internal migrants from adjacent cities and villages—the boys' parents. Although the neighborhood was not affluent, it was under active reconstruction. Most buildings were being renovated with money from the tourist industry and related service sectors. Other renovations were financed by remittances from international migrants who had "made it" abroad. From the degree of completeness and the quality of materials used to build the family homes, it was easy to distinguish those financed with foreign money from those built on Tunisian work.

Since the 1960s, mass tourism had been actively promoted by the state, becoming a major axis of economic and social modernization in Tunisia. Its impact was strong and pervasive, particularly in coastal areas. In 2010 it represented 6.5 percent of Tunisia's gross domestic product and directly or indirectly employed 12 percent of the population (Belloumi 2010). Attracted by such opportunities, the parents of the Tourist Shop Boys, including Fouad's father, had migrated to informal settlement areas on the periphery of Sousse and had obtained low-skilled jobs in the tourist industry as caretakers, gardeners, or builders. By moving to Sousse and working in the tourist-led modernization of Tunisia, they were able to support their families. However, their incomes were overtaken by those generated from their sons' involvement in the forms of "intimate labor" introduced by the neoliberal service economy that encompassed tourism (Boris and Parreñas 2011).

Fouad's place was a small house on two floors. The ground floor and walled private area surrounding it had almost been completed; money was being saved for the building of the other floor. I was received with a mixture of curiosity, respect, and diffidence on his father's part. Fouad's father was lying on the sofa because of a back injury incurred at work, while we all sat on the carpet below him. His symbolic dominance over us was undermined by his injury and by the fact that Fouad was the main earner in the family. As Fouad introduced me to his father, I understood why I had been invited: to further shift the household power dynamic in Fouad's favor. My presence embodied the new economy of intimate labor, which Fouad was infinitely more equipped to navigate than his father, who had worked as a hotel caretaker for many years. I had been invited into an intergenerational power struggle. The second, related reason I had been invited to the family home had to do with a more direct challenge to parental authority. My presence was a way for Fouad to win the right to go out that night. My profile was meant to undermine the father's curfew. It worked. After a couple of biscuits and rounds of tea, we were allowed to leave.

Fucking "Tourirists"

"There are no tourists here in Sousse. Only fucking tourirists. Five million people come to Tunisia each year, looking for sex and sunshine. They don't make any shopping. They buy nothing," Ahmed once told me.[2]

"What's the difference between tourists and tourirists?" I had to ask.

"Real tourists spend money. They go to the restaurant, buy stuff. They give. Tourirists are cheap. They stay in their all-inclusive cheap hotels and are only interested in sex. They come here for the Tunisian banana. We call them tourirists because to us they are like terrorists—they destroy everything for us."

I was impressed by this forceful appropriation of the Islamophobic terrorist stereotype to strike back at the impact of tourism from the Global North. That's how *Fucking Tourirists* became the working title of the second movie in my *Sex Work Trilogy*. The title was also inspired by Glen Bowman's seminal essay "Fucking Tourists," which analyzes how Palestinian men challenge geopolitical and socioeconomic inequalities by having sex with foreign female tourists (Bowman 1989).

In the first version of the film, I superimposed my tourist videos of Sousse's Medina and beaches onto a faded (to protect his identity) version of Ahmed's video interview. I wanted to capture the way his mobile orientation was assembled within an intimate environment where everything was commodified around the relational and material needs of the tourist industry. "I sell everything tourists want!" Ahmed told me half-jokingly one day, with a cheeky grin hinting more at his evening job than his day job in the tourist shop. But his suggestive humor left me cold. It was his more intimate and desperate reappraisal of the commodified affective and psychological landscape he inhabited that captured my attention as our relationship developed. On the balcony that night, when he laid himself

6. *Mother Europe*: The commodified everyday life lived by the Tourist Shop Boys.

bare to me, Ahmed's seductive buoyancy in the face of female tourists and his peers dwindled before my eyes. While the sun set on the Medina, he let me know about the economic pressure he was under.

"My mother wants me to stay in Tunisia. She needs everything. She needs me; she needs money. Only I give money for my family," Ahmed told me.

"What happens if you are not able to give money?" I asked.

"They tell me to leave. I don't care, because I have lots of friends and girlfriends, Tunisian girlfriends. . . . I have a Tunisian girlfriend, and she gives me money every day. Because she loves me very much."

It was the first time he had talked about her, or mentioned love outside the context of his work as a professional fiancé. I was intrigued by his implicit association between love and "giving money," and wanted to understand more about how it worked. "Do you love your Tunisian girlfriend?" I asked. His answer made me understand the way his economic pressures had pervaded his intimate world.

"No, I don't love anybody. Not even myself. I love only one thing, my mother. She is something special for me. I live now with tourists without this [pointing to his heart]. It's now with my mother. She keeps it clean for me. Everything I do is for my mother." He still had a sardonic smile on his face, but the tone of his voice was increasingly sad. "In the last month I could not give anything to my family. We have arguments all the time because of this. I spent 135,000 dinars. . . . For this work . . ." He looked toward the apartment, to make sure he could not be overheard. ". . . For these twenty days. Sixty-five thousand dinars for the flat, then for the food, the drinks, everything. You need to do all this if you want it to work. The plan. But the day I get the papers, I will stop all of this. I will leave her and go, directly. That is the plan," he said with a smile, his voice now brightening. "To get the papers and make money, in Europe. To have the money to have a car, a nice house. A relaxed life. A normal life. It is possible here, but it is very expensive. Impossible for me."

I wanted to know more about the plan. "How does it work?" I asked.

Ahmed explained that in order to be successful, he had to give the European woman a good "impression of love." That meant being able to provide a credible representation of a viable breadwinner, including paying for the flat and for food while she was visiting, and also going to work during the day. "To show her that you are a good man," he added. Being a "good man" also meant strategically refusing gifts and "going Dutch" with money, in order to perform love in accordance with the separation between economic and intimate spheres that characterized their tourist partners' cultural constructions of romantic love (Hoefinger 2011).

"What else do you have to do to prove that?" I asked.

"You have to introduce her to your family. I took her home to meet my mother last week, but she refused to talk to her. My mother does not want me to do this. Ivana is not the first tourist I bring home like this, you know . . ."

These practices are not dissimilar to those analyzed by research in the Caribbean that shows how the strategic performance of family inclusion and poverty can be used to encourage the generosity of clients (Padilla 2007, 157). The love performance of professional fiancés in Tunisia of course also includes lots of sex, which was presented as an indispensable trust-building device. "If you want Europe, you have to fuck her every day. Every day. That way she'll know you love her. If you don't, you are in trouble. I don't like fucking every day. It's too much, but it's important. If you want Europe, you have to fuck Europe, and a lot!" We laughed, but I felt sad for him: under the weight of so much pressure, with so many commodified conditions imposed on his being loved and respected by his family and peers.

I also felt worried about Ivana, particularly after I had heard the details of the plan. Having made doubly sure she was not listening, Ahmed lowered his voice and told me, "She is very sick, you know? The heart. Very bad. She has a doctor appointment in February to know if she makes the operation or not. I want to make marriage and the papers before." It was September 2004. I looked at Ivana talking to her friend. They were smoking on the other side of the large terrace. Her little daughter was playing in the large space between us. I felt both privileged and ashamed at having become aware of the plan. I started to think of ways to let her know what was going on, without betraying my allegiance to Ahmed. His behavior was framed by the impossible situation in which he was placed by the contradictory expectations and priorities of his family; his desire to lead a "successful," individualized, and normal life; the lack of opportunities to sustain his aspirations; and his agencing decision to leave Tunisia as the only solution, whatever it took. At the same time, I kept thinking how dangerous the situation was for Ivana.

It was not the first time I had felt an ethical unease about the Tourist Shop Boys' performances of love to female tourists, although I had never felt the urge to intervene until now. During fieldwork I often sensed that most tourist women's romantic "cultural scripts of love" as detached from economic interests exposed them to the danger of being manipulated (Frohlick 2009). My cultural scripts of love, while not framing it as necessarily devoid of instrumentality, do not understand love or its performance as primarily motivated by economic and other instrumental advantages. I guess that the consonance, albeit incomplete, between our cultural scripts of love made me identify with the women targeted by Ahmed and the other Tourist Shop Boys.

Elizabeth Bernstein (2007b, 103–4) analyzes "bounded authenticity" as "the sale and purchase of authentic emotional and physical connections." As I thought about Ahmed's life, I reflected on how emotional and physical connections were being negotiated through the metaphor of the "girlfriend experience" in the Global North. Was I witnessing a tacit and more unbalanced version of the consensual and transactional dynamics explored by Bernstein? A part of me thought so. Ahmed was arguably involved in a socioeconomically and geopolitically marginalized configuration of those same globalized dynamics. He was providing his female tourist partners with an experience of bounded authenticity and intimacy, which they framed as romantic love in order to avoid the stigma associated with relatively older women from the Global North desiring younger men from the Global South. His specific experience of the convergence between liquid

7. *Mother Europe*: Young men "fishing" for female "tourirists" on the Tunisian beaches.

modernity and neoliberalism also made him merciless. The fact that he was counting on Ivana's heart condition made me decide that I needed to warn her.

The opportunity came just a few days later. We all met for coffee in the city center. Ahmed received a text about an urgent matter and disappeared. Suddenly I was alone with Ivana. "Do you think Ahmed is good man?" she immediately asked. I was both relieved and embarrassed by her asking.

Her English was poor, so I struggled to find words and phrases that would be clear but nuanced. I rehearsed and condensed some of the "truths" with which I had been providing other doubtful female tourists. "Life is very difficult for him. He has many problems with money. He needs many things. He wants to change his life." And then I added something a little more specific: "In the end, it's your decision if he's good for you or not." I felt I had been cautious and somewhat enigmatic, but honest. That was all I could say, almost in one breath. She listened and looked away. I was relieved. At least she looked pensive enough for me to think she had heard me. I kept reassuring myself by repeating in my head that I had been as fair as I could be, given the circumstances. Everything I said was true. I would have been lying if I had told her I believed Ahmed was a bad man. So I didn't.

A few days later, Ahmed, Bilal, and I remained silent for a while after the end of the interview at my beach house outside Sousse. They had to go back to their tourist fiancées, and it was getting late. We shared a taxi into town. As the small villas being built for tourists paraded along the road to Sousse, I kept thinking about Ahmed's impossible situation. His social role as a loyal son supporting his mother clashed with his aspiration to what he called "a more free and easy life in Europe." These contradictory expectations, and the limited opportunities to meet them in Tunisia, pushed him toward tourists and the associated possibilities of "making money" through intimate forms of labor.

I thought about Ivana, about how she had looked away pensively after we had spoken about Ahmed a few days earlier. I came to the conclusion that she, like Ahmed, was in an impossible situation, trapped between a serious heart condition and the desire to live her life. Like Ahmed, I thought, she might feel that she has nothing to lose. "If they ask me for a finger, I give. Normal for me," Ahmed had told me just a few days earlier while sitting on the terrace of the flat he had rented for her, for his project, for his future. I could not help thinking that she shared a version of this feeling, and that it was this shared existential condition that had brought them together. I also thought that perhaps she had suspended her disbelief and become absorbed in Ahmed's love performance because she needed to protect herself from the stigma and shame associated with her intimate encounter with a younger man from the Global South.

I left Tunisia just a few days later. I was looking forward to leaving. I needed to separate from and reflect on what I had experienced. I received missed calls from Fouad in the following months. I called him back sometimes. But that stopped too after a while. Ahmed never called; it was not his style. Gradually we lost contact. As I edited the video and interview material into the film two years later, I reflected on its focus. I removed the superimposition of Ahmed's profile, and only kept his voice over the footage from my tourist camera wandering through the Medina and beaches of Sousse. I wanted the film to emphasize the commodified environment that framed his mobile orientation and his sense of worth and belonging. By using my holiday footage, I also wanted to underline the ambivalent tourist-researcher position I came to occupy in Tunisia. I decided to focus the interview voiceover on Ahmed's persistent and contradictory allegiance to both his mother and Europe, which seemed to be contending over his subjectification. In homage to the unresolved liminality and Oedipal tension that characterized his mobile orientation, I finally called the film *Mother Europe*.

As I was revising the notes from my Tunisian fieldwork while writing this chapter, I was able to follow up on some of its protagonists. Having lived in Austria with his former wife, Fouad is now back in Tunisia, and works at the same shop. He is still working as a professional fiancé. Ahmed made it to Mother Europe by marrying a British tourist, with whom he no longer lives. The plan involving Ivana did not work out in the end.

Existential Mobilities

"I don't have a father any more," Ahmed once told me. Looking back as I write this book, I realize that none of my privileged witnesses felt they had a father: not Fatjon or Tarek; not Florin or Ciprian. They did all have fathers, in fact. But they did not look up to them as authoritative figures and sources of protection and support, for different and interrelated reasons. Ahmed lost (respect for) his father the moment he had to pay his gambling debts:

> I like my father, but he is not good for us. He spends two thousand . . . three thousand . . . four thousand dinars playing cards every night. Sometimes he brings twenty thousand when he wins. But that happens once every ten times he loses. And then he prays. My mother prays. I don't pray. Not any more. If my mother asks me to do something, I'll do it. But I will not do anything my father asks. I do nothing for him.

As I listened to Ahmed's words I thought about Fatjon. "My father is very good, you know," he told me one night. "He made lots of money after Enver,[3] by bringing stuff through the border. He is a good father. He opened a supermarket with the money. When I left for Italy with my cousin, he told me, 'Do what you have to do, just don't get in jail.'" I imagined a thirteen-year-old Fatjon, looking even younger than when I met him, being asked by his cousins to sell drugs to young Italians. "They called me 'the Albanian,' you know. Everybody liked me. They respected me because I was a sweet kid, but very smart."

I also thought about Tarek. He never mentioned his father or mother, except indirectly when he said he felt he could not go home empty-handed. He told me that they used to work in agriculture, and that now things were difficult. Both Ciprian and Florin mentioned their fathers as people who needed rather than provided support. As with Tarek's parents, their working lives had either ended or been strongly undermined by the convergence of neoliberalism and postindustrialism in Eastern Europe and North Africa.

Ahmed felt he had been let down by his father, by his family, and by formal education. "I left school earlier because I did not like it. I wanted to study to work in tourism, but my father said no. My brother already works in hotels, so he wanted me to study as a mechanic. I said no, so I stopped going to school. And now look at me; I have the worst job in Tunisia," Ahmed said while sitting on my balcony next to Bilal. He looked away to the beach, just two hundred meters away.

"But you get to live a version of the life you want by hanging around tourists, no? And you make much more money than if you were a mechanic," I prompted him.

"Yes, but in order to get money, you have to spend money. Drinks, cigarettes, going out, clothes. It's part of work. For tourists. I told you, the only way for me is Europe. Europe or nothing," Ahmed replied.

The economic and social sustainability of the families of the migrant men selling sex I met during my research was often threatened by the devaluation of local salaries and pensions, the postindustrial transformation of local economies, or the loss of a parent. However, very few of them had migrated in order to survive. The majority of them were socioeconomically disadvantaged, but they were not from the poorest sections of Albanian, Moroccan, Romanian, or Tunisian society. They had access to the minimum social (contacts and information) and financial capital required to plan and implement their migratory projects. These considerations refer to what Hein De Haas defines as the "selectivity of migration," referring to the fact that it is generally not the poorest who tend to migrate the most because of the investments and networks required (De Haas 2007, 15). For the majority, the decision to migrate was the agencing of a mobile orientation, restarting a project of desired social mobility that had become unviable at home. In many cases these migratory projects, as I discussed in chapter 2, emerged at home in relation to transcultural media consumption, the often glorified narrated experiences of returning migrants and their combined impact on local youth cultures, lifestyles, and the associated models of successful personhood. In this respect, and most importantly, for most young men, migrating was an opportunity, rather than a risk. It was the only opportunity they felt they had to become the kind of men they had already been subjectified into at home.

The Tourist Shop Boys saw working in the intimate tourist industry as an opportunity to become "successful men" according to the contradictory selfrepresentations that framed their mobile orientations. These self-representations required them to support their families while becoming proficient, individualized consumers. Framing young people's decision to work in the intimate tourist industry primarily in terms of their sexual, economic, and racialized exploitability by older and privileged (female or male) tourists (Sanchez Taylor 2006) does not account for how their intimate labor allows them to express their mobile orientations. Their engagement in intimate labor should not be seen as simply maintaining and reflecting socioeconomic inequalities, as Boris and Parreñas (2011) observe, but as actually and successfully reversing those inequalities, on their terms. It can be seen as part of a traditional economy of intimacy, expressing a sense of filial obligation that paradoxically, to paraphrase Wilson (2004, 93), makes them inappropriate men in order to be appropriate sons. By working as professional boyfriends and fiancés, they are renegotiating their parents' "modern" (often internal) migratory trajectories and livelihoods in a late-modern, globalized, and individualized context characterized by the rise of service and intimate economies.

In a parallel way, framing female tourists' involvement with professional fiancés exclusively in terms of exploitation and manipulation by local "love rats" does not account for the ways their desiring subjectivities are implicated. The balance between agency and exploitation in shaping these relationships is set by the tension between the pressures exerted by neoliberal social transformations on young men's intimate and economic lives and the cultural scripts of love through which female tourists understand their intimate encounters with younger men from the Global South. By framing such encounters in romantic terms to avoid the associated stigma, tourist women can become less alert to the potentially dangerous consequences of the pressures to "become successful men" felt by their male, nontourist partners. As we have seen in Ahmed's case, the subjectifying pressure exerted by the globalization of neoliberal, socioeconomic ontology can translate into violent forms of intimate labor, as young men are placed in impossible situations by the commodified demands posed by their combined traditional and late-modern roles and obligations.

By linking Ahmed's experiences to those analyzed in Rome and Seville in previous chapters, I want to underline the shared dynamics and processes linked to the global onset of the neoliberal onto-epistemology and its embedded and commodified "social rationality of success" (Winnubst 2012, 86). The mobile orientations of Ahmed, Fouad, Tarek, and Fatjon reflect this commodified rationality as they attempt to become successful men; this is mirrored by the existential impossibility of their returning (or staying) home "empty-handed." It is important to acknowledge the ritual connotation of young migrants' mobilities and the existential salience of their mobile orientations, which explains why their autonomous practices and desires always exceed governmental attempts to manage migration (Papadopoulos, Stephenson, and Tsianos 2008; Mezzadra 2010). As discussed earlier, for *harragas*, migration is not only a possibility; it is an existential necessity to become successful men according to the ways in which they have already been subjectified. That *harragas* risk their lives on dangerous sea crossings is simply a fact. However, addressing their need to migrate only in terms of poverty, vulnerability, and irrationality misses the agentic and existential resonance that the possibility of going to Europe has within their mobile orientations, within their sense of self. In the next chapter I draw on these considerations to address understandings and experiences of agency among key targets of sexual-humanitarian policies, interventions, and selfrepresentations: migrant women working in the sex industry. I focus on how the deployment of ironic affect in interviews with victims of trafficking facilitates the emergence of "contextual and relational" experiences of agency (Ham 2017, 17) that are essential if we are to understand the agencing decisions that enable and shape their mobile orientations.

SIX

The Trafficking of Migration

Alina entered the room hesitantly. It was an awkward situation for both of us: a research interview at the police station. Diego, the antitrafficking unit liaison officer, had briefed me on the confidentiality of the situation. As he left the room to look for Alina, we recapitulated the ethical terms of the interview. I was not going to know her real name, and she should be free to talk about what she felt comfortable with. I was grateful for the opportunity, and I was excited too. It would be the first time I had met a "certified" UK victim, someone who had actually been granted victimhood status through the National Referral Mechanism (NRM), a framework set up by the government to identify and support victims of trafficking in the United Kingdom. There are not many around. Only a minority of people working in the sex industry are trafficked, and even then, it is extremely difficult to gain recognition and be protected as a "real" victim.

Data from the Salvation Army, the organization awarded the NRM contract in 2011 to support victims of trafficking (for £2 million per year), provide an opportunity to discuss where and how individuals come into contact with support services, but they do not account for the difference between potential and actual victims. Although the annual report for 2016 shows that the organization supported 4,314 "potential victims" of trafficking between 2011 and 2016—45 percent of them potentially exploited in the sex industry—it does not mention that only a small minority were likely to be officially recognized as victims (Salvation Army 2016). The likelihood of a very low conversion rate from potential to actual (i.e., recognized) victims of trafficking is strongly corroborated by the results of the multi-agency antitrafficking operations Pentameter One and Two, conducted between 2006 and 2009, which "after raiding 822 brothels, flats and massage parlours all over the UK, finally convicted of trafficking a grand total of only fifteen men and women" (Davies 2009). Of the 167 "potential victims" initially identified by Pentameter One and Two, only 11 (i.e., 6.6 per cent) were recognized as "genuine" victims.

Do these data show that only a minority of people working in the UK sex industry are trafficked? They do. Loud and clear. So do the observations and data from health and harm-reduction services that support sex workers. This information is readily available and has been for some years. Yet, like all evidence surrounding sex trafficking, it is routinely and resolutely ignored, because it does not fit the sexual-humanitarian epistemology (and the implicit neo-abolitionist, antiprostitution agenda) embedded in prevailing governmental and nongovernmental policies, both in the United Kingdom and increasingly in the rest of the Global North. This is the case even when the evidence reflects the lives of people directly implicated in trafficking and officially recognized as victims. Alina was one of them.

Rhetorical Evidence

On 1 July 2009, as I watched the parliamentary discussion of the Policing and Crime Bill 2009 on television, I believed for a few hours that scientific research might actually inform policymaking on sex work and migration. My heart leaped when I saw that the research findings of the *Migrant Workers in the UK Sex Industry* project,[1] which I had completed just a few days before, were part of the debate. Baroness Miller of the Liberal Democratic Party used them as evidence to argue against the criminalization of clients, which the Labor government was trying to implement as a way to fight trafficking. The Policing and Crime Bill wanted to give the police even more discretionary power to close down premises arbitrarily "linked to sexual exploitation." It also sought to criminalize those who paid for sex with a person "subject to exploitative conduct," regardless of whether the client was aware that the person providing sexual services was a victim of trafficking, thus making the purchase of sexual services a "strict liability" offence.

The police criticized the applicability of the proposed legislation. For instance, Commander Allan Gibson, head of antitrafficking at the Metropolitan Police in 2008, emphasized that the legislation would be hard to enforce, especially given the lack of evidence about whether the majority of women working in massage parlors and brothels had been trafficked; he said that targeted research needed to be undertaken on the issue (Travis 2008). UK sex workers and the organizations representing their rights were even more critical of the proposal to criminalize clients, which they saw as exacerbating workers' vulnerability to exploitation, violence, and trafficking by pushing the industry farther underground. This situation was by no means unique to the United Kingdom. Globally, the Swedish model—which inspired what ultimately became the Policing and Crime Act 2009—has been strongly criticized by sex workers' rights organizations and harm-reduction services on the basis of evidence that the criminalization of clients further marginalizes and invisibilizes sex workers, who then become more exposed to violence, exploitation, and trafficking (Levy 2014).

It was precisely in order to respond to the opposing claims of neo-abolitionist organizations, sex workers' rights groups, politicians, law enforcement agencies, and projects supporting sex workers that I decided to submit the project *Migrant Workers in the UK Sex Industry* to the UK's Economic and Social Research Council (ESRC) for funding. The timing could not have been more relevant: the research was carried out across the period preceding and immediately following the passage of the Policing and Crime Act. The project was undertaken between 2007 and 2009, and produced one hundred in-depth, qualitative interviews with migrant women, men, and transgender people working in London's sex industry. The majority of participants were approached directly through their work contacts and, when appropriate, through their friends and colleagues. All interviews were conducted away from work premises so that research participants would be less likely to censor their remarks for fear of being overheard by people who potentially controlled them. The methodological approach incorporated sex workers as researchers and advisors, which allowed the project to gather the experiences of migrant groups that are particularly hard to reach because they are often stigmatized and marginalized. As with all the other projects I directed, the research combined ethnographic observation of sex work settings with semistructured interviews in order to analyze the strategic contradictions and continuities between preferred selfrepresentations and actual behaviors.

The main and most controversial finding of the project was that only a minority of the one hundred migrant sex workers who participated felt that they had been forced or trafficked. Specifically, approximately 6 percent of female interviewees felt that they had been deceived and forced into selling sex. The purposive composition of the research sample, the hidden nature of sex work and (even more so) of trafficking, and the qualitative methodology adopted by the project did not allow randomization, which meant that its findings were not statistically representative. However, the fact that only a minority of sex workers in the United Kingdom were trafficked was later corroborated by research conducted on risk factors associated with sexually transmitted infections and experiences of physical and sexual violence among sex workers in London (Platt, Grenfell, Bonell, et al. 2011, 2), and also by research carried out by the police on the trafficking of migrant women in the off-street prostitution sector in England and Wales (ACPO 2010, 5). Both of those studies used official UN indicators to determine the prevalence of trafficking and coercion. The second most relevant finding of my research was that the majority of migrants had decided to work in the UK sex industry in order to avoid being exploited in other sectors. These two interrelated findings should be enough, I thought, to dismantle the neo-abolitionist, onto-epistemological conflation of migrant sex work with exploitation and trafficking. They made the headlines in many news stories across the United Kingdom and internationally. However, even though they were the result of rigorous, peer-reviewed research, they were ignored by policymakers, politicians, and neo-abolitionist academics, whose own research had been debunked by the international research community.[2] My findings were too dissonant from the neo-abolitionist and sexual-humanitarian affective epistemology, which had started to prevail at that time, to be acknowledged.

The parliamentary debate on the Policing and Crime Bill on 3 November 2009 ideologically shrugged off the scientific research evidence demonstrating the harm that would be caused by the criminalization of clients and the arbitrary closure of flats where sex was being sold. Data gathered by researchers and project workers through years of hard work were swept away by a sexual-humanitarian (and intellectually dishonest) rhetoric, which morally "affected" the debate in terms of being with or against victims of trafficking. These are the words uttered by Attorney General Baroness Scotland of Asthal, on behalf of the Labor government of the day:[3]

> We are faced with a choice tonight: do we speak for the victims, do we stand up for those who have no voice for themselves, do we stand in the breach for them—or do we provide a cloak of anonymity and protection for those who do not wish to face what they do when they purchase sex from a woman or a man, quite often of tender years, who has been coerced or forced into that position?

None of these rhetorical questions referred to the evidence of the proposed measures' impact on sex workers' lives presented by Baroness Miller, who spoke against the clause (Clause Fourteen) criminalizing clients. Scientific evidence and rational argument were dismissed on an affective and rhetorical basis. This is what Baroness Howarth of Breckland said, referring to the acute suffering she had witnessed just a few days earlier at an event organized by neo-abolitionist organizations, who routinely invite victims of trafficking and ask them to perform their tragic histories of abuse for fund-raising and political purposes:

> Last night I listened to the stories of these women, who are all hoping desperately that noble Lords will support Clause 14. It will stop providers enslaving women, or at least deter them, because even if you are a user and not the pimp, you are complicit; there is no other way of looking at it. If you see some of the young women whom I have seen, there is no way in which you could not know, as the most reverend Primate the Archbishop implied, that they are damaged goods. They need to get out of that damage and live a life.

The use of the commodifying phrase "damaged goods" to refer to victims of trafficking clearly reflects their objectified status within neo-abolitionist propaganda. More importantly for my argument, the rhetorical equation of clients with exploiters and pimps refuses the possibility of any legitimate space for the purchase of sex between consenting adults, which is legal in the United Kingdom. The manipulative conflation of any approach that recognizes the complex understandings and experiences of agency and exploitation of sex workers with complicity in sexual exploitation is a typical tactic of neo-abolitionist activists, who often evoke the existence of an unqualified "pimp lobby," including dissident academics and sex work activists, to discredit any dissenting voice. This moral blackmail can be a powerful rhetorical tactic, and it encourages politicians and other public figures to publicly support neo-abolitionist policies so as to avoid being seen as complicit with trafficking or modern slavery. Sadly, the 2009 parliamentary debate on the criminalization of clients was no exception. As rational argumentation was overwhelmed by epistemological violence and sexual-humanitarian rhetoric, Baroness Miller withdrew the proposed amendments, and the law was passed. The provision criminalizing the purchase of sexual services from a person "subject to exploitative conduct" was adopted on affective and rhetorical grounds, not on the basis of the scientific evidence that had been reviewed in Parliament. Somehow the rhetorical evidence, along with the affective performances of suffering produced by the exemplary victims mobilized by neo-abolitionist activists and politicians, made for a more persuasive argument than evidence produced by publicly funded social research.

Moral Gentrification

The majority (81 percent) of police forces across England and Wales have not used Section Fourteen of the Policing and Crime Act 2009, which criminalizes clients purchasing sex from anyone "subject to exploitative conduct." Where it has been used, it has been used inappropriately to address "curb-crawling," the practice of driving slowly along a road while looking for sex workers (Kingston 2014). However, Section Twenty-one, which allows the closure of premises linked to undefined instances of sexual exploitation, has been used more consistently. As a result, migrant and nonmigrant sex workers have been further marginalized and made more vulnerable to violence and abuse. This is exactly what happened around the 2012 London Olympics, which proved to be an incredible funding opportunity for the antitrafficking sector, and a difficult time for migrant and nonmigrant sex workers in London (Perry 2012).

The implementation of antitrafficking brothel-closure orders in London is an exemplary study in how "sexualised spaces" can get caught up, in specific, sex-gendered ways, in processes of "neoliberal urbanism, spectacularization and gentrification" (Hubbard 2012, 196). It is also a grotesque illustration of the tragic consequences of sexual-humanitarian interventions. The combination of flat closures and the heightened policing of street sex work through fines and Anti-Social Behaviour Orders pushed many migrant women into working alone and in unsafe areas to avoid police controls. This is what happened to Mariana Popa, a twenty-four-year-old Romanian woman who was stabbed in the chest on 29 October 2013 while selling sex on a thoroughfare in the East London borough of Redbridge. When Mariana Popa was killed, the Metropolitan Police were running an enforcement campaign, Operation Clearlight, against sex workers in Redbridge. To avoid detection by patrolling officers, women had started to hide in less visible places and to work alone, thus becoming more vulnerable to violence and crime (Taylor and Townsend 2014).

Just a few months later, on 3 December 2013, Operation Demontere resulted in the closure of several brothels within and around the perimeter of an ambitious regeneration program that aimed to "redevelop" Walker's Court, one of the few remaining Soho streets that specialized in adult entertainment shops and venues. Police officers had gathered intelligence against Soho's sex workers for more than eighteen months, deploying undercover agents. Not one trafficking case was identified as a result of this entrapment operation. What follows is a long excerpt from an interview with Valbona, a twenty-nine-year-old female Albanian sex worker caught up in Operation Demontere, whom I interviewed in March 2014.

> Nobody objects to us being here in the neighborhood. We spend our money here. We eat, shop, we live here! We get along with everybody, and we are treated with respect, like everyone else. There is no place safer than Soho to work. In December they treated us as terrorists. One girl was handcuffed and put with the face in the floor. They crashed the door as if there was trafficking, but which trafficking are they talking about? The door is open here, there is no trafficking. If people wanted to leave they can leave. I have never met a trafficked woman here in Soho and I have been here for years! They too could not find any thing. They raided every flat in Soho and found nothing! [. . .] They did not arrest me because I did not let them. I kept asking them: why do you bother us all the time? Why? I am not a victim of trafficking. I am a victim of the police, coming here all the time. Now because of you I am a victim. Not because of sex!

During the interview Valbona underlined several times that she felt safe working in Soho, and that she felt accepted and respected in the neighborhood, a moral zone that has historically welcomed migrants, sex workers, and other marginalized social groups. However, she also highlighted the negative impact of antitrafficking police raids on her livelihood and safety at work, as clients stopped coming, and sex workers came to distrust the police. In her words,

> Since the raids it's gotten worse. Not only clients are much less, they are beginning to come back now. But we have lost the trust of the police, completely. We do not have confidence and are taking risks because we never call them now. Not after what they have done.

The experience of being less safe as a consequence of Operation Demontere was shared by Mirela, a thirty-five-year-old Albanian woman who was also present during the antitrafficking raid:

> Lots of things have changed since December. Nobody comes here now compared with before! And now we don't call them any more when things go wrong. Not after what they did. And that is dangerous for us, because there are lots of weird and dangerous people around this business.

Besides confirming previous research evidence on criminalization's negative impact on the lives and rights of sex workers, Valbona's interview damningly revealed the merging of humanitarian, governmental, and economic interests that produces sexual-humanitarian interventions, particularly when the latter map the contours of gentrification.

> They had been planning it for a long time, you know? It is not by chance that it maps so well with the redevelopment. Just think about this. Of the two flats on X street, they raided twenty-seven and twenty-eight because of trafficking, right? Well, we appealed in both cases, but we won back only twenty-eight. The flat that is not in the development area. The other, and it was often the same people there. They confirmed that we were controlled. That there was control, but no trafficking. What does this tell you?

In the months that followed Operation Demontere, the English Collective of Prostitutes denounced the operation as complicit with Westminster Council's sanitization of Soho, and managed to obtain the reopening of two of the closed flats by challenging the closure orders in court (McLennan 2014). By pointing out that only the flats that were outside the regeneration area were reopened, Valbona establishes a direct link between the timing and motivation of the raids and the gentrification of Walker's Court and adjacent areas. The gentrification was being proactively promoted by Soho Estates, a company belonging to the estate of the late pornographer and Soho property magnate Paul Raymond, whose spokesperson claimed that the redevelopment was part of its plan to regenerate the area and drive out "anti-social and criminal uses" (Kay 2014).

The gentrification of Soho through antitrafficking raids gained new momentum after the implementation of the Modern Slavery Act 2015, which consolidated previous offences related to trafficking and slavery, and expanded the focus of immigration law enforcement from sex work to all forms of labor exploitation. The more comprehensive approach introduced by the new legislation has meant that an increasing number of migrants in a variety of sectors are now being targeted as potential "slaves" and prosecuted for breaches of immigration law, which can lead to deportation. This happened with ninety-seven nail bar workers, who were arrested for immigration offences between 27 November and 3 December 2016 as a result of antislavery Operation Magnify, which raided 280 businesses across the United Kingdom. Fourteen of the ninety-seven cases were referred to the NRM, but it remains unknown how many of these were offered support as victims of modern slavery (*Telegraph* 2016). However, the sex industry remains a primary site of concern in the fight against trafficking and modern slavery. About a month earlier, on 20 October 2016, the Metropolitan Police had launched the antitrafficking Operation Lanhydrock and stormed six massage parlors in Soho and Chinatown in Central London. Although ten women were referred to a special reception center as potential victims of trafficking, it is unclear whether any were referred to the NRM. As a result of the operation, twenty-four arrests were made. Seven people were arrested for "controlling prostitution for gain," while seventeen others were arrested on immigration grounds and detained by the UK Border Agency, which was present during the raids. In the process the police confiscated £35,000 of individual sex workers' incomes (Mullin 2016).

Sex workers were not the only sexual-humanitarian casualties of the "hegemonic gentrification" (Sanders-McDonagh, Peyrefitte, and Ryalls 2016) implemented by Soho Estates, which also resulted in the closure of many gay venues deemed too "sleazy" for the wealthy elite they wanted to attract. The mainstreaming of Soho, London's main moral region, should be seen as an epiphenomenon of the wider dynamics of moral gentrification engendered by the global onset of neoliberal onto-epistemology. By "moral gentrification" I mean the contemporary neoliberal convergence of moral conservatism and economic gentrification, created by the increase in socioeconomic polarization and the hegemony of sexual-humanitarian rhetoric and values. The global rise of sexual humanitarianism corresponds with the imposition on the rest of the world of a North-centric, privileged, and profitable morality that does not recognize the ethical validity of migrants' difficult agencing decisions to sell sex (and sometimes endure bounded forms of exploitation) in the short term in the name of a better future for themselves and their families. In the process, the world's remaining moral zones are being sanitized by a privileged (mis)understanding of migrant agency that criminalizes underprivileged livelihoods as "trafficking" in order to make way for the ethical and economic priorities of reinvented corporate and non-governmental moralities.

The Rise of Sexual-Humanitarian Global Sentimentality

There was widespread bewilderment at the circulation of fake news during the 2016 US presidential campaign, which led to the victory of property developer and reality TV star Donald Trump. But as Oxford Dictionaries declared the 2016 Word of the Year to be *post-truth*—a circumstance in which "objective facts are less influential in shaping public opinion than appeals to emotion and personal belief"—I found myself wondering what all the sudden fuss was about. For scholars studying people's involvement in sex work, the militant circulation of neo-abolitionist "alternative facts" that conflate sex work with trafficking and dismiss any dissonant scientific evidence has been an everyday reality for a long time. However, the systematic obliteration within politics, public debates, and policymaking of scientific findings that draw on the complex and diverse realities of people working in the sex industry cannot simply be explained in terms of adversarial political militancy. It is one of the most visible markers of a shift away from modern epistemologies, authorities, and ethics under liquid modernity, which offers opportunities for democratization as well as for the unqualified debunking of scientific evidence and expertise (Sismondo 2017). This late-modern shift is dangerous because it enables the horizontal—that is, non-hierarchical and potentially democratizing—circulation and validation of both "conspiracist" and "popularized" versions of social critique (Latour 2004, 228). It also encompasses the emergence of a commodified, "post-humanitarian sensibility" that, according to Lilie Chouliaraki (2013, 5), supersedes the modern division between "the public logic of economic utilitarianism, applicable in the sphere of commodity exchange, and a private logic of sentimental obligation toward vulnerable others, applicable in the sphere of individual altruism and increasingly in institutionalised philanthropy." An example of this complex and contradictory interplay between commodification, moralization, and humanitarian interventionism, which Elena Shih defines as the "anti-trafficking rehabilitation complex," is the "commodity activism" of NGOs from the Global North that market "slave-free" goods produced by former sex workers, providing them with "the same exploitative labour relations that they claim to detest" (Shih 2015).

In our post-humanitarian, liquid, and neoliberal world, the merging of altruism and profit produces profitable moralities, solidarities, and epistemologies that can be subsumed under the heading of the human rights economy (Bernstein 2016). The post-humanitarian and post-truth shift coincides with the increasing prominence in social representations of "spectacular" rhetorical and visual repertoires that inscribe specific social groups as victims within human rights discourses that are an expression of the Global North (Hesford 2011). In order to understand the governmental and affective implications of this, it is important to recall US scholar Lauren Berlant's (2001, 53) notion of "national sentimentality," a "rhetoric of promise that a nation can be built across a field of social difference through channels of affective identification and empathy." The interplay of these dynamics plays a key role in the emergence of new forms of affective governance that are highly manipulative because they transcend the rational and evidence-based apprehension of reality. The rhetorical and affective spectacularization of prostitution as trafficking is pivotal to the establishment of a global sentimentality and governance—defined, paraphrasing Berlant, as a rhetoric of promise that a global humanity can be built across fields of social difference—that is the direct expression of the sexual-humanitarian and neoliberal onto-epistemology of the Global North in general and the United States in particular.

The rise of sexual-humanitarian global sentimentality is a powerful, onto-epistemological shift in hegemonic ways of understanding, representing, and intervening in social transformations. It coincides with the onset of humanitarian forms of governance based on a strategically simplistic representation of the growing economic inequality of world societies in terms of the contrast between a unified "humanity" and individual victims to be cared for (Rancière 2004). The increasing inequalities produced by neoliberalism in the Global North and the rest of the world are being reframed and obfuscated by the circulation of moralized and profitable sexual stories and their embedded rhetorical figures of humanitarian speech, such as the victim of sex trafficking. At the same time, for many undocumented migrants working in the sex industry, stories of sexual trafficking also act as powerful humanitarian biographical borders between recognition as an individualized subject of human rights and deportation. They legitimize antitrafficking campaigns that actively reproduce hierarchical social imaginaries within which women are both sexualized and subordinate (Andrijasevic 2007). By negotiating the sex-trafficking biographical border, migrants working in the sex industry potentially obtain the benevolence and protection they need. But it is only when people convincingly perform and embody those biographical borders that they become intelligible and believable.

These theorizations and concepts are important for my argument in this book, and also for my decision to make experimental ethnographic films as a strategic vector to disseminate my research findings. As I watched the parliamentary version of the sex-trafficking moral panic unfold before my very eyes, with its intellectually dishonest "post-truth" exaggeration of the number of victims, its ignorance of migrant sex workers' complex understandings of exploitation and agency, and its unqualified praise for damaging, antitrafficking police raids, my heart sank. It took me a while to accept what had happened—to understand why scientific evidence had not made more sense than the rhetorical and affective "truth" mobilized by neo-abolitionist politicians and activists.

While grappling with these issues, my thoughts went to the migrant women working in the sex industry whom I had met since I started working on this issue—to the intricate experiences of agency, autonomy, and dependency emerging from their life trajectories. The evidence I gathered through different but interlinked projects shows that the vast majority of people selling sex do so in order to avoid the increasingly precarious working conditions produced by neoliberal policies and politics. Most would rather deal with the people who enable them to leave their countries and work in the sex industry than be deported through an antitrafficking raid, even when they think that their relationships and working conditions are exploitative. My thoughts also went to the young men working as third-party agents whom I had interviewed in Italy and Albania. Most of them were from the same socioeconomic background as the women working with/for them and were subject to analogous social pressures. Many had voiced their ambivalence about their management role in the sex industry. But these voices and ambivalences—which inform the lived experiences of the people directly involved in the sex industry and the meanings they assign to their mobile orientations and agencing decisions—do not "make sense" according to the affective and rhetorical strategies characterizing sexual-humanitarian selfrepresentations.

As I watched my research findings being systematically ignored by policymakers, I decided I had to contextualize them within the affective politics of global sexual-humanitarian sentimentality. I also wanted to present the facts and findings of my research as they emerged, while they were still embedded within the affective and intersubjective dimensions through which knowledge had happened between the other research participants and me. I wanted to challenge the sexual-humanitarian onto-epistemology by providing viewers with access to the complex and ambivalent selfrepresentations and affective dynamics I experienced while carrying out interviews with migrants working in the sex industry. A few weeks after I met Alina, I decided to make *Normal*, my first experimental documentary using actors to perform real research interviews.

Interviewing Alina

I definitely had not expected that Alina's interview would strike me as forcefully as it did, or that the experience would inspire me to make an experimental documentary to convey the intricacy of agency and exploitation emerging from her story. Alina had been trafficked into the UK sex industry in the early 2000s and had been deported back to Moldova about a year later in the context of an antitrafficking police raid. She then decided to return to the United Kingdom with the help of an Albanian former client. Initially, she worked in construction in order to make the money to continue her law studies, which was her childhood dream. Eventually she decided to work in the sex industry, as she realized it was going to be impossible to save enough money working in construction. She describes the period when she was working as an independent sex worker in a flat in London as a positive and assertive time in her life, thanks to which she could finally have a "normal life," by which she meant being able to afford to help her family, go on holiday, and live comfortably. After her flat was raided by the police for a second time, and confronted with the possibility of being deported again, she decided to inform on her original trafficker, and later obtained the right to stay in the United Kingdom.

Alina's story allowed me to better understand the difference between forced and voluntary involvement in the sex industry. What particularly touched me was the complexity of her mobile orientation, which was reflected in the contradictions between the different and evolving selfrepresentations that she deployed in response to my questions. After hesitantly entering the room and sitting down, Alina started to size me up. She wanted to know where my accent was from, and appeared reassured to know it was Italian, not Romanian or Albanian. I began the interview by recapitulating the ethical terms of engagement: she should tell me only what she was comfortable with and feel free to refuse to answer any question—or to lie. Alina laughed at the mention of the possibility of lying in a research interview. I laughed too, and added that I was going to address her history from a migration perspective, focusing on people's multiple reasons for moving, rather than on the details of her history of trafficking and forced engagement in sex work. "I am trying to protect both you and myself from stirring up feelings that might be hurtful and unnecessary. I mean, this is not a legal interview. And I am not a therapist either, so I am not qualified to deal with traumatic details," I said, or something along those lines. She nodded approvingly, and I asked her my first question, about her family history and background in Moldova. It was the beginning of a classic migration life-history interview.

Alina came from a "good" family: her father was an architect, and her mother was a nurse. Things had been going relatively well until her father died when she was only thirteen, and the local currency was devalued in the context of Moldova's postcommunist transformation. In order to sustain her family, Alina dropped out of school and started working in the open-air market in the capital, Chisinau. A woman she met there put her in touch with people who would enable her to go to the United Kingdom, and who subsequently forced her to work in the sex industry:

> She used to come at the market and she heard me complain about my life. . . . So one day she said, "Would you like to go to the UK? You could be an escort and sex is up to you. . . . You will learn English . . ." At the time, I was very sad about not being able to study and also . . . I never thought someone could lie just like that. . . . I was young and naïve, and I came from a small village. [. . .] Anyway, I went. It was the year 2000. Everyone was leaving for a better life at the time.

As Alina told me her life history, I could hear in her narration the presence of competing selfrepresentations. I could feel sexual-humanitarian versions of herself that she had had to produce for different certifying audiences while she was trying to have her suffering recognized in order to avoid deportation and obtain the right to live and work in the United Kingdom. The emphasis she gave to specific aspects and details in the narration made me aware that she was formulating her story according to the affective and narrative tropes of the sex trafficking story, a humanitarian biographical border that potentially allows irregular migrants working in the sex industry to stay in the United Kingdom as victims of trafficking. Sex trafficking stories are powerful narrative technologies in the certification of humanitarian truth. They produce an affective atmosphere of compassion, enabling the certification of victimhood and credibility that is needed to cross sexual-humanitarian biographical borders.

Alina's mobilization of rhetorical figures of sexual-humanitarian speech was both authentic and performative. It reflected the ironic sensibility characterizing current post-humanitarian times, whose merging of utilitarianism and solidarity makes people aware of the workings of humanitarian rhetoric and representations (Chouliaraki 2013). Although Chouliaraki's conceptualizations refer to people's ironic competence as spectators of humanitarian campaigns, I draw on her analysis to describe how this ironic post-humanitarian sensibility also frames how knowledge happens in the context of research on sexual-humanitarian biographical borders. While explaining how crucial decisions had taken place at different stages of her life history, Alina presented me with an ironic and self-reflexive assemblage of two main discursive repertoires. The first, which I define as the migration script, framed her decision to leave home and work in the sex industry as a response to economic, political, and sociocultural causes. The second was the sex-trafficking biographical border. As these two selfrepresentation repertoires offered access to different experiences and understandings of agency, I used irony as a strategy to switch the intersubjective, affective, and cognitive frames she offered to make sense of and explain her life history to me. In this way I heuristically challenged the affective atmosphere of neo-abolitionist compassion created by the sex-trafficking biographical border whenever I felt that it might be silencing more complex experiences of agency than those presented. In doing so, I made Alina aware that I was a benevolent and ironic spectator of her post-humanitarian self-representation.

I also adopted humor as an intersubjective and intimate approach, in order to establish an ironic affective atmosphere that would allow contradictory meanings, narratives, and experiences to emerge. Humor is an emotional and relational strategy used by sex workers to manage awkward situations and negotiate boundaries between themselves, clients, authorities, and researchers (Sanders 2004). During my many years of ethnographic observation of migrants working in the sex industry, I have witnessed many instances when nonmoralized and non-normative aspects or events in people's lives were transmitted through irony and humor. Being able to smile or even laugh about dramatic, if paradoxical, aspects of the lives of people selling sex is often the only way to open a safe space where it is possible to talk openly about delicate personal matters without being emotionally overwhelmed.

Alina provided me with a first opportunity for humor when she started talking about the desire to run away from her violent boyfriend as one of her reasons for leaving Moldova: "I had a boyfriend at the time. He used to beat me up; . . . I mean all men are violent over there, but he was really over the top, like once he left me with no teeth in the mouth."

"What a charmer . . ." I interjected. I smiled carefully.

"Yes . . . indeed!" she responded with a surprised smile. I could feel some relief on her part. She had not anticipated this intersubjective and affective possibility, but she welcomed it: "And you can't even go to the police, as they think you must have done something wrong to be treated like that. . . . I was also ashamed to tell people at the village, as the mentality is that once you get a man, you have to stay with him forever. . . . You have got to make it work. . . . I mean I also wanted to get away from him."

"No kidding!" I added, this time smiling less timidly. She responded with a light giggle.

The construction of an ironic affective atmosphere through humor allowed the gradual emergence of more plural narratives and experiences within and outside the sex-trafficking biographical border. It also allowed me to establish a relationship of trust. By mobilizing humor in a normative interview situation inside a police station, I was able to present myself as someone who "got it"—that is, someone who was not an "outsider" in relation to what goes on in the sex industry. A turning point was when we both inadvertently challenged one of the most important tropes of the trafficking humanitarian biographical border: the narration of "the first time" one sells sex under coercion. (I analyze this narration in more detail in chapter 9). Alina started by describing the horrible situation in which she found herself:

> The first day, . . . it was terrible, I cried all day. . . . Sex is seen as dirty and disgusting at home; I had not even seen a man naked before. I was embarrassed! I kept thinking that this job was not for me. . . . Just think that I did not even know what a blowjob was! Can you imagine that? My life and my family were going to be in danger because of that!

At this point we both "just" laughed. The paradoxical situation of being in grave danger because of not knowing what a blowjob was both encompassed and transcended compassion. It shifted the affective atmosphere toward a more ironic and plural discursive field. We quickly composed ourselves after this moment of unexpected laughter, but the overall balance in the composition of the affective atmosphere remained ironic, allowing a plurality of narratives, experiences, and subject positions to emerge.

For instance, in the excerpt that follows, Alina describes the "rushed and unsophisticated" way she was detained and deported the first time, when she did not report her (female) trafficker. She also explains how she came to the decision to go back to the sex industry, as well as the constraints and opportunities she faced when she was finally "rescued" and supported by antitrafficking interventions and projects.

> ALINA: In 2000 there was a raid in one of the flats. I was arrested together with lots of girls. I spent two months in prison in Heathrow. . . . It was a detention center. . . . It was very rushed and unsophisticated in those days. I spent two days in a cell, for what? The immigration people were tough; they did not even ask you if you were OK. I had met a nice Albanian customer in Soho; he felt sorry for me, and he came to visit. . . . I was deported with no money at all. I even had to ask my mother for the money for the taxi from the airport. I felt guilty, ashamed. I had sold my body for nothing. I kept thinking, "What have I got left?" I felt guilty and worthless, and I started thinking to go back. . . . I also wanted to meet her again, the lady, and to see whether I could do something about it.

NICOLA: How did you manage to go back?

ALINA: With the help of my Albanian friend. I borrowed money from him and from the maid and bought a fake passport. The Albanian guy helped me with that. . . . He was nice. I paid him back by working in construction, but then I decided to go alone. . . . It was impossible for me to keep working in construction. Very heavy physically, and also the environment was difficult. I was the only woman amongst builders. So I got a newspaper, and I responded to an advert for a job in a flat in Heathrow. It was something else. I was free to work when I wanted and with whom I wanted, and to do what I was comfortable with, with customers. I used to keep half of the money and I was earning more than £700 . . . on a bad day. . . . I remember that was a good life! I could finally rest, help my family, go to nice places, . . . even have holidays! There were other girls there, with pimps. Most of the Lithuanians and some of the Polish had Albanian pimps. . . . But I was free. With my fake passport I could have a good life. I got fed up in the end, though. I was tired of being scared of the police. . . . And I wanted to study.

NICOLA: So how did you get where you are now, what happened?

ALINA: Well, what happened is that one day the immigration police came, and I mentioned what had happened to me before. They had my fingerprints from the previous time, . . . so I had to explain. As I mentioned the name of the trafficker, they let me off the issue of having false papers and released me. I had to sign in once a week, and that was it. I now have got refugee status and an indefinite leave to remain recently. This time, the experience was much better, I mean with the police. I was explained everything and was supported.

Because of the intimate, intersubjective relationship that had arisen between us and the ironic affect it generated, Alina felt free to demarcate clearly between trafficking and voluntary engagement in the sex industry. Through our ironic exchange, she was able to explain that both of her decisions to migrate had been motivated by her desire to have a better life and help her family in the context of constrained opportunities. Most importantly, she explained how the ability to decide which clients to take and which sexual services to offer, and the ability to enjoy the income produced by her sex work, enabled her to have a "good" and more "comfortable" life, which she saw as "something else" in relation to her previous experience of trafficking.

The ironic affective atmosphere and intimate intersubjectivity framing our interview allowed her to show that the ability (or inability) to profit from the money made from sex work and the working conditions attached are what defines exploitation, rather than sex work per se. Alina was also able to mention the possibility of supportive relationships between women and their clients, some of which were characterized by solidarity and respect. Hardly the Manichean world presented by the neo-abolitionist and sexual-humanitarian onto-epistemology. However, Alina's story is also an exceptionally positive one, as she managed to gain recognition and protection as a victim in the end. Many women caught up in antitrafficking raids do not have their status as victims recognized, and they are detained and deported in the process, just as Alina was when she was first arrested in the context of sexual-humanitarian antitrafficking interventions.

For instance, Candy, a nineteen-year-old Romanian woman who followed her boyfriend to the United Kingdom and ended up being forced to work in the sex industry, had a much more difficult time getting her victim-of-trafficking status recognized. Her situation in relation to trafficking was much more complex than Alina's: other women accused her of being part of the organization that had trafficked her. Candy's story highlights the role played by "love" in the experience of being trafficked, which was corroborated by the accounts of many other female research participants. It is to this complex intricacy of agency, love, and exploitation that I now turn.

SEVEN

Love, Exploitation, and Trafficking

Candy, Anca, and Viorica

I met Candy, Anca, and Viorica at the premises of an organization supporting victims of trafficking in Manchester. The three women were between the ages of nineteen and twenty-one, and all came from the same area of Romania. They were involved in a significant (and at that time ongoing) trafficking investigation in the United Kingdom, which eventually led to the sentencing of twenty-three-year-old Jonut and his father to twenty-one and six years respectively for sexual exploitation and controlling prostitution for gain. As part of the process, Anca and Candy had each served a seven-month sentence for controlling prostitution for gain.

When I arrived at the support organization, Anca and Candy were already waiting for me. Cheryl, the project worker who had arranged the interviews, met me at the door, quickly introduced us, and went to prepare hot drinks while we waited for Viorica to join us. While we waited, I told them I had been to Romania quite a few times in the context of doing research for Save the Children on the migration of minors and young people. I mentioned that I had even been to their village, and I made a few jokes in Romanian, hoping to elicit an ironic affective atmosphere right from the start.

The ethical framework of the ESRC-funded project *Migrant Workers in the UK Sex Industry* allowed participants to receive fifty pounds in acknowledgement of their contribution. Cheryl had already indicated over the phone that the women were excited at the prospect of some extra money to spend on clothes, given that their weekly allowance of forty pounds offered little room for glamour. Viorica arrived rather flustered, and as she sat down, she asked Anca and Candy in Romanian whether there was really going to be any money to be made out of "this fool" (i.e., me). Seeing Anca, Candy, and me laughing embarrassedly, Viorica froze and said to them, "Oh shit, tell me he does not understand Romanian!"

"I do," I answered, also in Romanian, laughing.

As Viorica started to apologize, I reassured her that no offence had been taken, and introduced myself properly. We were all able to laugh together. I could not have hoped for a quicker or more spontaneous way to elicit an ironic affective atmosphere, or a better kick-start to our intersubjective relationship.

The day I spent at the organization in Manchester was one of the most intense and productive moments in my life as a researcher. Anca, Candy, and Viorica had all been brutally exploited in the UK sex industry. However, they had been involved in different relational dynamics, and had come to be trafficked through different routes and with different degrees of awareness. Anca presented herself as Jonut's distant cousin. She was already working in Spain (in agriculture) when she decided to join him in the United Kingdom to "make more money." Candy thought she was Jonut's fiancée when she fled her home in Romania to be reunited with him in Manchester. Jonut and a friend of Viorica's kidnapped her back in Romania and subsequently took her to the United Kingdom. Viorica was seventeen at the time. While interviewing the three women, I was confronted with a labyrinth of convergent and divergent descriptions of the same story and its embedded relational dynamics. Each of them had been trafficked and sexually exploited, but the different ways they had become entangled with the management of the women who were trafficked after them formed the basis of mutual accusations of pimping. The trafficking ring in Jonut's family was brought down when two women who had recently arrived from Romania refused to give in to the threats and violence to which Jonut and his father subjected them, and alerted the police. In their eyes, Anca, Candy, and Viorica were simply part of the chain of command. It was on the basis of this assumption that the three women had been accused of controlling prostitution for gain, a charge to which Anca and Candy had pleaded guilty.

Challenging Candy's Trafficking Melomentary

I decided to include Candy's story in my experimental documentary *Normal* because it had the potential to reveal how love performances can be effective embedding mechanisms for controlling and exploitative dynamics. My decision was also motivated by the fact that her life trajectory was the closest example I had encountered to the "Natasha" script, a popularized and spectacularized account of trafficking that typically presents naive, young, Eastern European women as seduced, deceived, and forced to sell sex by their fiancés (Zhang 2009).

Current post-humanitarian and sexual-humanitarian times coincide with the emergence of new hybrid genres that straddle the gap between fiction and documentary filmmaking through melodramatic—and therefore fixed—narratives and rhetorical devices. The absence of statistical data on trafficking, the availability of antitrafficking funding, and the need to produce evidence on trafficking for auditing and marketing purposes have fueled the emergence of a (sexual) "humanitarian media complex" that produces neo-abolitionist affective evidence by strategically using trafficking victims' testimonials (Lindquist 2010). The "subgenre of anti-prostitution films" (Shah 2013, 550) has become a strategic vector for the global production and dissemination of the neo-abolitionist conflation of prostitution and trafficking. According to Carole Vance (2012, 207), the resulting new genre of "melomentary" frames empirical evidence on sex trafficking according to strategically predetermined plot lines and subject positions that define women as innocent victims and men as evil villains, thus offering "no place for empowered 'victims'" and "no intervention other than rescue." In this respect, sexual-humanitarian melomentaries should be considered as closely related to neo-abolitionist antitrafficking campaigns, which raise both funds and awareness through the constant repetition of stereotypical representations of victimhood and of mythical, fixed narratives of coercion into prostitution and humanitarian redemption (Andrijasevic and Mai 2016).

The sexual-humanitarian merging of fact and fiction concerns not only the production of hybrid genres but also the way fictional films are used in public debates as if they were factual documentaries. For instance, the Swedish fiction *Lilya 4-Ever* by Lukas Moodysson (2002)—about the brutal trafficking of sixteen-year-old Lilya from Russia to Sweden—has been extensively used as a tool of "awareness-raising" (and politicization) for the issue of trafficking (Suchland 2013, 264). Its documentary aura resides not merely in its loose association with a tragic real story but in its onto-epistemological and affective resonance with the "self-evident" neo-abolitionist (post-) truths circulated by sexual humanitarianism. The Natasha script is perhaps the most recurrent sexual-trafficking story among fictional and documentary accounts of the relationship between migration and the sex trade. Its fixed, melodramatic, and spectacularizing rhetoric obfuscates the intricate and contradictory experiences of agency and exploitation that emerge from sex workers' actual life histories.

It was in order to bring this complexity to the fore that I decided to include Candy's story in my film. During her interview, I tried to challenge fixed, sexual-humanitarian selfrepresentations by making good use of the ironic affective atmosphere we had established at the beginning of our encounter, which allowed multiple and contradictory narratives to emerge.

"I fell in love, basically . . ."

That was Candy's shorthand explanation for how she came to be trafficked. "How was he?" I asked quickly, before the demonization of the trafficker prescribed by the trafficking sexual (humanitarian) story could kick in, and she could present Jonut as a stereotypical "loverboy." *Loverboy* is a term coined within antitrafficking academic and gray literature to define young men who manipulate and force young women into prostitution by making them believe they are in love with them (Leman and Janssens 2008).[1]

Candy looked surprised. "What do you mean?" she replied, a perplexed expression on her face.

"I mean, what did you like about him; was he sexy, was he funny?"

Her eyes sparkled. She had not expected this question, but a part of her visibly welcomed it. Her tone and presence became more engaged.

CANDY: He was gorgeous. . . . I mean, I knew him from before, as he had a reputation of being a bastard with girls, like sleep and tell. . . . He was in the UK all the time, and I met him through friends. . . . He was nice to me, in the beginning. . . . His father had a reputation for bringing girls out to work in the sex trade, but not him.

NICOLA: What did you like about him, in particular?

CANDY: Well, he was different from all others. He had a nice car, he was well dressed. . . . My parents always gave me what I wanted, so I did not want to be with boys who had no money, and I had to pay coffee for. Maybe because I was spoilt, but he was different, he was nice, good-looking, he had money and the respect of everybody.

Whenever she finished a sentence, Candy would look at me coyly as if to check whether I had believed and understood what she said in the way she wanted me to. Sometimes I did, sometimes I did not—and she knew it. Every time she framed an answer according to the Natasha sexual story, new questions came into my head: "How could she not know that she was going to be in deep trouble? Could she really think that Jonut was not working with his father? Why is she so disparaging of her penniless peers?" In challenging Candy, I was not disputing the credibility of her answers or the reality of her experience of trafficking, but the fixed tropes and rhetorical figures she was offered by the sexual-humanitarian onto-epistemology with which to tell her life history.

I had to better understand her current feelings for Jonut and the way their relationship had evolved since she was trafficked. "I do want him to get caught, but I would not want anything bad, I mean physically bad, to happen to him," she replied to my question about whether she wanted the UK police to find Jonut. At the time of our interview, Candy was actively cooperating with the authorities by agreeing to keep talking to Jonut (who was in hiding in Spain) by phone so that they could track him down. She had obviously decided not to protect him any more and to look after herself. But she was also sad about how things had turned out between them. A part of her still felt for him, even after everything he had done to her. The saddest moment in our conversation was when she told me she felt completely betrayed by him when he first forced her to sell sex.

> When we finally get to the bus station, he was with Anca, which I found strange. Because he was very happy to see me, as he was in Romania, I thought nothing of it. Later I phoned my mother, and we had a big argument over the phone . . . when I told her I was in England. Then we went to meet his father, and that's when it all came clear to me. I could see very well what was going on, and he actually told me: "You knew what you came here for, you came on your own, so I am not expecting problems from you," and then he said that the following day I would have to go to work with Anca. I wanted to go home. We had a big argument: "If you go home, your mother will know. . . . I will tell them you did it anyway." I felt I could not escape, . . . that I had no choice. I could not go home. . . . I felt that my father and mother would never talk to me again, . . . especially after I was then arrested and spent seven months in prison for controlling. Anyway, in the morning Jonut told me to get changed and go to work. I refused, and he beat me up, a lot. I hated him and myself as I realized how right everyone had been about him, and I did not want to believe them. His father told me that if I tried to do something, he would have hurt my family back in Romania.

I did not interrupt her, and we remained silent for a moment after she finished speaking. I guess we were both trying not to be overwhelmed. I could feel her sadness affecting me, and I wanted to remain critically engaged in the interview process. I also wanted the interview to remain an emotionally safe space for her and for me. At the same time, I had to understand more about the kind of love that had made all this happen, given that Candy had presented "love" as the reason she had got into so much trouble. "How were things between you and Jonut after he forced you to sell sex?" I asked.

> It became a game, a sick game between us. But we have loved each other. Sometimes he would treat me worse than other girls because he loved me. He would sleep with them in front of me to punish me if he understood that I liked a client more than another. Other times we were very close, and I felt that we were together again.

Candy replied to these questions calmly. I listened without interrupting, and tried to resist the aura of credibility with which her looks and her flirting endowed her narration. Candy was beautiful, and she was aware of the credibility and innocence her beauty evoked. Her flirtatious attitude, and the way she kept checking that I believed her, encouraged me to think that there was more to her story than could emerge through the Natasha script with which she selfrepresented. I started to suspect that, forced or not, she had been more involved in the management of Jonut's business than she wanted anyone to know. She had been convicted for controlling, after all. I decided to ask more strategic questions about her feelings for Jonut and her involvement in his business.

CANDY: Once we went to Holland with Jonut and met a Romanian guy there from our area. He came to the UK with us, as he wanted to steal, but then he got caught and decided that he wanted to work with girls as well. Then he brought two girls, two crazy girls. . . . After one month the police came to the sauna, and although she could not speak English, she must have been able to say something, because they took her immediately to the station, dressed as she was. . . . She told them many lies anyway—that we all beat her up and stuff like that, but it was not true, and I was arrested . . . and spent seven months in jail.

NICOLA: Are you surprised that the police believed the girls? It sounds a bit implausible that you did not take that chance to denounce Jonut? One could easily see it as a business trip you were part of?

CANDY: It was not a business trip. I had to go with him and do what he said, otherwise he would hurt my family. Yes, there were fights with the girls. . . . I mean it was natural to have fights, but I did not beat them up and force them to do anything like they say. I was forced to do what I did by a man. I am not a pimp! That was not my position!

NICOLA: What was your position?

CANDY: I was a prostitute, a victim.

Candy stopped talking and composed herself. She told me all this at once, while still checking whether I believed it or not. What I believed most was that she was telling a version of her story that she could live with and that offered her the chance of a future; that was what my next question was about. "I want to go back home to Romania. I do not want to be alone here, in England. At least there I would have my family, . . . but the police keep telling me that it might not be safe for me to be there, that I know too many things and that I have to wait for Jonut to get caught." Candy continued: "I would like to work as an interpreter, translating Italian, Romanian, English languages. That would be my dream. And I would like to marry a very rich man and have two children."

The flirtatious way Candy said she spoke Italian, and her final remark about wanting to marry a rich man, corroborated my feeling that she was flirting for her life. She needed to be believed and to move on from the terrible situation in which she found herself. No part of me judged her for having stuck to her sexual-humanitarian guns when describing what happened, but I was left with the impression that a lot of relevant truth had been left out. As the interview came to an end, I think we both felt that she had gone a lot further than she wanted in cooperating with Jonut's business in order to protect herself, her family, and her romantic dream of social mobility with him.

My affectively and intersubjectively grounded experience of heuristic disbelief was corroborated by the interview with Viorica, which immediately followed that with Candy. As soon as she entered the interview room, Viorica asked me: "Tell me the truth, did Candy flirt with you? Before, in the interview, did she?" I did not want to lie or break confidentiality, so I decided to say nothing. "I can't tell you anything about the other interviews, I am sorry," I replied. But something in me must have given it away; affect transmits in mysterious ways. She looked me in the eye, an ironic smile lighting up her face. "I knew it!" she said triumphantly. We both knew she was right. And I had not told her anything. Not in words, at least.

During her interview, Viorica distanced herself from her (forced) entanglement in the management of sex by effectively blaming the other two women for having made themselves vulnerable to trafficking. Her use of sex-gendered stereotypes, assumptions, and accusations reflected Sykes and

Matza's (1957, 667) neutralization theory, particularly the "denial of responsibility" strategy by which criminalized activities are presented as "due to forces outside the individual and beyond his control."

> Look, they liked the guy and were crazy about him. They are different from me; I mean, Anca used to sleep around with boys in Romania, going to discos and stuff; she used to wear makeup by the age of twelve to thirteen. . . . They both liked being around young men back in Romania. They gave blowjobs and stuff. . . . Everyone knew. When you want to do these things, you are basically a whore. They both wanted to be free and to get attention, and that's how they got in trouble. [. . .] I did not belong to that world back in Romania. In England it is different; girls wearing makeup by the age of twelve, wanting to be free, . . . but back there it is not appropriate. And about Jonut, I told you they were both in love with him and were jealous because he kind of liked me more. Maybe because I resisted him, and I was different from them. Anca liked the guy, otherwise why would she come back from holiday? Freely? I mean, she actually pimped me at some stage; she told me what to do. . . . Both Anca and Candy had abortions, and both of them wanted to keep the baby in order to hold onto the man. . . . As for Candy, she likes boys with lots of money. . . . I think she knew that Jonut was doing that job. . . . But maybe she did not think it was going to happen to her because she was his girlfriend. . . . At least I think she knows.

In this except, Viorica discredits Anca and Candy according to the "whore stigma" selfrepresentation repertoire, claiming that they were already "whores" in Romania because they wanted to be "free" and be "around young men." At the same time, she asserts a sense of superiority through being liked more by Jonut. She accuses Candy of having known that her boyfriend was a pimp, but then admits that she only thinks so; she cannot say for sure. I shared some of her perplexities regarding the credibility of some aspects of Anca's and Candy's stories, but how could I know for sure? How could anyone know for sure? These considerations highlight the structural limitations at work when interviewing people who are negotiating sexual-humanitarian biographical borders. In the interviews I undertook with Anca, Candy, and Viorica that day in Manchester, I found echoes of their previous and ongoing interviews with the authorities, during which they had to defend themselves against accusations of complicity in their own and other people's trafficking. As the three women were still defending their cases in court, my ironic attempt to access multiple truths collided with sexual-humanitarian onto-epistemological power. All I was left with were affective and cognitive contradictions that gave me glimpses of more complex experiences of agency and exploitation.

When each interview drew to a close, I gave the interviewee the money that constituted acknowledgement of her participation in the research. This was also an opportunity to discuss the economic support given to victims of trafficking by the organizations supporting them through the NRM. The handing over of the interview money gave research participants the opportunity to talk about the limitations and conditions attached to the recognition of their credibility, which was predicated on their ceasing to sell sex. Although the three women had come to be trafficked in different ways and felt well supported by the organizations taking care of them, they also felt that the amount of money given to potential victims, combined with the impossibility of continuing to sell sex, made it difficult for many "girls" to feel "free."

Alina, whose situation I discussed in the last chapter, had also been adamant in this respect, claiming that although "people there are very kind and they know what they are doing," there was "no freedom at all." In her words,

> Some girls go actually back to work to be free. You cannot pass from having what you want when you want to forty pounds per week and only training, training, training. . . . And also, working without a pimp is a completely different story, and they should allow that, rather than telling people to stop selling sex.

I was taken aback when I heard this remark, unsolicited, from someone who had been trafficked and was directly involved in supporting other victims of trafficking through her advocacy work. I think the ironic affective atmosphere framing our interview played a role in allowing this divergence from the sexual-trafficking story to be uttered. I was even more astonished when I heard similar and equally unsolicited critiques and observations from Candy, Anca, and even Viorica, who claimed to have had no responsibility at any stage of the process that had led to her being trafficked. In this excerpt, Anca explains that, although many of the young women she met were controlled,

> cases like ours show them that they can be free, that they do not need anything from these guys. Their eyes need to be opened, and they need to hear and see that they can have a better life than the one they have; . . . that they can work alone if they want. I mean, after all, I believe that this is a job that

> is not for everyone, but that some people can really do it as a job. I would like to find a way to help more people, to tell these girls that they do not need to have a man.

I was surprised to hear these important nuances and distinctions—stating that prostitution is work—uttered by women who were trying hard to gain recognition as victims of trafficking for sexual exploitation and whose involvement in the sex industry had been marked by extreme experiences of violence and abuse. Nevertheless, Alina, Anca, Candy, and Viorica were adamant that, according to their experience, trafficking is different from sex work and that it is possible to decide to engage in sex work freely and independently. They were also clear that, tragically, that had not been the case for them—including Alina, who was forced to work in the sex industry when she first came to the United Kingdom.

For Love and Trafficking: Tackling the Intricacy of Autonomy and Exploitation

I thought a lot about my afternoon with Anca, Candy, and Viorica during the two years that followed. I reflected on the intricacy of love, agency, and exploitation that emerged from their interviews, from their lives. The strategic role of cultural constructions of love in trafficked women's experiences of exploitation surfaced as an issue in each of the three interviews. Anca explained to me that most of the young women she met who were trafficked in the sex industry had heard "bad stories" about their boyfriends, but that none of them thought it was going to happen to them. In her case, she felt she was going to be safe because Jonut was part of her family (he was a distant cousin), but in most other cases "the love thing is important," she claimed, because "they believe the words of love and then get lost in them a bit."

I found similar experiences in thirty interviews with off-street (massage parlors, saunas, brothels, etc.) migrant sex workers, undertaken as part of an evaluation (which I directed) of services provided by SHOC (Sexual Health On Call), a sex work support project operating in the London boroughs of Haringey and Enfield. The majority of the women interviewed were from Eastern Europe, specifically Romania (twenty), Albania (two), Lithuania (two), the Czech Republic (one), Latvia (one), and Poland (one). Most interviewees were between the ages of twenty and twenty-six, the youngest being twenty, and the oldest, forty-nine. All respondents were contacted during outreach services organized by SHOC.

From my overall analysis of the interviews, the picture emerged of a strong prevalence of consensual practices in the present day: all but one of the women interviewed felt they were free to work in the sex industry. At the same time, my analysis of these interviews identified multiple and competing discursive strategies that were deployed to avoid what I define as "trafficking stigma"—the stigma of being seen as controlled, pimped, and/or trafficked within the sex industry. The term *trafficking stigma* does not refer to the specific articulation of *whore stigma* that women associated with sex work abroad, including victims of trafficking, face when they return (or are deported) to their countries of origin (Plambech 2014). Rather, trafficking stigma operates in relation to the canons of successful selfhood disseminated by the global hegemony of neoliberalism, with its celebration of individualism, consumerism, and autonomy. The commodified "social relationality of success" (Winnubst 2012, 86) globalized by neoliberal onto-epistemology resonates strongly within the moral orientations and agencing decisions of migrant women and men working in the sex industry, many of whom are subject to the specific 'stigma of failure' when deported back to their countries of origin (Schuster and Majidi 2015, 642). By distancing themselves from trafficking stigma, the women I interviewed in Haringey were undertaking a double operation. On the one hand, they were strategically dissociating themselves from aspects of their emotional and migratory histories that did not allow them to selfrepresent as successful, autonomous, neoliberal subjects who were able to benefit from the results of their own hard work. On the other hand, they were avoiding any association with criminalized activities that might expose them to the dangers of targeting and deportation if sexual-humanitarian initiatives saw them as controlled, exploited, and trafficked.

Many women selfrepresented as able to avoid control by agents. In the process, they condemned other women to trafficking stigma, framing them as responsible for their inability/unwillingness to free themselves from exploitative situations and, indirectly, for their own failure to live as autonomous and successful, neoliberal selves. In the process, the stigma associated with vulnerability to emotional and economic dependency on men was often displaced, both onto other women and onto previous phases of one's own life. For instance, twenty-three-year-old Jessica from Romania revealed that she used to work with "a pimp" in Spain—her first experience of emigration—but said she was now happy with her current boyfriend.

> I used to work with a pimp, but I did not know he was the pimp. He paid for my passport and the travel. He told me I was going to be a cleaner for

> his sister, and then when I was there, he told me, "Now you have to do sex work." Now he is in prison. Actually, he was a good pimp; he did not slap me or didn't put out a cigarette on me as many pimps do. The deal was to work for one week for him. I used to make €14,000 per month, and he used to pay me €1,000. [. . .] I now live with my boyfriend. He is a good guy; he does not ask anything, and buys presents for my son!

As researchers, we were confronted with a labyrinth of competing self-representations, which aimed to establish hierarchies of economic and emotional autonomy in relation to trafficking stigma. Some women presented themselves as "really" loved and respected by underlining the emotional and economic naïveté they perceived in other women. For instance, Alketa, a thirty-year-old Albanian woman, claimed that many of the women working in brothels were trafficked, which she equated with having a partner who was aware of their work in the sex industry:

> Do you think that the girls that you know are not trafficked? They have to behave like us. The clinic where you work should give more advice saying: "Do the best for yourselves! Don't believe that your boyfriends love you!" Do you know what I think? That love does not exist if the boyfriend knows what job you are doing. Absolutely not! I had a boyfriend; I came here with him because I thought it was safer, and he was an arsehole. My current boyfriend does not know, and it is better like that; he is lovely. He is from my town, and we are going to get married, once I get the papers.

Alketa selfrepresents as currently autonomous by revealing that, although the boyfriend she first migrated with "was an arsehole," her current boyfriend "is lovely." She also tells us that she is going to marry her current boyfriend, who "does not know" about her job, after she gets her British passport. Having listened to the mutual discrediting of many Romanian sex workers according to trafficking stigma, I could not help but retain a heuristic suspension of belief.

The following excerpt from an interview with Tatiana, a twenty-four-year-old woman from Lithuania, further complicates the picture. She describes her previous boss, who did not want her to leave the flat, as behaving like a "pimp," while also claiming to hate her boyfriend, who is economically dependent on her.

> I don't know anything about trafficking, but I do know that there are pimps. Like the boss I told you before—he was like a pimp. He didn't want me to

> quit that flat. He used to threaten me. He used to say that if I left, he would have said to my boyfriend—because he knew that my boyfriend does not know what I do. [. . .] I hate my boyfriend, I hate him, . . . I hate him so much! I usually buy for him two packets of cigarettes per day. . . . I am the only person bringing money home. And children need to go to school. They need everything. . . . I afford everything for my boyfriend and the children.

Tatiana's statements further underline the intricate cultural constructions and practices associated with "love" and "exploitation" within which migrant sex workers make sense of the advantages and disadvantages of working and living in partnerships with men (Mai 2009b). Contrary to prevailing understandings of the nexus between migration and the sex industry as trafficking, the ethnographic material examined here reveals complex arrangements between third-party agents and sex workers with different degrees of agency, which have been corroborated by other research evidence (e.g., Marcus, Horning, Curtis, et al. 2014). However, the further criminalization of "pimping" brought about by its reframing as domestic and international trafficking meant that female sex workers often seemed to mirror sexual-humanitarian organizations and institutions in mobilizing the concepts of "trafficking" and "pimping" arbitrarily as "floating signifiers" to distinguish their experiences from those of victims of trafficking, and to demarcate hierarchies of autonomy among women selling sex (Grupo Davida 2015). In the process, some women's selfrepresentation in terms of current autonomy was challenged by other women, who claimed that many of those interviewed for the study were trafficked purely on the grounds that they were living with partners in relationships of economic and emotional interdependency. Thus, while distancing themselves from trafficking stigma, many women operationalized the term *trafficking* to encompass very different experiences of third-party management that did not fit the definition of trafficking per se.

The interview excerpts discussed above show that in the contemporary international arrangement of sex work, the boundaries between advantage and disadvantage, love and exploitation, remain complex and ambivalent. In many cases, as Alketa exemplified, women's understandings of whether their partners were good husbands and fiancés or pimps changed according to how their men reacted to their work (Nencel 2005). Criteria to distinguish husbands from pimps included whether they were working, whether they needed money, whether they were faithful, and whether they were (too) violent. Most women selfrepresented as autonomous when they were able to work, get paid, and be treated appropriately in the sex industry. However, the definition of "appropriately" was embedded in evolving, sex-gendered selfrepresentations, roles, and relationships. The perception that one was being exploited economically was often inextricably enmeshed with the perception that one had been betrayed in a romantic relationship; different romantic arrangements carried different economic implications.

Debts, Arrangements, and Bounded Exploitation

During my research on Eastern European migrants working as sex workers and agents in Italy and the United Kingdom, I identified two main kinds of sentimental and economic agreement between women and men: the "fiancée agreement," according to which the man keeps all the money "for the family" because the couple is going to marry and is romantically involved; and the "work partnership agreement," in which the man and woman split the money fifty-fifty, and romantic involvement is not necessarily present (Mai 2013). Fiancée status involves a merging of economic profits, while a less binding sentimental relationship does not. Therefore, fiancées who found out about their fiancés' economic and sentimental involvement with other girlfriends/sex workers wanted half the money back, and sometimes also took revenge by reporting their lover and agent to the police as a "trafficker." If the original agreement (whether as a fiancée or as a girlfriend/partner) was kept, the situation would not evolve into a conflict leading to a police report.

The life histories of migration and involvement in the sex industry I collected show a diverse range of experiences within both the "fiancée" and "work partnership" modes of relationship. For instance, Daniela, a twenty-four-year-old woman from Lithuania, thought she was "lucky" that the Albanian man who had bought her at the beginning of her stay in the United Kingdom "fell in love" with her and never forced her to sell sex or asked for money.

> In the end this man is the best man in my life, because he had never been a pimp, the man who bought me; he was hard-working. Because all his friends are pimp, they told him "Why do you need to work?" So buy one girl and you don't need to work, and you be rich. He worked in the restaurants; he do any jobs. He had good money, which he spent on me! I was lucky, but after a while we had separate as his parents wanted a good Albanian girl for him to marry, and also all his friends were making pressure on him to make me work and we had to run away.

Daniela's story is not unique in illustrating the pressures on men to conform to hegemonic (and criminalized) models of masculinity. Nor is it unique in revealing men's manipulability by women and peer groups, which I explore in more detail in the next chapter. In many cases, women were able to work within structures of authority and control, and despite being immersed in patriarchal and heterosexist values, they could manipulate their environments and relationships to their relative advantage. Katerina, a twenty-nine-year-old Albanian woman, by stating that "everyone can leave a pimp," underlined the fluidity of the relationships between working women and their men:

> All the girls have pimps. We all work with pimps. We have all had a pimp, but everyone can leave a pimp. Everyone can leave the job. Only the silly girls can really think that they love them. Pimps ask to work and money, saying "I love you," but nobody is forced to work.

These considerations are important for antitrafficking social interventions, which can only be effective if they take into consideration the complexity of the experiences of the people they aim to help and also acknowledge the emic categories and concepts expressing their worldviews. In many cases, women live with men they feel are "nice" to them but are also temporarily unemployed and know that their "girlfriends" work in the sex industry. Does this make them pimps? Whether and to whom the label *pimp* can be applied is a matter of debate and carries important consequences. Who should decide who is a "pimp" and who is not? In whose interest is this categorization made? These are important concerns for policymaking and social initiatives targeting migrant and nonmigrant sex workers, because it is in the name of criminalizing and generalizing assumptions that damaging interventions are deployed.

My research findings confirm that, contrary to the obliteration of consent introduced by neo-abolitionist scholarship and policymaking, migrant sex workers can and do agree to enter "indentured" forms of mobility, including the possibility of working under the management of a third-party agent, in order to meet the economic and administrative (i.e., becoming documented) objectives they set for themselves (Parreñas 2011, 7). This was definitely the case with the Nigerian women selling sex in Paris in 2015 whose stories I condensed into Joy, the protagonist of my ethnofiction *Travel*. This film, which I co-wrote with eight Nigerian women with experiences of sex work,[2] tells the story of a young woman who agrees to work under the management of Blessing, a slightly older woman. Blessing arranges Joy's travel to France and her job in the sex industry for €30,000. Although Joy expects the sex work to be escorting rather than street-based, she decides to endure exploitative working conditions as long as Blessing respects the original deal. When Blessing wants her to pay an extra €10,000, she seeks help from a local sex work support association, which informs her about the possibility of obtaining asylum as a victim of trafficking. Joy decides to report Blessing as a trafficker and to apply for asylum. Her decision is based on the fact that it was Blessing and not she who had betrayed the original deal, which was sworn with a juju oath back in Nigeria. She obtains asylum and starts working in a hotel as a cleaner, but the money is not enough to support herself and her family in Nigeria. She therefore decides to go back to the sex industry and work independently.

The plot of *Travel* reflects the findings of ethnofiction workshops and semistructured interviews undertaken as part of the *Emborders* project between 2014 and 2015. These findings show that Nigerian women agree to enter deals involving "bounded exploitation" – that is exploitation within set temporal and economic limits - in order to reduce the socioeconomic hardship—which they describe as "suffering"—of their families (and themselves) in the long term (Mai 2016b). Many young women are aware before they leave Nigeria that they are going to work in the sex industry to repay those who are enabling them to get to Europe, although they are often unaware of the harsh working conditions frequently attached to street work. Young Nigerian women also tend to be subjectified as responsible for the support of their families according to sex-gendered roles and expectations that frame them as "more reliable and loyal to the family" and "more willing to support their relatives financially" (Ratia and Noterman 2012, 147). However, the possibility of embodying their existential and social role as family providers tends to override their perception that they are being "cheated," even when they discover the exploitative working conditions they have to endure in Europe. Nigerian sex workers tend to recognize themselves as victims of trafficking only when they feel that their third-party agents have betrayed the original deal and that they are being prevented from alleviating their own and their families' socioeconomic "suffering."

These findings confirm previous research with female Nigerian sex workers in Europe, which shows that they endure exploitation in the hope of a better life (Peano 2013) and that they challenge the agreements sanctioned by customary law (juju) when those who enabled them to come to Europe fail to respect them (Guillemaut 2008). They also corroborate existing studies of Nigerian women's involvement in sex work, which have analyzed the inextricable mix of support and constraint that characterizes the relationships between girls and madams as part of an indentured migration system (Plambech 2016). These considerations are reflected in *Travel*. Joy decides to report Blessing only after she realizes that the latter has not respected the original oath and that that there is no other way for her to fulfill her mobile orientation, which is arranged around her existential mandate to help her family. It is then that she decides to apply for asylum, which will give her the right to work independently and reside in France, as well as offering humanitarian protection. And it is in order to help her family and support herself that she goes back to the sex industry. Once she is documented, Joy tries to work in a different sector (hospitality). However, the possibility of higher earnings and better working conditions in a situation of greater autonomy leads her to decide for a second time to work in the sex industry, which she prefers to working as a hotel chambermaid.

This chapter analyzes the complex ways in which sexual-humanitarian selfrepresentations and borders are reflected in interviews with migrant sex workers and victims of trafficking. By eliciting an ironic affective atmosphere and sensibility, and by adopting participative ethnofictional methods, I tried to challenge sexual-humanitarian selfrepresentations and stories in order to access the complex mobile orientations and agentic decisions of migrants working in the sex industry. The dynamics analyzed in this chapter show that it is respect for (or betrayal of) the economic and/or sentimental arrangements framing women's involvement in the sex industry, rather than that involvement per se, that determines whether they feel exploited, pimped, trafficked, or not. They also show that the concepts of trafficking and pimping often get confused (and are confusing) in women's understandings of their own and other women's involvement in the sex industry. At the same time, other distinctions emerge more clearly. The vast majority of female research participants, including those who were deceived and coerced into selling sex, think that sex work is different from trafficking, and that it can be experienced as work both when women work independently and when all the parties involved—including third parties—keep to the original agreement. Women's sentimental and economic relationships with those who facilitate their social mobility through migration and sex work are characterized by a fluid intricacy of love, support, and exploitation. This meaningful, affective, and intersubjective intricacy is obscured by the trafficking (sexual) humanitarian biographical border, which makes access to rights conditional on the performance of rhetorical figures of humanitarian speech. It is also obscured by sex workers' displacement of trafficking stigma onto other sex workers in order to selfrepresent as "normal," "successful," and "rational" neoliberal subjects, and to avoid being surveilled, controlled, and deported by antitrafficking and other sexual-humanitarian interventions. In the next chapter I explore how these dynamics are reflected in the mobile orientations and agencing decisions of young male traffickers and third-party agents, who tend to share the same sex-gendered selfrepresentations, intersubjective dynamics, and socioeconomic pressures as the women they manage, albeit from a privileged sex-gendered position.

EIGHT

Interviewing Agents

Toxic Betrayals

I never got used to the sound of bars slamming shut behind my back. I had to remind myself several times that those bars were not there for me as I was escorted to the section of Rebibbia prison in Rome where traffickers were detained. People who had committed crimes that other prisoners considered particularly infamous were detained on a special wing to protect them from "rough justice." In Rebibbia, infamous crimes included the facilitation and exploitation of prostitution, any form of sexual abuse of minors, collaboration with the police by Mafia deserters, and police corruption.

As the prison guard explained the rationale behind the protective grouping of prisoners according to hierarchies of infamy, I was reminded of the moral taxonomy structuring Dante's *Inferno*. The ninth and last circle of Dante's representation of Hell includes historical and mythological figures who have committed what he considers the "most evil" form of treachery: the betrayal of a special relationship of trust. There are four concentric zones, or "rounds," of traitors in the ninth circle, corresponding to the betrayal of family or community ties, guests, and benefactors, according to his ordering of evil. The most evil form of betrayal, that of benefactors, is consigned to the fourth round, named Judecca (after Judas Iscariot, the betrayer of Christ). This is where Satan appears, presented as the incarnation of evil for having betrayed the ultimate benefactor (i.e., God). As I was escorted to the library of the infamous wing, where my interviews with traffickers were to take place, I perceived a moral rationale behind the isolation of detainees according to unspoken degrees of betrayal.

I had agreed to work as a consultant researcher for an International Organization for Migration (IOM) pilot project, which aimed to sketch a "psychosocial profile of Albanian and Romanian traffickers." My main reason for doing so was to gain access to Albanian and Italian prisons, in order to talk to people who had been convicted of trafficking. I wanted to compare their experiences with those of the third-party agents I had met on the outside during my research. The main aim of the IOM project was to gather at least thirty interviews (ultimately thirty-three) with men involved in the arrangement and management of sex work across international boundaries.[1]

In this book I use the term *third-party agent* to indicate people who facilitate and manage the sex work of others. I prefer this to terms such as *pimp* or *trafficker*, which foreclose the analysis of negotiated and constrained experiences of agency, including the cases of "bounded exploitation" analyzed in the previous chapter. These concerns are particularly significant in the context of the sexual-humanitarian governance of sex work and migration, which makes a neo-abolitionist conflation of pimps with traffickers and constructs them as a "dangerous class on a global level" (Horning and Marcus 2017, 6). My avoidance of terms such as *pimp* and *trafficker* is not intended to underestimate the exploitative and abusive nature of some practices and relationships between sex workers and third-party agents. It aims rather to create a plural and heuristically open discursive space within which the mobile orientations and the related experiences of agency of people selling sex or managing the sex work of others can be understood in their full complexity.

When I agreed to undertake the research, I was aware of the stereotypical and implicitly stigmatizing implications embedded in the *psycho* element of psychosocial profiling. In one of the first meetings with the IOM project manager, I successfully resisted this aspect by pointing out that I was not a psychologist and was only going to be meeting most of the interviewees once. I was let off that hook quite easily. Interviewing people in jail posed specific methodological and ethical challenges. Whereas in Italy the people facilitating the prison interviews allowed roughly an hour for each of the two participants they had identified, in Albania I was generously allowed to "interview" around fifteen people in one day. The people who had arranged interviews in Albanian prisons obviously thought I was going to conduct some kind of survey, rather than qualitative interviews. The combination of the huge number of research participants and the short time available did not allow more than thirty minutes for each interview. Although this time constraint potentially hampered the emergence of an ironic intersubjective intimacy—or indeed any intersubjective intimacy at all—in many cases I was able to elicit complex narratives. This was mainly because the interviewees wanted to talk to somebody else, somebody who did not belong to the judiciary, family, or criminal networks that surrounded them. Despite the methodological limitations, the material gathered allowed me to identify betrayal as a strategic dimension for interpreting the complexity of intersubjective and socioeconomic transactions between third-party agents and sex workers.

The majority of detainees, particularly in Albania, did not accept their sentences. They saw the interview, and therefore me as the interviewer, as an opportunity to reassert their innocence. I often had no choice but to listen to the discursive pleas of interviewees who desperately wanted their truth to be heard, if not believed. And so I did listen. I listened on and on, for days on end, until I was full of discourses and faces and could take no more. In the stuffy library of Rebibbia prison and in the chlorine-smelling staff room of the Albanian penitentiary, I listened to people who wanted to shed their infamy like a disavowed skin, and I allowed myself to be reached emotionally and affectively.

Recalling how I felt and behaved while interviewing "infamous" criminals, I think I allowed the pain and knowledge of the other to happen to me (cf. Das 1998, 192). I had no choice. I "just" let myself be exposed to the rage and suffering of my interviewees. As they sat before me one by one, I felt affectively overexposed. I was a few centimeters away from them. I could smell their skin, feel the vibrations of their voices, their breathing. I felt their shame and their sense of injustice. I resonated affectively with the ways they had betrayed and been betrayed, socially, economically, and psychologically. I felt empathy with the poverty and desperation that had motivated some of their actions. I felt their rage at the inequality of access to legal representation, at the judicial corruption that freed the most ruthless and incarcerated the most dispossessed. I felt my own rage at the cruelty and contempt with which some of them behaved toward "their" women, at what they had become able to do to them, at how deeply they had been able to betray them. I found in myself a profound sense of justice when I felt intimately happy that some of them were incarcerated. But mostly I felt privileged—for not having needed to make those decisions; for having had the opportunity to be with them at the center of the infamous circle of Inferno where they were locked away; and for being able to leave after the end of the last interview.

It Wasn't Me

In the majority of cases, particularly in Albania, detained interviewees tended to explain their involvement in trafficking by resorting to three "techniques of neutralization" (Sykes and Matza 1957, 667) to deny or minimize it. The first, which I call the "fragmentation discourse," enabled the interviewee to present himself as completely innocent by focusing on his involvement in just a small part of a wider plan that fitted the trafficking paradigm. When resorting to the fragmentation discourse, an interviewee would typically claim that he was only doing a favor for a friend, either by accompanying his wife or fiancée from one city to another or by providing her with accommodation. The friend is blamed for any wrongdoing, while the interviewee presents himself as having got caught up in trafficking "by accident." The second discourse, which we might call the "I only helped her" discourse, emphasizes the agency of the women involved by claiming that they were willing to sell sex and that the interviewee was only helping them to get what they wanted in exchange for money and/or sex. The third discourse, the "fit of jealousy" discourse, displaces the focus away from the interviewee's involvement in trafficking by claiming that their female accuser was prompted by jealousy or revenge for having been left behind and/or betrayed. All three of these discourses were corroborated by a broader fourth, which we might call the "corruption discourse," which was used to delegitimize the judiciary and the police, while emphasizing the willingness of the interviewee's female accusers to sell sex. Typically, the "corruption discourse" described magistrates and police officers as unjustly accusing the interviewees and as forcing women to report their friends and lovers, in order to extort money and further their own careers.

The main challenge in interpreting these competing and overlapping discursive practices was that the project was not granted access to judiciary evidence, as it was supposed to focus on the experiences and perceptions of third-party agents. In Albania this lack of information was partially compensated by informal conversations with the people in charge of providing prisoners with social and psychological support. The director of social services, a witty and confident woman in her early thirties, informally allowed me to consult some of the judiciary files on the people I had interviewed. "So, Dr. Mai, how did it go today?" she asked as I went to meet her after the first interview session, just before the lunch break. "They are all innocent, aren't they?" she added with an ironic smile.

"Yes, . . . With a few exceptions," I replied. I was surprised and relieved that an ironic sensibility had been offered so spontaneously. I usually had to do all the affective labor for that to happen, and found it particularly difficult to circulate any ironic affect in the disciplinary atmosphere of the jail.

"Well, just to show you how unfounded their accusations are, I would like to show you the dossiers of two of the people you spoke to this morning," she added, taking two bulky folders and putting them on the table. "Please have a good read, and then join us for lunch when you are done. Of course, no pictures or note-taking of any kind is allowed."

Lunch was thirty minutes away; I only had time to browse quickly through the two dossiers. They were massive. The evidence was thorough and overwhelming. What had been presented to me as an involuntary and tangential involvement was actually a substantial and strategic participation in a lucrative business, usually run by a group of friends and relatives. These contradictions between the defensive and "neutralizing" selfrepresentations emerging from interviews and the judiciary evidence in the folders were confusing and revealing.

Another important source of productive contradictory information was the interviews, both in jail and outside, in which respondents decided to talk openly about their own lives. These became an indirect critique and commentary on the silences and omissions that characterized the majority of the other interviews.

The most important aspect of the interviews I undertook with male third-party agents, both inside and outside prison, were the gaps and contradictions around gender roles, and the way these affected the relationships between the men and women involved. The nature of the relationships and economic arrangements between women and men in the sex industry affects the management techniques used by agents and, indirectly, their ability to avoid being reported to the police. Most male agents' accounts contained two main competing (and often overlapping) discursive and practical repertoires through which they understood and managed sex work. The less common repertoire was based on an essentialist madonna/whore dichotomy that rigidly differentiated working "whores" from morally viable romantic partners. According to this interpretation of the patriarchal madonna/whore dichotomy—whose ideological and emotional resonance in the world of sex work has been well documented (O'Neill 1997; Pheterson 1993)—only virginal, "good" women are worthy of being loved (and married). However, within the narratives of Albanian and Romanian men managing women who work in the sex industry, a less violently heterosexist and patriarchal repertoire gradually prevailed. This was the "economic necessity" discourse, discussed in previous chapters, which allowed both men and women to ambivalently accept the moral viability of their involvement in the sex industry in terms of survival, while remaining within the coordinates of patriarchal heteronormativity. In the excerpt that follows, a twenty-one-year-old Albanian man I interviewed in an Albanian jail frames women working in the sex industry as "good women" who are providing for their children and families.

> They were good women, many of them divorced or separated; . . . they were between twenty-seven and thirty years old, . . . usually from Romania and Moldova. Most were working to maintain their children and their families. I remember a Moldavian teacher . . . when I asked her why she was doing this job, she said, "It is better so. . . . I earn a lot of money, for my children. What else could I do?"

This "economic necessity" discourse destigmatized female sex workers and inscribed them as "good women"—that is, mothers and nurturers—within the patriarchal social order. Its destigmatizing effect was often also extended to women who wanted to improve their economic situation more generally, particularly among young men who did not use violence to manage their female work partners.

The majority of the third-party agents who framed women's involvement according to the "economic necessity" discourse resorted to more consensual and fluid management techniques. This usually prevented them from betraying the original relational and economic arrangements they had made with the women they managed, and consequently from being reported as traffickers. In chapter 7, I identified two main kinds of relational and economic agreement between women and men in the United Kingdom and Italy: the "fiancée agreement," according to which the man keeps all the money because the couple is going to marry and is romantically involved; and the "work partnership agreement," in which the man and woman split the money fifty-fifty, and romantic involvement is not necessarily present (Mai 2013). When both partners abide by one of these two modes, there is no feeling of exploitation on the woman's part. However, when the terms are transgressed—for instance, if the male working partner does not love and respect his fiancée, or if he actively reframes a "work partnership" as love (i.e., by pretending to be a fiancé when this is not the case, in order to maximize his profits)—problems arise, and women feel exploited.

These dynamics are not unique to sex work management embedded in romantic relationships. For instance, as explained in the previous chapter, my research findings in 2015 (and the ethnofiction film they informed) showed that most Nigerian women selling sex in Paris had agreed to endure "bounded exploitation" in the sex industry in order to fulfill their roles as providers for their families. It was only when the original deal with their third-party agents—in these cases older women—was not respected that the trafficking biographical border started to make sense to them. Similarly, it is the betrayal of women's economic or romantic arrangements with men, rather than the mere agreement to work for/with them, that characterizes women's perceptions that they are "being exploited" and motivates them to report their third-party agents as "traffickers."

The interplay between prevailing sex-gendered selfrepresentations, relational and economic agreements, and sex work management techniques outlined above greatly influenced the life trajectories of third-party agents. All of the research participants who had not been convicted referred to having abided by the "fiancée agreement" and "work partnership agreement." The economic and romantic dimensions appeared to be inextricably merged in men's accounts of relationships with their work partners, whom they described as either their girlfriends or their work partners, depending on the kind of agreement they had with them. Recourse to violence happened on a relatively small scale and predominantly in the context of "fiancée agreements." In these cases, it was presented as part of "normal" relations of love and affection, a necessary way to substantiate the female partner's feeling of being cared about and loved. The few male interviewees who adhered closely to the essentialist tenets of the madonna/whore dichotomy tended to manage their female partners predominantly through the use of violence, which led to them being reported and arrested for trafficking as a result. In the remainder of this chapter, I focus on the different experiences of Besnik and Adrian, young men from Albania and Romania respectively, to explain these dynamics.

Besnik: The Normalization of Trafficking in Post-Communist Albania

Besnik, a twenty-eight-year-old man from a small town in northern Albania, was the most exemplary embodiment of the heterosexist and violent madonna/whore approach. In the five years preceding our interview, he had trafficked three women. He had managed them exclusively through violence and deception, forcing them to sell sex in Greece or Italy. In each case he had been reported and convicted for trafficking back in Albania. And in each case he had bribed the lawyers and judges and served only a fraction of his sentence, a practice confirmed by research on Albanian trafficking during that period (Tabaku 2008).

I met Besnik through a friend of mine who was working as an interpreter. They came from the same area, but their lives had taken different paths. Besnik was born in a mountainous area of Albania that became infamous for the involvement of young men in trafficking of all kinds, including for the sexual exploitation of women. In Besnik's village of origin, and in the peri-urban rearticulation of his village that internal migration had created around Tirana in the post-communist period, his peer group saw "working with girls" as the best method to "make money" in a way they perceived as "normal."

BESNIK: My project after school? I had a good project. Normal. To make money, because here in Albania that was the priority, then and now. I started working with a girlfriend.

NICOLA: What kind of work did you do in Albania?

BESNIK: I have never worked in Albania. I never liked working here because there is no money to be made. Only Italians and other foreigners make money here. So I went to Italy a couple of times. I joined a friend of mine who had already been there. It was about five years ago. I went with a speedboat from Vlorë. It was very frightening. I paid US$3,600 for two people. Me and my ex-girlfriend. I worked eight months with her, and then she got me locked up in prison.

NICOLA: Was she your official fiancée here in Albania?

BESNIK: No, we only met. Normal. I convinced her to go to Italy; she did not want to. Not only her, the others too. If they don't want to come willingly, then I force them.

The way Besnik became involved in trafficking matches existing studies of the evolution of Albanian organized crime during that period: criminal groups were small scale, and were based on friendships and family relationships (Tabaku 2008, 102; Arsovska 2015, 152). However, the difference between Besnik and the Albanian and Romanian third-party agents I had met outside prison in Rome could not have been presented more starkly. The majority of the latter were able to intercept and manage aspirations to social mobility among young women from their areas of origin as a way to motivate them to work in the sex industry. By adhering to more consensual economic relations, and by managing the women within the discursive repertoire and practices of a romantic relationship, they were able to avoid being reported as traffickers, which was why they had never been detained. I decided to ask Besnik what he thought about it.

NICOLA: I think your management method is typical of the early years after the end of communism. I met quite a few younger men who use a love relationship as a way to manage women. Isn't managing women through love in the context of a relationship safer? If you use violence, you put yourself at risk, as the woman will escape as soon as she has a chance. . . . Why don't you use this method?

BESNIK: I don't use it because it is more dangerous. If you are together with them [women], you can fall in love. You have to use love as little as possible and violence as much as possible, because the more you use violence against women, the more you are going to hate them.

NICOLA: So you would not consider using a love relationship as a method . . .

BESNIK: Only at the beginning, in order to get them abroad and then put them to work. That's my method; it works for me.

NICOLA: You don't want to mix love and work?

BESNIK: The more violence you use against a woman, the more you are going to hate her. If you get the most beautiful woman in the world and then love her, you are going to fall in love with her, and then you won't be able to put her to work in Italy.

NICOLA: But there are guys who do it consensually, by managing women through a love relationship.

BESNIK: There are very few who use mutual understanding; it's very rare. Normally, once women are in Italy, they get nothing but work and beatings. That's the way to do it. Normal; it's better.

Besnik told me all this while sitting at a table in the garden of a hotel in a semiperipheral part of Tirana. I was struck by his recurrent mention of the word and concept "normal." It seemed to refer implicitly to the way the management of sex work had become normalized on the outskirts of Albanian postcommunist society. I was alarmed and excited to be with him, drinking coffee, in a "normal" situation, as he would probably put it. I had never had the chance before to meet an embodiment of the stereotype of the Albanian trafficker. His answers echoed those of many other young men who worked as third-party agents. But Besnik was much blunter and clearer, which was why I decided to include him as one of the six strategic characters in my documentary. I also provocatively named that documentary *Normal* to capture the normalization of criminal behavior that emerged from his life history, as well as to convey the ways in which privileged, commodified, and individualized lifestyles were normalized by the onset of neoliberal onto-epistemology in postcommunist contexts.

Like most of the male agents I met in prisons, Besnik had only completed the twelve years of compulsory education, attending school on and off. Many violent third-party agents decided to abandon their studies because of their fascination with a high-consumption, big-cash lifestyle, which could only be achieved by prioritizing "making money" in the short term over a longer-term investment in education or "straight" income-generating strategies.

> The idea [of working with women] came when I was still at school, during the last two-three years. All my classmates, they talked about it. That played a role. Normal. Then a friend of mine went there [to Italy] before me. . . . He worked a lot and had lots of women. So that became my project, to get one woman to start with and see how it goes.

As this excerpt shows, Besnik thinks peer pressure played an important role in motivating him to work as a third-party agent. The excerpt also shows the relative normalization of involvement in the management of sex work among specific groups of young Albanian men, which he understands as having "more or less" become a "way of life" to make "easy money." Besnik sees this work as part of his "normal" lifestyle and his self-image as a successful man; he describes himself as a "gangster," "someone who knows how to manage, who has many women and because of that he employs other people." When asked whether he thought his "way of life" contradicted traditional Albanian values, he says he does not see it as particularly "modern," the latter being a term that acquired the connotation of "alternative" (to traditional family values) in the postcommunist context (Mai 2004b):

BESNIK: I don't think my lifestyle is very modern. I take my work very seriously. It's not a game. It's something I do with pleasure. I have a very good private life. I have nice friends who don't do these things; they have honest jobs.

NICOLA: Why did you choose this lifestyle, then?

BESNIK: It's when I saw many of my friends that made money. One is returning from Italy tomorrow. He has a three-floors villa, two cars, and much

> more. . . . But in the beginning I did not start because of the money. It was more about becoming more of a gangster, someone with a name, with money, that people don't mess with.

The excerpt above highlights how the emergence of trafficking was embedded in the criminalization of everyday life during the early years of Albania's postcommunist transformation, which was characterized by the rejection of established values and authorities, as well as by the collapse of the centrally planned economy. In 2000, a World Bank report analyzed the emergence of vulnerability—defined as "the new conditions of social weakness suddenly created by the turmoil in society, which are qualitatively different from poverty"—during the process of Albania's postcommunist transformation (La Cava and Nanetti 2000, 1–2). The report identified several vulnerable groups in Albania, including young men at risk of criminal behavior and young women at risk of prostitution. These groups emerged from the overlapping of two conditions of vulnerability: social exclusion, which marginalizes people through rejection from mainstream society; and gender abuse, which marginalizes women through the threat and use of violence. According to the same report, at least 25 percent of young men between the ages of eighteen and twenty-five were engaged in criminal activities. At highest risk of becoming criminals were uneducated young men living in the peri-urban areas of coastal cities and the capital, where drug smuggling and trafficking in women and children were concentrated.

My ethnographic and interview material in Albania confirmed these earlier findings. The following are excerpts from interviews with two young Albanian men from a poor, peri-urban neighborhood in Tirana. Neither man was in prison.

> Yes, I mean, it is the main thing young men and women do here. . . . It is a very poor neighborhood; there is no work at all. So it is quite easy to think you can do it too, when everyone else is doing it. It becomes sort of normal. But I hated it; it is not for me; I am very lucky to have found this job now.

X: Of course I was not the only one, . . . I mean, you need to know one thing. . . . Here, all the people who were able to build something which is not . . . how can I put it . . . which is not basic, like a good restaurant or . . . a good car . . . and a nice house . . . that is how they did it!

NICOLA: But I cannot believe that everyone is doing it, come on . . .

X: Not everyone, but many more than you will ever know, I think at least 35 per-

> cent of the young people I knew in my neighborhood started working with women.

These claims are further corroborated by Besnik's estimate that between 30 and 35 percent of young men in Albania were involved in the third-party management of women. Together, these perceptions and estimates show that this livelihood had become a normalized lifestyle and a survival practice for many young men in relatively marginalized areas of Albania.

As I reflected on these social dynamics during my interview with Besnik, I was reminded of a young man I had met in jail just a few days earlier. I had not even had time to register his pseudonym. He was twenty-three years old, good-looking, and incredibly angry. He had only been able to find casual work as a builder. He sat down in front of me in the little room where I was interviewing detainees, both irritated and curious. "I don't want to talk about anything," he said. "I just want to tell you that I did nothing wrong. I am here because judges want to make a career on our backs. I got fifteen years for nothing. I did what every young person does when he has no work. I only finished state school. I did the only thing I could do. Normal." And then he left.

Immediately after him, another twenty-three-year-old had come in. Petrit was not angry, but ashamed. He was from the city of Berat. "What am I going to say?" he asked me rhetorically.

"I don't know," I answered with a sigh. I really didn't. After a day spent interviewing infamous detainees, I found myself speechless before the normality through which they had come to be involved in criminal and violent activities. He did not even look me in the eye. I did not try too hard either. "Tell me what you want," I said.

He told me briefly that his father was old and ill. That his sister was, "thank God," married, and his mother was left alone to take care of the fields and the house. And, after a short pause, that his brother was in jail for the same story. They shared a cell. This was when he first looked me in the eye, to see how I would react. I tried to remember whether I had talked to his brother, whether I could identify a resemblance. He seemed too ashamed, and I was too tired. He continued:

> I have only been in school for a year. From what I remember I have always worked, . . . loading, unloading stuff, . . . the fields. . . . Then one day, while I was away, a friend of mine from Gramsh arrived at my place and stayed there for one night with a girl. My parents let him stay, as they are old and naive.

> And so was I. I did not know what my friend was up to when I accompanied the girl to Tirana. I did not know the risks. . . . Anyway, when my friend was accused of trafficking, the judges thought that I was part of the plan, and here I am. But I did nothing. I was only naive.

"The fragmentation discourse again," I thought, and said nothing. He was the last interviewee of the day, and I had little energy left. As he stood up to leave the room, he finally said something he and I both partially believed: "Only those who are less guilty and cannot pay lawyers end locked up in Albania." Then he left.

As I drove home that night, all I could think of was that I wanted to swim in the sea and have a glass of wine. I guess I wanted to wash the whole affective and physical experience away. My skin felt sticky with betrayal and infamy. I stopped at my favorite pizzeria on Golem beach, near Durrës. What had been a low-rise bungalow nestled discreetly beneath a maritime pine forest just a few years earlier was now a three-storey building, towered over by hotels under construction. Still, it did the trick. After a long swim, a nice meal, and a glass of wine, I drove back to Tirana. While driving, I mentally reviewed the people I had talked to during the day: the prisoners, the guards, the director. I suddenly remembered the dossier I had consulted just before lunch. I remembered a picture of the leader of a criminal gang. I had interviewed him. He was also from Berat, and looked a lot like the last interviewee. "His brother," I thought. It had been the thickest folder of all, and the least "fragmentable."

Every time I immersed myself in the affective atmosphere of infamy surrounding the management of sex work, whether I was right at the heart of a prison in Rome or Albania, or sitting comfortably on a hotel terrace in Tirana, I emerged exhausted by a compound experience of social, economic, and affective betrayal. The social betrayal experienced by third-party agents in the face of poverty, social immobility, and judicial corruption meant that only the "less guilty" and "less connected" remained in jail. My fear of betraying my own ethics and integrity by allowing myself to remain heuristically open toward infamous acts and toward people I often felt should be (and mostly were) in jail for what they had done. But what affected me most was the betrayal of women's trust, of their investment in their romantic and economic relationships with their agents. I was not alone in this. As I understood during the research, it was this form of betrayal, rather than violence per se, that had got agents reported as traffickers by "their" women.

Besnik saw this happen to him every time he forced a woman to sell sex. Although he presented himself throughout the interview as a hegemonic and successful male, with his references to having made it as a gangster, by the end of the interview, he was starting to put some of his cards on the table.

Knowing the severity of traditional Albanian morality in relation to what he was involved in, I guessed that he might have paid a huge price for his actions. I asked him about his family. His voice, demeanor and posture gradually changed. His monolithic performance as a hegemonic and successful male started to liquefy, very slowly. "I talk to them, but not much. Normal; they don't like what I do. But this is my way of life. We have not spoken, or spoken very little, for about two years. I have my own house, and I meet my brother every now and then, but that's it." Besnik said this all in one go, and cleared his throat. Immediately afterward, he looked away, suddenly sad and distant. His sadness at having been rejected by his family and his nervous tic were the only glimpses of more complex self-representation beyond the Albanian gangster stereotype.

By then we had been talking for almost an hour and a half, and I needed to know about his plans for the future. "In ten years? I hope I'll have five or six good whores working in Italy. I don't think I will open a venue like my friend did. . . . Even if he did well out of it. I don't have the patience to deal with clients, waiters . . ." As Besnik put the empty glass down and looked at his watch, I also felt we had come full circle and that it was time to go. Whatever small glimpse into his vulnerability had been opened by his sadness at the loss of his family had quickly closed down. I was exhausted by the amount of affect I had had to mobilize to get and keep the interview going. I emptied my glass too, and thanked him for his time. I meant it, but I was really glad it was over. It was one of the most interesting and disturbing interviews I had ever undertaken. Unlike in Kathleen Blee's (1998) research on self-defined racist and anti-Semitic groups in the United States, fear had not been a relevant affect in our intersubjective interaction, although it had not been defined by empathy either. I did not feel afraid in his presence, possibly because my interpreter friend was there too. I was revolted by his behavior and the way he talked about women, and I struggled to conceal it for the sake of the research.

Before we parted I gave him the fifty-euro note, which he readily accepted. I then left, while the interpreter lingered for a few seconds. As the taxi was leaving the square in front of the hotel, I looked back and saw Besnik walk straight into the casino opposite. "Easy money goes quickly," a phrase I had heard over and over again while researching sex work, passed through my mind. As the car sped toward the city center, I found myself thinking how many agents wasted their money gambling. Quite a few, particularly those who managed sex work through violence. I could not help thinking that a part of them, a vulnerable part they kept well hidden from themselves, could not hold onto the money they had earned through trafficking, out of some disowned sense of guilt. I also thought about how violently Besnik stopped himself from loving the women he exploited and wondered whether his gangster selfrepresentation was mostly a facade covering a much more vulnerable and indeed "normal" personality. But then I could not think any more. I felt dazed by the violence and infamy that had emerged from the interview with Besnik. I had come too close to the real horror of trafficking, to its eerie normalization.

Adrian: Liquid Agent

Adrian was a twenty-two-year-old Romanian man who worked as an agent in partnership with Milena, a young woman from his area of origin. His life history perfectly exemplifies the transition toward more consensual forms of management in later postcommunist times. Adrian had learned the hard way to stop using violence, as he saw most of his friends being arrested for having betrayed the terms of their agreements with the women they managed. Unlike many of his peers, he was able to reflect on the sex-gendered roles he performed and the relationships he engaged in. During his interview, Adrian explained clearly that the strategic function of the agent is not only to offer protection and logistical support, but also to work as a professional fiancé, which (as described in chapter 5) means performing a credible phenomenology of love that endows both his female working partner abroad and her family at home with a morally, economically, and relationally sustainable framework.

> A woman working like this, with the job that she has, you have to wash even her socks and underwear when she comes home. If there is only one morsel of food left, you have to give it to her. So that she trusts you and does not betray you. So that she can see for herself that she is better off with you than other girls, that she sees that, . . . that she does not find reasons to denounce you. "This one never spat in my face, never tore my hair away, never burnt me with cigarettes, never beat me up or shouted at me. Some girls come to work with black eyes, burnt with cigarettes, with torn hair, . . . whereas I

> am treated like a princess." [. . .] I mean, my way is not to be violent. . . . If I don't give her what she needs, like nice clothes, some company, a bit of love, protection, take her to medical controls, . . . I mean, for example, if she catches something, she will think, "What did I catch this illness for, for money? And not even for money I gave to my family and my children, but for this one, who treated me like a chicken . . . and then threw me in a bath of acid." Her mentality, you see, her heart will burn. . . . She will think, . . . she will open, . . . and she'll go to denounce you.

Perhaps Adrian's ability to respect the sentimental and economic agreements he made with Milena and the other women he managed stemmed from his own experience of betrayal by his parents, who arranged his marriage to a neighbor's daughter when he was fifteen. Although this practice was not uncommon in the Roma community he belonged to, he had expected his parents to be less traditional and more "open." In his family they "never had women wearing long skirts, and there was never any mention of marrying off children so early."

Once in Italy, Adrian was also betrayed by his expectations of a better life, which he had glimpsed by watching Italian satellite television back in Romania. Confronted with the reality of living in a Roma camp on the outskirts of the Eternal City, and with the stigmatized livelihoods available to him—including begging, stealing and selling sex—he again felt angry and disappointed. He decided to try begging and stealing from tourists, but he kept getting put into, and escaping from, minors' centers. Unaccompanied migrant minors like Adrian experience social protection as infantilizing in relation to their priority of making money, a dynamic I discussed in chapter 2. It was at this point that he started managing sex work, like many of his peers. When asked about his work with Milena, Adrian was like an overflowing river.

> The girl I work with, I met her back at home; she is from my same town. She contacted me in a disco while I was home for a visit. She was doing the same job that she is doing here, and she wanted to make more money in Italy. She is twenty-four years old; I met her about three years ago. She kept on phoning me; she said, "Everyone is taking the piss because they know what I do, better that I come there; you don't have to be implicated, but people know you, and they respect you, and we can work together if you want. This is not to say that I am an idiot, and that I am going to give you all the money." I told her, "Look, I help you, I consider you a friend; if you want to work with

> me, that is fine, so that you can say that you are my girlfriend in Romania and also in Italy, so that you are respected because you are with me, so you won't have any problems with the other boys roaming around." It was not about the money at first, but then the end I thought, OK, there is no love between us; I could as well work with her. Who is that stupid that would not see an opportunity in this?

I guess that was the question he was waiting for, the one that allowed him to selfrepresent his desired mobile orientation as a hegemonic neoliberal man who "made it" by exploiting every money-making opportunity that came his way: a clever and rational agent, a skilled entrepreneur, and conspicuous consumer, efficiently calculating risks and returns against the danger of being perceived and reported as a trafficker. But there was much more to Adrian than the calculating agent he selfrepresented in the interview. His life history exemplifies the transition from violence-based, third-party management techniques to more consensual practices that took place in the sex industry during the 2000s. This shift in management techniques reflects the late-modern melting of established sex-gendered roles and authorities that Bauman (2000) describes as a defining aspect of "liquid modernity." Like his peers, Adrian "liquefied" trafficking into a late-modern practice that capitalizes on the commodification of intimacy and the social rationality of success engendered by neoliberal onto-epistemology.

Adrian's transition from violence to consensuality was a response to the opportunities and constraints encountered by his peers, and to the transformation of sex-gendered male roles, power, and authority toward a higher degree of fluidity in late-modern times. He was not the only third-party agent straddling these dynamics of fluidification of traditional models of masculinity, which have recently been documented and studied in contemporary Albanian society (Çaro, Bailey and Van Wissen 2018). This excerpt from an interview with Fatmir, a twenty-five-year-old Albanian agent working in Rome, shows the specific forms of intimate labor that enable the relationship between male agent and female partner to work.

> I told you, I care about her; she is like a sister to me. . . . Of course I fuck her, but this too is part of the trade. When she comes back from work, you have to fuck her, so that she feels that she does not disgust you for what she does. And if you are good enough to let her understand that, then she is yours. I know it sounds bad, but I also care about her; sometimes it is work, but most of the times it isn't. . . . I mean, she is basically a lover and a friend; she actually became the person I trust more in all this.

These words highlight once again the intricacy of need, desire, advantage, and affection that underpins relationships between men and women implicated in the sex industry as agents and workers respectively. Many interviewees who talked openly about their relationships with their female work (and often also sentimental) partners described their seduction techniques as strategic assets of their selfrepresentations as "men in control." In these circumstances they selfrepresented as rational and calculating agents, according to the rhetoric of rational entrepreneurship that shapes neoliberal late-modern canons of subjectification (Marques 2010). However, the degree of "sentimental detachment" emerging from ethnographic observations provides a much more liquid picture.

For instance, the instrumental nature of their romantic commitments to their working partners sometimes appeared to contradict aspects of the relationship and the power relations embedded in it. This was how Fatmir replied when asked to compare his relationship with his fiancée in Albania to the relationship with his girlfriend and working partner in Italy:

> I have two relationships in this moment, one with the woman with whom I work and another with a woman from my country, whom I am going to marry. I love them both. The only difference is that one woman is helping the other to be better, economically. One woman is my lover, with whom I make money. The other is my future wife; who is happier than me? With the woman from my country I build my family, while with the other, I build my future for me, for her, and for her future family. [. . .] When I met her [the lover], I really liked her. . . . She told a friend we have in common that she was looking for somebody to take her to Italy, and I took her. Now I am very fond of her. She is like a sister who helps me. Well, we actually help each other. Of course, I have to fuck her, as it is part of the job, to show her I love her, but the truth is that I am really fond of her. Here we feel free; if one night we want to go out to have a good time, we do it; she does not go to work, we get out and get drunk, we dance, and then go home to fuck, like a normal couple.

In many cases, as shown in chapter 7, men were torn between contradictory masculine roles, expectations, and established mobile orientations. For them too, working in the sex industry as third-party agents was a way to fractally mediate between normative selfrepresentations as married and providing sons at home, and the desire to embody the individualized and hedonistic young man having fun with his girlfriend abroad, "like a normal couple."

On the one hand, the emphasis on women's autonomy in their decision to sell sex under their management can be seen as strategic discursive move for agents, as it detaches them from the stigma and criminalization associated with "pimping" and "trafficking" (Gleeson 2004). In a symmetrical way, by emphasizing their lack of consent to sell sex under the management of a male migrant, women detach themselves from the whore stigma (Andrijasevic 2010). By performing themselves as "victims of trafficking," women can also avoid the threat of deportation. For instance, by highlighting her subjection to her agent, Candy, the nineteen-year-old woman I presented in chapter 7 and portrayed in my documentary *Normal*, discursively downplayed her own criminal conviction for controlling prostitution for gain. However, the fluid selfrepresentation of relationships between women who sell sex and men who manage them emerging in the ethnographic material I analyze in this and in the previous chapters cannot be explained solely in terms of interdiscursive dynamics that seek to avoid stigmatization, criminalization, and deportation (Sandberg 2009). Rather, these more fluid, sex-gendered selfrepresentations point to the transformation of the associated roles and practices into less exploitative and more consensual forms in later postcommunist times.

The opaque coexistence of manipulation and genuine support that characterizes relationships between agents and sex workers highlights their shared socioeconomic vulnerability, which is related to commodified conditions of subjectification in contemporary times. Young migrants' existential priority to "make money" transcends the economic dimension and reflects an objectualized moral economy where the social stigma attached to returning home "empty-handed" overrides the danger of being exploited (Lindquist 2007, 227). The reiterated reference in migrants' selfrepresentations to neoliberal canons of commodified normality as a vector of their mobile orientations highlights the predicaments of subjectification offered by globalized, neoliberal late modernity. The interviews with Dorina, a twenty-six-year-old woman selling and managing sex in Italy, and Cesar, her twenty-five-year-old fellow Romanian agent/boyfriend, show the fractal tension between individualization, commodification, and the resilience of traditional sex-gendered selfrepresentations at home:

DORINA: We both come from a bad place. We always had to do things that we did not want to do; . . . now I feel I don't have to lead that shit life any more. Where I come from is a shithole; there is nothing to do, and the mentality is very old. If you want to have a good time, you have to become somebody's whore; otherwise they get you to marry and create a family, and then you are old as they are. I thought that the situation was better here [in Italy] than over there, and it was true. Everybody was saying the same thing. One way or another, everyone who came here made money, and so when I met him, . . . and I understood he was making money, I decided to come here too.

CESAR: To live in Romania nowadays, . . . you do not really need money to live, but to prove to others that you are better than them. Sometimes you live like shit, but outside people think you are OK. [. . .] Look at me, I am full of gold and so is my girlfriend. Look at Romanian women or girls; they are always full of gold because they need to prove to somebody that they are doing well. [. . .] The problem is this always having to prove something to people and also at home, to your family. They expect everything from you, and when you go out, you need to be able to show that you can afford fashionable things; otherwise you are not worth a fucking thing.

Dorina and Cesar's life histories and decisions highlight the shared, commodified socioeconomic and cultural conditions of men and women who decide to migrate in order to "make money" as workers and agents in the sex industry. They also highlight how established sex-gendered roles are both reinforced and challenged in the process. Their mobile orientations are the expression of a fractal mediation between the aspiration to an individualized and more hedonistic lifestyle, the stigmatization of women wanting to have "a good time," and the performance of standardized and commodified deeds of economic success and privilege "at home."

These broader dynamics are reflected in the relationship between Adrian and Milena. In order to feel morally entitled to make money in the sex industry, Milena needs to selfrepresent as Adrian's fiancée to protect herself from the (partially internalized) whore stigma associated with her willingness to sell sex in the name of social mobility. In turn, Adrian needs to tacitly and fractally manage on Milena's behalf the emotional and economic transactions that dare not speak their names at home. He is able to do that not only because he needs to stay safe, but also because he now objects to the use of violence against women. Asked whether he felt bad about having resorted to violence against women in the past, he replies,

I do feel guilty because I took advantage of a person, . . . of her pains and unwillingness to work, her fears and stress. As I imagine her when she is with a client and she is afraid that he will hurt her, that he wants to kidnap her, or rob her, "God knows where he takes me, . . ." I feel guilty because for a period, with this girl, before I started doing things the way I told you, . . . seeing guys beating up girls and stuff like that, I did the same. In general . . . I did

> not think about her. For instance, I only thought about buying her clothes for work, which would attract clients, not for her. In other words I used to be "a bad guy" too, in the past.

These self-reflexive considerations show that Adrian is a "liquid" third-party agent. His understanding of sex-gendered roles reflects the late-modern fluidification of traditional and modern values, institutions, and authorities under the pressure of neoliberal forces of commodification and individualization (Bauman 2000). Adrian is no stereotypical "loverboy" pretending to love women in order to manipulate them and force them to sell sex. Unlike Besnik, he does not need (or rather, he no longer needs) to despise and beat the women he works with in order to manage them. He manages his working partners by respecting their deals and by facilitating their mobile orientations according to the shared commodified and individualized terms of subjectivity engendered by neoliberal late modernity.

Toward Fluid Antitrafficking?

Interviews undertaken in early postcommunist times showed that Albanian men involved in third-party sex work management considered the women working for them—whether wives, fiancées, or relatives—their private property. Most of them failed to understand why the police would be interested in their private economic activities at all (Ballauri 1997). This was the case with Besnik, whose calm demeanor as he recounted the violence he inflicted on his victims confirmed the extent to which trafficking had become normalized in his milieu. "If I felt bad about it, I would not do this job. . . . When they start crying, it only makes me more angry," he replied to my question about whether he felt any remorse for what he did to the women he trafficked.

While I listened to Besnik, and possibly as a way to maintain my empathetic heuristic disposition, I thought about my own early analyses of social dynamics in early postcommunist Albania. The cultural construction of capitalist democracy as a utopia of individualized freedom and material luxury removed the restraints posed by institutional and social authorities, thereby allowing young men to use "their" women as sources of income for the accumulation of capital in deeply patriarchal settings (Mai 2001a). Albania's postcommunist transformation was accompanied by the rejection not only of communist ideology but of values and practices related to a collective ethical dimension. It was also accompanied by an uninformed idealization of the West as an easily accessible universe of material plenty.

Post-communist societies experienced a high degree of ambivalence regarding old and new sociocultural, moral, and economic values and priorities. Young people asserting their identities during this period of heightened social transformation were caught between the desire to conform to commodified and individualized late-modern lifestyles, the economic imperatives of family survival, and the enduring hegemony of patriarchal and conservative values at home.

One of the outcomes of all this was a reinvention of strategic aspects of cultural heritage, particularly patriarchal, sex-gendered roles, to meet emerging social needs and identities (Schwandner-Sievers 2000, 256). Young men who became involved in the management of international sex work in the early postcommunist years did so predominantly through violence, because they were assembling their mobile orientations in a context characterized by traditionalized selfrepresentations and values. These emerged from the convergence of heterosexist traditional models, the socioeconomic and cultural uncertainties and opportunities created by postcommunist transformation, and the weakness of the state in enforcing the law and guaranteeing dignified livelihoods. The decline of parental authority, the fragmentation and polarization of the socioeconomic situation, and the cultural construction of democracy as a place without prescriptive rules where luxury could be easily attained all constituted fertile ground for criminal behavior (Fuga 1998). Many young men had low expectations for their economic futures and little faith in the state's ability to solve their problems. The reactive rejection of traditional values of honesty and morality (because of their association with the communist heritage and with experiences of inequality and corruption at home), the lack of economic opportunities, and the corruption of state officials motivated such men to see criminal behavior as a positive way to help themselves and their families.

However, my ethnographic observations and interviews after 1998 in Albania, Greece, Italy, Romania, and the United Kingdom showed that violence and coercion were no longer the only or prevailing techniques used by young Albanian and Romanian men to manage their sex-working partners. This was a consequence of the process of individualization in their societies of origin; the transformation of sex-gendered selfrepresentations, values, and mores among young people; and the introduction of antitrafficking legislation that allowed young women to report their business and sentimental partners if they felt they were being exploited. These distinctions and nuances are important, because later postcommunist times were characterized by a transformation of international sex work into relatively less exploitative and more consensual practices (Schwandner-Sievers 2010). The violent methods adopted by young men such as Besnik should be seen as one traditionalized, sociocultural outcome of a complex situation—and not the only possible one.

Romanian sociologists Sebastian Lăzăroiu and Monica Alexandru (2003) contextualize Romanian women's involvement in trafficking within the moral and economic fluidity that followed the communist period and within the wider phenomenon of migration. In their view, victims of trafficking, and migrants in general, can be considered "social innovators" (Lăzăroiu and Alexandru 2003, 21) who take more risks than those who stay put. Their mobile orientations are responses to a social and economic environment where migration abroad has become a widespread strategy to cope with social, cultural, and economic transformations. Indeed, compared with other migrants, the female victims of trafficking described by Lăzăroiu and Alexandru (2003, 22–23) are "More independent, rather open to experiments, and willing to accept uncertainty and risk. [. . .] They do not feel close to their family and they do not believe that the family is the most important thing in one's life. They do not value education as a means to succeed and [. . .] have a high propensity to break rules."

These observations also apply to men involved in the arrangement and management of sex work across international borders. Many of them similarly challenge and reproduce established, sex-gendered roles, parental and institutional authorities, and regimes of social mobility by managing sex work abroad. The evidence I analyze in this chapter shows that the mobile orientations and sex-gendered roles embodied by third-party agents mirror those of the women they manage and reflect shared onto-epistemological, socioeconomic, and geopolitical transformations in the societies of origin and destination of their migratory projects. The individualized profiling of potential "traffickers" does not address how socioeconomic marginalization and polarization exacerbate the vulnerability of both young men and women to involvement in irregular and/or criminal activities. Nor does it address how trafficking has been transformed into relatively more consensual agreements and practices by the implementation of antitrafficking policies and the fluidification of sex-gendered roles and relationships.

These changes have brought about new conditions of vulnerability and agency, which call for a less Manichean interpretation of the subjectivities and relationships involved in the arrangement of sex work across (and within) international borders. Antitrafficking initiatives seem to be tailored only to traditionalized, extreme, and exceptional forms of abuse and violence, rather than to the individualized, diffused, and ambivalent situations that characterize the realities of the majority of migrant sex workers. The research findings I present in this book challenge the usefulness of the concept of trafficking and the related concept of modern slavery for grasping and addressing the complex understandings and experiences of agency and exploitation of migrants working in the sex industry. They show that women tend to use the instruments of protection offered to them when their agreement with their third-party agent is not respected, rather than in order to escape from sex work or third-party management per se. The main problem with the mainstream trafficking paradigm is that it is predicated on a neo-abolitionist denial of the possibility of voluntary sex work (Ditmore and Wijers 2003), allocating humanitarian protection on the basis of hierarchies of "innocent" victimhood (Ticktin 2017). The relationships between the women and third-party agents involved in international sex work are often interpreted in convoluted and illogically pathologizing ways that do not reflect the socio-economic priorities embedded in migrants' mobile orientations. For example, the concept of the "Stockholm syndrome," referring to a situation where a hostage shows signs of loyalty to the hostage-taker, has often been used in a vernacular way by neo-abolitionist scholars and activists to obliterate the possibility that women might consent to sell sex independently or under the management of a third-party agent (Adorjan, Christensen, Kelly, et al. 2012). Similarly, the concept of "retrafficking," referring to people who are forced back into the sex industry, is often conflated with the desire of repatriated "victims" to "remigrate" abroad (Jobe 2010, 14), as the experience of Alina (discussed in chapter 6) illustrates. This antitrafficking terminology does not account for the socioeconomic priorities of the majority of migrant sex workers, for whom migration and sex work are strategic ways to fulfill their mobile orientations. It is consistent with a social intervention paradigm—and with profitable, privileged moralities—that would be delegitimated by the possibility of voluntary engagement in sex work, either independently or under the management of another person, and that evoke scenarios of false consciousness to defend their *raison d'être.*

The aim of these considerations is not to deny that social and psychological vulnerability can be implicated and exacerbated in sex work, but to encourage a redefinition of the priorities of social intervention so as to respond to evolving challenges. To meet these challenges and changes, policymaking on sex work and trafficking should adopt forms of "collaborative governance," embracing rather than rejecting the complexity of their encompassing "policy field"—the surrounding socioeconomic, cultural, and geopolitical context—and establishing an "authentic dialogue" with the dissonant epistemological approaches drawing on the lived, complex, and multifaceted experiences of sex workers (Wagenaar, Amesberger, and Altink 2010, 263). This means that antitrafficking and antislavery efforts should dissociate themselves from neo-abolitionist ideologies and adopt labor-based approaches offering "greater hope of long-term prevention and change" rather than prioritizing harmful and inefficient criminal justice approaches (Chuang 2014, 644). They should accept the reality and possibility of voluntary prostitution, including through debt and under the management of others, which does not necessarily amount to trafficking in the eyes of those directly involved: migrant sex workers. Only if antitrafficking and antislavery efforts stop being complicit with sexual-humanitarian and migration law enforcement will migrant (and nonmigrant) sex workers see current interventions as supportive rather than repressive and harmful (Maher Dixon, Phlong, et al. 2015) and be able to participate fully, on their own terms, in the fight against exploitation and trafficking (Bergquist 2015). Understanding and working with migrant sex workers' complex agencing decisions, mobile orientations, and their embedded existential priorities is the only way to actually prevent their exploitation, whether they want to quit or continue working in the sex industry.

NINE

Ethnofictional Counter-Representations

Making *Normal*

At the beginning of my research on the sex industry, I was not immune to the sexual-humanitarian, melodramatic, and neoliberal conflation of migrant sex work with trafficking. I was forced to reject it gradually, bit by bit, by multiple reiterations of the mismatch between the knowledge happening before my eyes and the spectacular selfrepresentations engendered by sexual-humanitarian rhetoric. For instance, the most revealing thing about my interview with Alina was when she was moved. By "when" I do not mean the *fact* that she was moved, but the *moment* it actually happened. In sexual-humanitarian accounts of trafficking victims, the affective (and affecting) atmosphere of neo-abolitionist compassion usually thickens around the recounting of the first time a person sold sex (as mentioned in chapter 7 in relation to Candy's interview). "The first time" is a powerful trope within the rhetorical spectacularization of migrants' involvement in the sex industry in terms of trafficking. It rearticulates the long-standing patriarchal leitmotif of loss of virginity by framing women's involvement in the sex industry as their entry into the stigmatized terrain of female promiscuity (Nencel 2005).

Alina's interview (described in chapter 6) challenged this patriarchal trope of "the first time" and its neo-abolitionist framing. In line with the intimate, intersubjective dynamics that allowed us to laugh about the paradox of being in danger for not knowing what a blowjob was, Alina's account of her "first time" was marked by ironic rather than tragic affect. Most important, the tragic climax of her story was not about becoming a "loose woman" by having sold sex *per se*. It was about coming home with nothing to show for it. For her, the ultimate humiliation was the betrayal of her mobile orientation, which had been shaped by the existential and subjectifying mandate to support her family. "I had to ask my mother for the money for the taxi from the airport," was the deepest and most painful mortification for Alina. It was this humiliation, and the lack of local alternatives to fulfill her family-provider mandate, that prompted her return to England.

Alina's tacit challenge to sexual humanitarianism by being moved in the "wrong" rhetorical place was mirrored by Catalin, a sixteen-year-old Romanian minor selling sex in Rome, when he talked about his "first time":

> A guy came by in a car, and he asked me if I'm passive or active. I told him I was active, and he took me to his home. He made me take a shower, and he gave me shoes, underwear, trousers, everything. When I came out of the shower, he sucked me off and then I fucked him. He gave me thirty euros and he took me back.

When asked how he had felt about it, Catalin replied: "Fine, how else should I feel? I fucked, I came, and I earned thirty euro!" The sexual-humanitarian approach framing all minors as sexually exploited is further destabilized by another passage from Catalin's interview:

> My wife knows what I do. She keeps telling me that she's afraid of the clap and AIDS. My parents also know about it. My mother says it's better than stealing, as at least I don't get to jail. She keeps the money for my house in Romania. I give her some of the money and the rest I keep for me to buy shoes and T-shirts.

Catalin's situation could be framed as parental abuse and exploitation according to sexual-humanitarian onto-epistemology. Was he being exploited or supported by his mother? Such questions remain enigmatic because they are asked across dichotomies that express different socioeconomic, affective, and onto-epistemological frameworks. Experiences of parenthood, childhood, and love based on economic support in a context of poverty collide with a privileged, sexual-humanitarian, and North-centric epistemology that frames economic activity and intimate relations as "separate spheres and hostile worlds" (Zelizer 2005, 20). Let me reiterate that "Global North" is not a geographical expression: it refers to the diffused geopolitical center from which hegemonic, onto-epistemological regimes produce sexual-humanitarian global sentimentality through the demonization of sex work in underprivileged and affluent countries alike. This sexual-humanitarian global sentimentality frames as inherently exploitative any intimate relationship—including friendship, parenting, and marriage—that becomes directly or indirectly associated with sex work. In doing so, it criminalizes as "pimping" the ways these intimate relationships are implicitly or explicitly mediated, with varying degrees of consent, through specific economic transactions in what is constructed as "the rest of the world."

The onto-epistemology of trafficking and slavery, disseminated by (sexual) humanitarian spectacular rhetoric, clashes with migrants' own narratives of self-realization and autonomy through sex work. It was this clash that led me to research the nexus between migration and the sex industry. Social intervention and research automatically address the migration of minors through legal and social protection categories such as "errant mobility," "unaccompanied minors/separated children," "asylum-seeking children," "child exploitation," and "trafficking." When the person selling sex is younger than eighteen, prostitution studies increasingly refer to the "commercial sexual exploitation of children" (CSEC), since the term *child prostitution* implies that the activity might be voluntary (O'Connell Davidson 2005). These dynamics are particularly pronounced in the United States, the generating center of sexual-humanitarian rhetoric and epistemology, where the framing of all minor sex work as "domestic trafficking" has legitimized carceral forms of protection and control that do not address the "intersecting racial, economic, and gendered root causes of the problem or the devastating effects wrought by neoliberal economic policies" (Musto 2013, 272). Moreover, these sexual-humanitarian categories do not exist in the social, cultural, and economic worlds of migrant and nonmigrant children, some of whom can and do decide to sell sex with varying degrees of agency, as recent research in the United States shows (Marcus, Horning, Curtis, et al. 2014). The research findings I present in this book also show that many migrant male minors and young adults express a sense of agency by selling sex, which they see as a more economically rewarding way to make money, as this excerpt from Catalin's interview shows clearly:

> There are younger, thirteen- to fourteen-years-old boys. They have clients too and they work. We all come from the same village and know each other. We know this is a good job. What am I going to do in Romania? Wait for someone to ask me to throw away his old table for a couple of euros? What am I going to do with a couple of euros?

Yet minors' existential priorities and understandings of agency are systematically ignored by governmental and nongovernmental policies, as well as the sexual-humanitarian rhetoric of victimhood that frames all minors as victims of CSEC. These infantilizing and North centric understandings of adolescence eliminate important differences in how the passage to adulthood is negotiated within and across different social and cultural settings. For instance, as discussed in chapter 3, outside the Global North (and in marginalized and disadvantaged contexts within it) adolescents are seen primarily as bearers of duties rather than of rights (Whitehead 2007). Social interventions need to address these differences if they genuinely want to respond to their target populations' priorities and socioeconomic vulnerabilities (Mai 2011).

I am not making these observations because I want to present the sex industry as a suitable or desirable environment in which migrant or nonmigrant minors can realize their mobile orientations, which it is not. But by ignoring the fact that adolescents between the ages of fourteen and seventeen can and do decide to sell sex, sexual-humanitarian rhetoric and interventions can further contribute to their marginalization and stigmatization by ignoring the socioeconomic inequalities that frame their mobile orientations and agencing decisions to work in the sex industry. As mentioned in previous chapters, many migrant minors experience protective residential centers as a waste of time: they feel they should be out "making money" instead. Catalin's experience of sex work as agentic challenges the protectionist rhetoric and interventions deployed by sexual humanitarianism. So does the displacement of Alina's affective climax from the sexual-humanitarian rhetorical trope of "the first time" to the moment of deportation and economic destitution. These onto-epistemological dissonances reposition North-centric notions of agency and morality around the opportunity to offer economic and affective support to people and relationships that matter in one's life, including parents, lovers, agents, and friends. At the same time, Alina's and Catalin's mobile orientations and their embedded agencing decisions are constrained by the commodified terms of subjectivity and the socioeconomic polarization engendered by the global onset of neoliberal late modernity, which is characterized by the erosion of labor rights and the expansion and proliferation of intimate forms of labor. Only fighting these diffused, socioeconomic dynamics, rather than attempting to "rescue" individual victims through harmful and criminalizing social interventions, can truly enhance the agency of migrant and nonmigrant sex workers (including minors selling sex) and reduce their vulnerability to exploitation in the sex industry and in other sectors of employment.

How can we represent the complexity of migrants' trajectories within the sex industry? How can we avoid reproducing the neo-abolitionist affective strategies that characterize hegemonic, sexual-humanitarian selfrepresentations while expressing related experiences of suffering and exploitation? How can we give voice to migrants while protecting their identities? When I finally resolved to present my different and interrelated research findings in a single piece of work, I decided to start by making a documentary film rather than a book. I wanted it to be about the intricacy and complexity of experiences of exploitation and agency among migrant sex workers and third-party agents, and about the ways their contradictory selfrepresentations in interviews both challenged and reproduced sexual-humanitarian melomentaries and other filmic representations of migrant sex work as trafficking. Ideally, I wanted to present my work through the shared visual, affective, and intersubjective dimensions that had made knowledge happen; I wanted the audience to share my embodied gaze and perspective as a researcher. Most importantly, I wanted to challenge directly—that is, through filmmaking rather than writing—the "post-truth" affective politics of neo-abolitionist compassion mobilized by sexual-humanitarian filmic selfrepresentations.

I had many questions, but only a few answers. While I thought about a format for the film, the main question became, How can I question, filmically, the politics of the representation of all migrant sex workers as either victims or villains in hegemonic, sexual-humanitarian melomentaries on sex trafficking? Or, to draw on Rancière (2006), what aesthetic form might enable me to challenge the sexual-humanitarian "distribution of the sensible," the way materialities, subjectivities, and relationships are made socially visible and intelligible? I knew what I did not want. I did not want to have the original interviewees talking about themselves in front of the camera. This decision was taken on affective, ethical, and methodological grounds. I felt uneasy about the idea of pointing the camera at real research participants and asking them the same questions as might be asked during unrecorded, private interviews. I did not want to have that power, that intrusive presence in the complexity of our exchanges. It would have erased the contextual and relational way in which knowledge had actually emerged between us. What is more, the complexity of their mobile orientations would easily have become silenced by "safer"—that is, preferred and sexual-humanitarian—selfrepresentations. This was the initial reason I decided to use actors to perform real interviews instead. But I also wanted to use actors to question—by adopting a naturalistic aesthetic while making the fictional device visible—the criteria of authenticity that shape sexual-humanitarian melomentaries and their manipulative representations of all

8. *Normal*: The six characters. Clockwise from top left: Adrian, Candy, Besnik, Alina, Cynthia, and Catalin.

sex workers as victims. There was one thing I knew right from the start: I wanted the film to be called *Normal,* in homage to the contradictory normalization of commodified and individualized neoliberal lifestyles that framed the characters' decisions to migrate and work in the sex industry.

In identifying a cinematographic solution to my epistemological problems, I was inspired by the filmography and ethnofictions of Jean Rouch. The term *ethnofiction* refers to Rouch's successful attempt to capture the "ethos" of lived research experiences by transcending "the distinction between fiction and nonfiction, participation and observation, knowledge and sentiment" (Stoller 1992, 143). Starting from the notion that fiction is the only way to penetrate reality, Rouch developed a visionary body of filmic and ethnographic work in which he used cinema to create knowledge in participatory and shared ways by including his research subjects as coauthors and actors. His filmmaking was part of his epistemological approach, his way of knowing. For instance, in *Moi, un Noir* (1958) and *Jaguar* (1967), which both explore young men's involvement in labor and seasonal migration in Côte d'Ivoire, Rouch uses cinema to create as well as represent an ethnographic reality. Hence, when producing ethnofictions, the main issue is not to downplay the presence of the cinematographic device in order to minimize its impact on the observation of the real. It is to find a cinematographic device that has the potential to elicit and represent reality in the most heuristically significant ways. This was definitely the case with my first film, *Comidas Rapidas,* in which the process of filmmaking became part of a shared socio-anthropological research method and experience.

My main challenge with the ethnofictions that followed my early short films *Comidas Rapidas* and *Mother Europe* was to find a filmic device that would allow me both to express and to analyze the penetration of sexual-humanitarian selfrepresentations and borders in migrant subjectivities in post-humanitarian times. Understanding and representing the sexual-humanitarian merging of factual and affective evidence required the creation of a critical space through the introduction of a further level of fictionalization. Inspired by the self-reflexive reframing in the 1980s of ethnographic truth as inherently fictional and partial (Clifford and Marcus 1986), I decided to challenge further, building on the work of Jean Rouch, the enduring predominance of "observational realism" within the criteria of authenticity and objectivity at work in ethnographic films (Loizos 1997, 82). I decided to use actors to represent characters that embodied socio-anthropological truth for several interrelated reasons. First, the use of actors foregrounds the affective and intersubjective exchanges through which knowledge happens; this challenges the paradoxical, residual allegiance to "classical" (and positivistic) canons of "scientific" representation that still inform "observational cinema" (MacDougall 2003, 118). Second, as mentioned above, my push toward further fictionalization mirrors and responds critically to the merging of fiction and factual filmmaking that characterizes the hybrid genres produced by the (sexual) "humanitarian media complex" (Lindquist 2010), described in chapter 7. Third, my fictional take on ethnofiction also responds to real experiences of stigmatization and criminalization among migrants working in the sex industry, whose voices and complex experiences of agency can be more forcefully and ethically heard through socio-anthropological characters that protect their identities.

While attending classes for the MA in filmmaking at London Metropolitan University, I took a placement module at the Giles Foreman Centre for Acting. The center's approach draws on method acting, a range of introspective techniques that allow actors to reproduce within themselves the feelings and reasonings of the characters they are portraying in order to produce a realistic performance. The method draws on the seminal work of early twentieth-century Russian theater actor and teacher Konstantin Stanislavsky, which was further developed by Lee Strasberg, Stella Adler, and Sanford Meisner in the United States after World War II. Although many different approaches and interpretations have developed since, at the core of method acting is the axiom that in order to achieve a believable performance, an actor needs to establish a deep connection with the character by mobilizing personal emotions and memories.

While teaching us how to prepare characters, Giles Foreman encouraged us to explore their material, sensuous, and embodied worlds, their goals, fears, and needs. Which clothes would they wear? How would they move, look, and talk? How would they feel and react, in known and unknown circumstances? What decisions would they make? What drew us to the characters? Why? These were some of the main dimensions we were asked to consider while preparing a character. The process culminated in the most inspiring and relevant preparation activity of all for my ethnofictional purposes: an interview exercise during which the actor had to respond "in character" to questions asked by the whole class.

While attending acting classes, I was impressed by the overlap between the techniques, skills, and dimensions involved in the preparation of characters and those required for qualitative, in-depth interviewing and ethnographic research. Building a character is a self-reflexive and accurate process that can be incorporated into the scientific representation and analysis of reality. I decided to use this exercise with actors to reproduce the embodied, affective, and intersubjective dimension through which knowledge arose during my interviews. I started with Adrian, the young, Romanian third-party agent presented in the previous chapter. I based the preparation of his character on the transcript of a real interview, which I complemented with selfrepresentations, practices, and relationships that emerged from ethnographic observations with his peer groups, in order to produce a sociologically and anthropologically "true" typology. "Adrian" became an ethnofictional model of a liquid third-party agent.

I met Mattie (Matthew) Crowley, the actor who played Adrian, while training at the Foreman Center. I had noticed his attention when I pre-

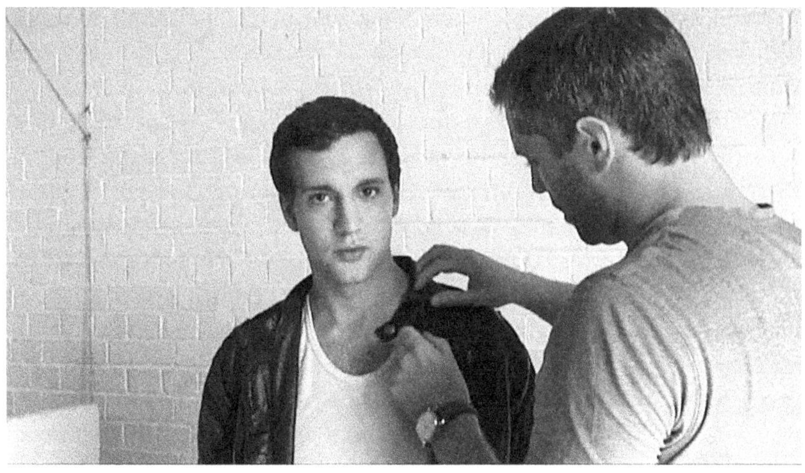

9. *Normal*: "Adrian" getting prepped for shooting, showing the cinematographic device at work.

sented my film project to the class, as well as his virile manners, which reminded me of the many third-party agents I had met during fieldwork. I felt that he had not only the *physique* but also the potential to develop an affective and intersubjective *présence du rôle*. He must have felt it too, which is why he volunteered for the project straight after class. He had been looking for a chance to engage with a complex character, and Adrian was a perfect opportunity. We started by reading and commenting on selected academic and gray literature, and by watching documentaries on trafficking and sex work, which we discussed in relation to Adrian's character.

Explaining the life circumstances and mobile orientations of a male, Romanian third-party sex work agent to a young British actor was an act of scholarly filtering, condensation, and analysis in itself. In order to allow Mattie to embody Adrian, I had to explain to him what Romanian third-party agents' presence looked and felt like, which forced me to translate sociological and anthropological truth affectively, spatially, and discursively. But it was only after we started rehearsing the script, when the intersubjective and affective dimensions kicked in, that Adrian became true in my eyes. Mattie's performance started to feel sensuously believable in relation to my experiences when interviewing Romanian third-party agents.

This is how *Normal* gradually came about—through a mirroring and reproduction of the affective and intersubjective dynamics that had produced knowledge during fieldwork. Although actors came to be involved in the film in different ways (some were acting-school classmates, others were selected though casting), the method I used to achieve ethnofictional realism and to reproduce and transmit socio-anthropological truth was the same. In all cases, although not to the same degree, an intimate, intersubjective, and affective platform was created between the actors and me that mirrored the platform that had allowed knowledge to happen during fieldwork. I decided that we were ready to shoot whenever I felt in rehearsals that we had recreated the dynamics of affective resonance and dissonance and the intersubjective relations that emerged during semistructured interviewing and ethnographic observations. The result was a strategic assemblage of ethnofictional characters and interviews that reproduced the way "true" socio-anthropological knowledge happened in the field. As a result, all of the characters in *Normal* both reproduce and challenge research participants' preferred selfrepresentations, including the fixed and rhetorical sexual-humanitarian understanding of victimization and suffering; that is why their stories were chosen from among hundreds of socio-anthropologically similar ones.

Normal, and my ethnofictional approach more generally, offers an artistic, political, and heuristic challenge to sexual-humanitarian onto-epistemology. On the one hand, by replicating the socio-anthropological truth and presence of "real" interviewees and by adopting a naturalistic aesthetic approach, my ethnofictions reproduce the presence of the real protagonists, whose lives and experiences mirror the "normal"—that is, normalized by the hegemony of sexual-humanitarian selfrepresentations—sexual stories of melomentaries. On the other hand, the complex knowledge being represented challenges the binary simplifications of sexual-humanitarian rhetorical tropes such as "the first time," and the teleological fixity of the "Natasha" and "loverboy" selfrepresentations. Most important, the tension between the effect (or rather affect) of the real produced by the naturalistic aesthetic of the ethnofictional artistic device and the awareness of the fictional nature of that device produces an affective and cognitive interruption of the neo-abolitionist politics of compassion. As people drift in and out of the suspension of disbelief produced by the ethnofictional device, a critical distancing space is introduced that allows the affective challenging of sexual-humanitarian onto-epistemology. Whereas *Normal*, which was completed in 2012, reproduces the complex ways in which knowledge happens during research interviewing, my later ethnofictions *Samira* (2013) and *Travel* (2016) represent the process of knowledge generation during ethnography. It is to this later ethnofictional work, and to the research process and findings underpinning it, that I turn in the next section.

Assembling *Samira* and *Travel*

Both *Samira* and *Travel* resulted from the *Emborders* art-science project, which I undertook at Aix-Marseille University between 2014 and 2015.[1] *Emborders* used ethnographic research and ethnofictional filmmaking to question the effectiveness and scope of sexual-humanitarian initiatives that targeted migrant sex workers and sexual minority asylum-seekers. The project's findings demonstrate that sexual-humanitarian categories risk exacerbating migrants' vulnerability if they do not acknowledge the agencing decisions that frame their complex experiences. At the center of the *Emborders* project is the consideration that in sexual-humanitarian times, migrants dealing with institutions have to become proficient at crossing biographical borders. They do so by learning how to narrativize themselves (Najmabadi 2013) in order to be recognized and validated as genuine rights-bearers.

Each of these two ethnofiction films explores a strategic biographical border operationalized by sexual humanitarianism: the sexual minority asylum-seeker and the victim of trafficking. *Samira* presents the story of Karim, an Algerian man selling sex *en femme* by night, who has obtained asylum as a transsexual in France but now wants to return to Algeria as the heterosexual male head of his family. *Travel* tells the story of Joy, a Nigerian migrant woman who sells sex in Paris after obtaining asylum as a victim of trafficking. Both stories challenge the teleological trajectories of salvation produced and disseminated by sexual-humanitarian selfrepresentations. Their protagonists do not fit stereotypical, sex-gendered notions of victimhood; by continuing to sell sex after obtaining humanitarian protection, they also do not adhere to the neo-abolitionist happy endings (with characters no longer working in the sex industry) that characterize melomentaries and other products of the "subgenre of anti-prostitution films" (Shah 2013, 550).

The life history of Karim, the Algerian man in Marseille who sells sex by night as Samira (presented in the introduction), offered an ideal opportunity to study the forms of narrativization and performance implicated in the negotiation of humanitarian biographical borders. Karim's life unfolded between the contradictory requirements of being an "Algerian transsexual" in France and a "man" in Algeria. The *mise en scène* of his mobile orientation posed questions that both included and transcended those that had emerged during the production of *Normal*. How can we represent the negotiation of sexual-humanitarian biographical borders? What form can ethnographic cinema give to the different aspects of subjectivity that emerge in the process? These questions added themselves to broader aesthetic and ethical ones. How to protect Karim's identity, given the degree of stigmatization experienced by sex workers and sexual minority refugees? How to avoid voyeurism, given the desire to show "the real" that characterizes both documentary and fictional filmmaking?

The experience of undertaking ethnography with Samira had been challenging. It had prompted me to focus on what Sarah Ahmed (2003, 72) calls the "ethnography of failure": learning to know what we fail to know about what we study. The way Samira selectively kept me at bay during two years of ethnographic observation forced me to acknowledge intersubjective distance as a heuristic situation where knowledge (still) happens. It was not that she did not like seeing me, but she never let me get as close as I wanted.[2] I could only see what she wanted me to see, and only when she decided to show it—including the night she invited me upstairs and told me about her plan to return to Algeria as her father's oldest son, the heteronormative new head of the family. In order to get papers in France, Samira had to selfrepresent to French authorities according to the "transsexual" humanitarian biographical border, which frames transsexual refugees as people who would face persecution and abuse from their families and wider society if they were to return to Algeria.[3] However, during our

10. *Samira*: The sexual-humanitarian version at the Office for the Protection of Refugees and Stateless People.

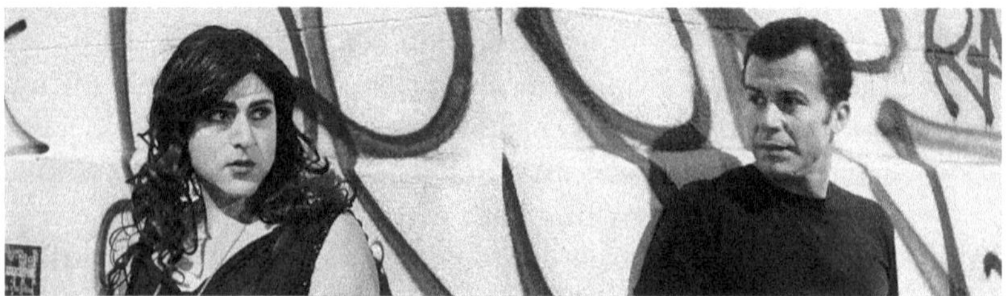

11. *Samira*: The ethnographic, "street" version.

prolonged ethnographic exchanges on the street corner where she worked, Samira told me repeatedly that she felt she was a man just like her father, and that she had left Algeria to have a good life, to enjoy her life and sexuality. It just did not add up with the sexual-humanitarian version she had told the French authorities in order to claim asylum.

It was only when she finally invited me upstairs and took off her wig at the end of a difficult night (she had been annoyed by a fellow Algerian transsexual and felt unsure about the viability of her plan to return to Algeria) that she showed me her passport, her asylum application, and her Facebook profile. She also showed me pictures of her wedding with a (lesbian) French-Algerian woman, thanks to which she hoped to return to Algeria and embody the man she had never been but was supposed to be. That was when I understood that she had not lied, to me or anyone else. She told everyone the version of the truth that different intersubjective and power settings allowed to emerge.

While I was conducting fieldwork on the street where she worked, Samira told me about her complex trajectory within and outside Algerian heteronormative masculinity—a trajectory that I found fascinating. While at the Office for the Protection of Refugees and Stateless People (OFPRA), she told the French authorities the suffering part of her life history, which they needed to hear in order to establish that she was a genuine refugee. Knowledge happened with Samira in contradictory, fragmented moments of selective exclusion, in which different sex-gendered scripts and biographical borders collided and converged. It was in order to represent this fragmented process of knowledge production that I decided to tell Samira's story by juxtaposing the selfrepresentations that emerged in different situations, relationships, and settings: the ethnographic observations on the street and in Samira's home, the medical visit, the interview with the OFPRA case adjudicator, shopping in the city center, sitting at a café next to the street market.

To convey the complex, intersubjective relations in each of these settings, I decided to present Samira's story on two screens.[4] This cinematographic solution has two main functions. First, the two screens allow viewers to observe Karim and Samira as they negotiate different and interrelated power dynamics, as well as the dualisms and normativities that fragment and aggregate subjectivities in relation to sexual-humanitarian borders. Second, by reminding viewers of the fictional nature of the film, the visibility of the cinematographic device aims to foster a critical engagement with the different selfrepresentations through which Samira's story is told and with sexual-humanitarian biographical borders more generally.

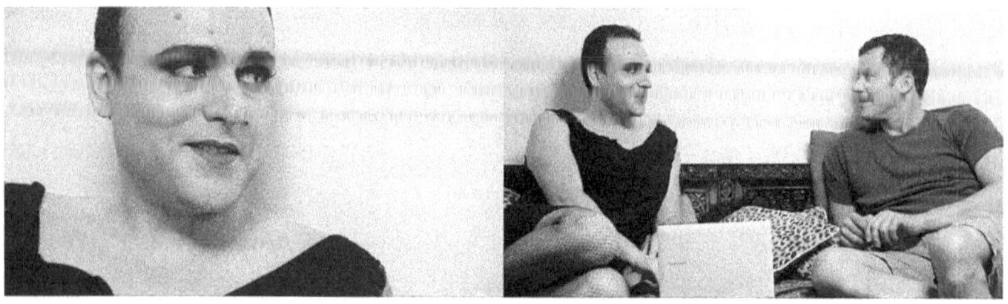

12. *Samira*: The ethnographic, "at home" version.

13. *Samira*: Karim watching ferries leaving Marseille for Algiers.

To make up for the silences and omissions produced by the selective exclusion through which knowledge happened between us, I assembled the parts of Samira to which I lacked direct access from narratives and situations that emerged from ethnographic research with others in the same socio-anthropological group: Algerian transsexuals living and selling sex in Marseille. Samira never explicitly mentioned the story she told to OFPRA; I could not observe the unfolding of her life during the day, or be present during her visits to the doctor. However, she did describe those situations and exchanges to me. All that was left for me to do to gain a fuller picture was to join the ethnographic indices she gave me with the narratives and experiences of her peers. While on the street, Samira did not tap into her suffering or vulnerability. On the contrary, she expressed her perplexity about my life decisions, my identification as homosexual, and my lack of interest in the possibility of reentering heteronormativity. That was not exactly how she put it, but the message was loud and clear. "You cannot have the life of a queer, you know?" she told me over and over again. "You have to get yourself a wife and some children! Who is going to wipe your arse when you're old otherwise, your boyfriend? Dream on."

The socio-anthropological truth of *Samira*'s ethnofictional assemblage does not reside merely in its basis in a real-life history corroborated by further research evidence. It is also grounded in the fact that the same dynamics of intersubjective distancing I had experienced during fieldwork were reproduced with the actor portraying Samira, to my extreme surprise. Right in the middle of rehearsals, the actor, Karl Sarafidis, left Marseille and returned to Paris to work on the character on his own. I experienced with him the same quality of frustration and anxiety I had experienced with the original research subject. Only then, when I thought I had lost control of the situation, did the preparation of Samira finally begin to make sense, affectively and intersubjectively. The ethnofictional Samira was on her way to becoming socio-anthropologically "true."

In the second ethnofiction arising from the *Emborders* project, *Travel*, I used ethnofiction more explicitly as a "creative research practice" and a methodology based on "improvisations that are aimed primarily at exploring the existence of the protagonists" (Sjøberg 2008, 239). The ethnofiction was carried out in collaboration with Bus des Femmes, a (non-abolitionist) peer organization that supports sex workers with an integrated approach, including outreach, sexual health services, counseling, language courses, social integration services, and an articulate anti-trafficking program. The organization allowed me to participate in outreach activities (during which I administered the questionnaire on the criminalization of clients discussed earlier in this book), and also arranged interviews with young women who were applying for asylum and subsidiary humanitarian protection as victims of trafficking. Bus des Femmes' activities included theater workshops and other cultural initiatives, and my offer to run regular ethnofiction workshops was readily accepted. The association supports both French sex workers and migrant sex workers from a variety of countries of origin. However, the increasing presence of female Nigerian sex workers in the streets of Paris, and consequently in the casework of the Bus de Femmes, prompted them to focus their language and cultural activities on Nigerian women's realities and needs. Indeed, the making of *Travel* was in continuity with the recent production of a play based on improvisations of scenes reflecting Nigerian women's everyday lives, which Bus the Femmes had also supported. The fact that the roles in the film were going to be played by actors as well as participants proved key to getting Nigerian women involved, as most of them feared exposure as sex workers to their friends in France and their families in Nigeria.

From September 2014 until June 2015, at a local community center adjacent to the Bus des Femmes, I ran weekly participative improvisation and writing workshops with eight of the original members of the association's theater group. The ethnofictional workshops started by reviewing some of the existing improvisation scenes, which were soon complemented by new ones emerging from the unfolding fieldwork and semistructured interviewing. Gradually, the new scenes were organized around a collective character and history, which allowed participants to express their individual stories of migration and involvement in the sex industry while protecting their identities. The ethnofiction workshops were in synergy with the intermediate phase—aptly named "Patience"—of the association's antitrafficking program, during which women who felt they were exploited were encouraged to reflect on their experiences of migration and sex work, and to reassess them through the onto-epistemological prism of trafficking. This involved a gradual process of self-disclosure and reflexivity, through which the initial agreements that enabled women to come to Europe were reframed by migrant women in relation to their experiences of exploitation in the sex industry and the opportunities for protection and regularization offered by the possibility of obtaining subsidiary protection or asylum.

Subsidiary protection is offered for the duration of a specific and temporary threat; asylum can give refugees permanent protection because of systematic persecution in relation to an inalienable aspect of their personal or social identity. The difference between subsidiary protection and asylum became very salient during my fieldwork. In March 2015 the National Asylum Court case of one particular Nigerian woman, the preparation of which I was able to observe at the lawyers' office, set an important legal precedent by determining that Nigerian victims of trafficking from Edo state could be recognized in France as a social group deserving asylum rather than subsidiary protection under the 1951 Geneva Convention. My research involved interviewing six women who were at different stages of the "Patience" process. During fieldwork, I also interviewed the person responsible for the association's antitrafficking program, a lawyer specializing in human trafficking cases, and the antitrafficking area coordinator of OFPRA, the French national institution in charge of granting humanitarian protection and asylum to refugees.

At the center of the association's antitrafficking program was the possibility of supporting women who claimed to be victims of trafficking through the construction of a "good file": that is, a case that could be safely brought to the attention of the authorities without compromising the credibility of the association presenting it (Jaksic 2013, 211). The construction of a good file is a complex process: the antitrafficking program coordinator listens to the women's evolving claims and poses questions to potentially orient their reassessment of their migratory projects and experiences toward the trafficking paradigm, which is the legal framework potentially providing claimants with asylum. During this onto-epistemological reorientation, Nigerian women reassess the allegiances, arrangements, and constraints that made the original migratory project possible in light of the lived and transforming experiences of the present and the future opportunities and dangers posed by presenting themselves to the authorities as victims of trafficking. My film aimed to represent this complex and evolving onto-epistemological reframing by showing how Joy's understandings of agency evolved in relation to her lived experiences of exploitation and the opportunities for protection and regularization through asylum and subsidiary protection.

The workshops that took place between October 2014 and June 2016 resulted in the story of Joy, a young woman from Edo state in Nigeria, who decides to sell sex independently to support her family after gaining asylum in France as a victim of trafficking. Joy's character and story emerged gradually within the safe space of the ethnofiction workshops. It was created through "projective improvisations," discussed by Peter Loizos (1993) in relation to Rouch's *Moi, un Noir*. Projective improvisation allowed Joy's eight coauthors to reveal "something fundamental about real lives" (Loizos 1993, 50), challenging the stereotypical way their migration and sex work experiences were equated with trafficking *tout court* in hegemonic, sexual-humanitarian selfrepresentations. Through the collective fiction of Joy, the ethnofiction workshop participants expressed their individual stories of migration and involvement in the sex industry while protecting their identities and private histories. To reflect the workshops' participative nature, the role of Joy was played by four different actresses, including some of the coauthors. This was also a way to convey the collective salience of Joy's history, which the eight coauthors saw as the expression of the lives of all Nigerian women working in the sex industry.

The title of the film evokes the ways Nigerian women's sex-gendered understandings of their migration and work trajectories revolve around the emic notion of "travel," which refers to women's movement abroad in order to support themselves and their families. Another emic notion that is strategic for understanding the negotiation of agency within Nigerian women's migration experiences is "suffering," which refers to the struggle to find sufficient economic and social resources to sustain the family. As existing research confirms, many Nigerian women explain their decision to leave home (travel) as related to an excess of "suffering" for themselves and their families, claiming that their suffering had become "too much" to endure at home (Ratia and Noterman 2012, 149). This is important to my argument: the notion of "too much" also emerges in relation to the amount of suffering Nigerian women are prepared to tolerate as part of the agree-

14. *Travel*: Joy negotiating biographical borders at OFPRA.

ments they make in order to migrate to Europe, and it also plays a key role in their decision to seek humanitarian protection in France (Mai 2016b).

The film begins with the ethnofictional scene that opened this book, when Joy challenges my question as to whether she decided to work in the sex industry. Although *Travel* does not go on to tell Joy's story in a linear way, that is how I summarize it here for the sake of concision and clarity.

While Joy is "suffering" to make ends meet in Nigeria, a returnee from Italy comes to her small, family-run beauty salon. The returnee puts her in touch with Blessing, a woman living in France, who is able to help her go to Europe for the price of €30,000. Although Joy is made aware that she is going to sell sex in France, she understands that she is going to be an escort rather than a street-based sex worker. Meanwhile, in France, Blessing is evicted by her flatmates and colleagues for wanting to bring a younger woman to France to help her pay her own debt, which casts her as a "madam"—a derogatory term for a third-party sex work agent. The film highlights the fluidity of the relationship between "girls" and "madams" as we then see Joy shopping for sexy clothes in Paris alongside Blessing, who later does her makeup and instructs her on how to behave and stay safe with clients as they sit together in the van from which they both sell sex in the Bois de Vincennes.

Instructed by Blessing, Joy tells OFPRA a fake sexual-humanitarian story—that she is a lesbian from (predominantly Muslim) Kano state—that wins her the right to stay in France until her case is heard, during which time Joy continues to work alongside Blessing to repay the €35,000 debt she contracted with her. It is only when Blessing kicks her out of the van, hoping to get her to pay an additional €10,000, that Joy feels exploited because her original deal is not being respected. She then seeks the help of Bus des Femmes. Joy is initially reluctant to report Blessing as a trafficker, because she wants to respect the oath she swore in front of the local juju (Ayelala) shrine in Nigeria.[5] However, she ultimately decides to do so when Blessing escalates the situation by threatening her family back home. The film shows her talking to the antitrafficking officer at Bus de Femmes, who helps her reframe her history of voluntary migration into a story of trafficking so that she can make sense of what has happened, and make a case that will be successful in court.

Once in court, when asked why she now selfrepresents as a victim of trafficking, Joy responds that it is because Blessing did not respect the original oath, rather than underlining that she was deceived or forced. Joy also explains to the judges that she will become a social outcast if she is deported, as Nigerian women sent home "empty-handed" are extremely stigmatized and marginalized.

Joy's case is successful, and she is granted refugee status on the grounds that she belongs to the social group of women victims of trafficking from Edo state. She can now work legally as a cleaner in a hotel, but soon realizes that she cannot support herself and her family on her small salary.

The film's closing scene evokes its opening. Joy encounters the researcher (me) again while she is working independently in the sex industry. She explains that she now feels free and that things are "more better than before" because she can decide when to work and with whom, and, most importantly, she can keep all of the income generated by her sex work.

15. *Travel*: Joy discussing her story with the association's antitrafficking officer.

16. *Travel*: Joy defending her case in at the National Asylum Court in Paris.

17. *Travel*: Joy working as a hotel chambermaid (still taken during shooting).

18. *Travel*: Joy telling the researcher that working independently in the sex industry is "more better than before."

The plot of *Travel* expresses the findings of both the ethnofiction workshops and the semistructured interviews undertaken during the *Emborders* project. These show that Nigerian women accept short-term "bounded exploitation" (Mai 2016b)—that is, exploitation within set temporal and economic limits—and resort to "indentured mobility" (Parreñas 2011, 7) to support themselves and their families in the long term, which is an existential priority of their mobile orientations. Most importantly, the *Emborders* findings demonstrate that Nigerian women see themselves as victims of trafficking and reassess their own migratory trajectories according to the related sexual-humanitarian biographical border, depending on whether the agreements they made back in Nigeria and the working and economic conditions they encounter abroad allow them to meet the priorities and needs informing their mobile orientations.

Like *Samira*, *Travel* presents its protagonist's story by juxtaposing on two screens the multiple versions and narrations of the self that emerge in different situations, relationships, and settings. In both films, ethnographic street observations, medical visits, and interviews with OFPRA are juxtaposed with shopping trips in the city center or visits to cafés. Each situation highlights contradictory or coherent aspects of Karim's or Joy's subjectivity and history. The two-screen display and ethnofictional approach adopted in *Samira* and *Travel* aim to portray and emphasize the contradictory ways humanitarian categories and LGBT taxonomies originating from the Global North are appropriated and rejected by migrants. *Travel* and *Samira* show that each version of the self presented by Karim and Joy is authentic. Every subjectivity is incoherent: the real privilege is not to have to be verified, recognized, or believed in relation to the biographical borders enforced by sexual-humanitarian protection.

When discussing my ethnofictional work with the public, I often encounter an implicit critique of its supposed claim to "realness" and scientific representation. Obviously, I do not think my ethnofictions show real people or real situations, which are represented through a fictional device. But I do think that they bring to life characters and situations that are ethnographically, sociologically, and anthropologically "true," for a number of interrelated reasons. On a positivistic level, I could defend the heuristic "trueness" of my ethnofictional work by highlighting its accurate reproduction of "real" research interviews and ethnographic dynamics. However, I think that the ethnofictional characters and situations I portray are and feel socio-anthropologically true because they resonate affectively and sensuously with the real dynamics, relationships, and circumstances through which knowledge emerged during fieldwork. Most importantly, my ethnofictions are socio-anthropologically true because they also affectively and cognitively challenge, on the basis of research evidence, the sexual-humanitarian "post-truth" simplification of migrant sex workers' mobile orientations, which conceals the responsibility of neoliberal policies for the socioeconomic constraints that limit the agentic potential of their decisions. It is to the broader social implications of these dynamics for the sustainability of the global democratic polity that I turn in the final chapter.

CONCLUSION

Challenging Sexual Humanitarianism

Social interventions that address migrants as vulnerable—and hence as entitled to social protection—are embedded in contradictory migration and human rights regimes. These regimes emerge from the tension between the expansion of migration and human rights at an international level and the restriction of those very rights to migrants on the basis of citizenship at a national level. The convergence of these factors is the background for the onset of humanitarian forms of governance that are based on a normalizing and reductive representation of the increasing inequalities of world societies. This representation rests on a unified vision of humanity expressing the values, moralities, and priorities of the Global North, while criminalizing dissenting states and groups, whose individual victims then become the legitimate "raison d'être of humanitarianism" (Agier 2010, 30). This North-centric governmental epistemology corresponds to a neoliberal moral economy that mobilizes strategic forms of humanitarian "compassion" in order to legitimize military and social interventions to protect the "security" of privileged citizens in the Global North (Fassin 2005).

The interplay between the increase in globalized migrant flows and the onset of humanitarian forms of governance produces biographical borders between the Global North and the rest of the world (Mai 2014). In the process, state benevolence and fundamental rights are allocated on the basis of humanitarian criteria of absolute and innocent—that is exceptional and exemplary—victimhood that are credible and intelligible only if performed according to a well-rehearsed politics of compassion (Ticktin 2017). This reframing inaugurates a "politics of humanity" operating a repoliticization, rather than depoliticization,[1] of social issues (Guilhot 2012) by making the complex inequalities that characterize world societies onto-epistemologically both intelligible and subject to intervention according to neoliberal, (sexual) humanitarian, and individualizing selfrepresentations. In the process, secularism is selectively constructed as the prerogative of the Global North and is deployed discursively against strategic, sex-gendered others to erect new geopolitical divisions and hierarchies. The new public focus on gender and sexuality in the Global North is consistent with the emergence of a new regime of neoliberal governmentality, "sexual democracy" (Fassin 2010), which strategically pathologizes and essentializes the gender and sexuality of minority ethnic and migrant groups in order to define geopolitical hierarchies and police their moral and spatial boundaries.

In this book, I have defined the strategic, humanitarian problematization and targeting of sex-gendered migrant groups as "sexual humanitarianism." This concept refers to an onto-epistemological formation that includes scientific research, documentary and fictional representations, policymaking, and social interventions. It produces a unified and hierarchical understanding of humanity according to essentialist and North-centric interpretations of gender and sexuality that are increasingly influenced by the convergence of neo-abolitionism, neoconservatism, and neoliberalism. Within this onto-epistemological formation, moral panics exaggerating the extent of sex trafficking play a key role in the establishment, on the basis of "affective identification and empathy," of a sexual-humanitarian, neoliberal, global sentimentality, which I defined, paraphrasing Berlant, as a "rhetoric of promise" that a global humanity "can be built across fields of social difference" (Berlant 2001, 53). Such spectacularizing sexual-humanitarian selfrepresentations present trafficking and modern slavery as a strategic "common denominator" in relation to which a neoliberal, globalized morality binds together diverse socioeconomic groups, actors, and forces "around corporate capitalist ideals of freedom and carceral paradigms of justice" (Bernstein 2007a, 136; 144).

The spectacular rhetorics (Hesford 2011) characterizing sexual-humanitarian selfrepresentations obfuscate the causal relationship between migrants' involvement in the sex industry and the social inequalities and conflicts produced by the globalization of neoliberal policies. At the same time, mainstream media selfrepresentations of everyday life in neoliberal late-modern times tend to both glorify and normalize privileged affluence, which further invisibilizes the global spread and local breadth of socioeconomic inequalities. Citizens of the Global North are prevented from reflecting on the ways they are affected by the "commodification of intimacy" introduced by the neoliberal service economy, within which "intimacy or intimate relations can be treated, understood and thought of as if they entered the market" (Constable 2009, 50). Distancing themselves from "absolute" figures of sexual-humanitarian suffering and intimate commodification—such as victims of sex trafficking—distracts them from their own increasing and more mundane exploitability and commodification in neoliberal times (Mai 2013). In the process, while some forms of "self-commodification," such as sex work, are spectacularly singled out as exploitative, the more diffused and structural forms of labor exploitation engendered by neoliberal global capitalism remain unquestioned (O'Connell Davidson 2014, 529).

These observations point to the need for scholarly work to focus on the wider political and socioeconomic forces that reframe migrant sex workers as victims of sex trafficking, regardless of how sex workers themselves understand their own needs, priorities, and decisions. They also contextualize sexual humanitarianism within the globalization of neoliberal onto-epistemology, in light of which the real focus of antiprostitution interventions can be seen as "eliminating the visible manifestations of poverty and deviance [. . .] from urban spaces rather than the exchange of sex for money per se" (Bernstein 2007b, 164). It is to capture this hypocritical invisibilization of mundane and diffused socioeconomic polarization and exclusion in the name of the fight against sexual exploitation that I have introduced the concept of "moral gentrification." This concept refers to the ways in which sexual-humanitarian social interventions criminalize and moralize underprivileged livelihoods in order to clear the space they occupy for estate developments and other highly profitable commercial investments, including their own humanitarian economies.

In order to understand the conditions of agency produced by this complex onto-epistemological interplay, I have elaborated the concept of "mobile orientations": socioculturally framed alignments between objects, mobilities, and selfrepresentations that frame the emergence of subjectivities. These orientations are mobile, both because they reflect young people's existential aspirations to social and spatial mobility through migration, and because they evolve and change alongside those people's migratory projects. Mobile orientations are arranged by agencing decisions—that is, contextual decisions that express the constrained agency of subjects in response to the new possibilities and challenges introduced by the late-modern "liquefaction" of modes of production, gender roles, authorities, and moralities (Bauman 2000). By bringing objects to the core of people's sense of self, the concept challenges the liberal assumption that "subjects are constituted in splendid isolation from their material circumstances" (O'Connell Davidson 2005, 149). The fact that mobile orientations are arranged by agencing decisions in response to the opportunities and predicaments posed by neoliberal policies and politics also challenges the neo-abolitionist "conflation of agency with choice" (Shah 2014, 198), and highlights the "relational and contextual ways" (Ham 2017, 17) in which agency works in contemporary times. For all of these reasons, mobile orientations offer a strategic vantage point from which to analyze migrant sex workers' pragmatic understandings and experiences of agency on the basis of their "wants and needs," rather than viewing them through the "passionate zeal" (Parreñas 2011, 268) of neo-abolitionist and antiprostitution activists. Without the strategic lens of mobile orientations, the decisions and relationships that migrant sex workers experience as agencing can easily be misread as catalysts of exploitation according to sexual-humanitarian onto-epistemology.

Moral panics about migrant "sex slaves" obfuscate the reality that only a minority of migrants working in the sex industry are forced or trafficked, as well as the "potentially negative consequences of humanitarian interventions" (Lindquist 2010, 234). The research findings presented in this book show that by migrating and working in the sex industry, young women and men take risks and opportunities to counter their own increased precariousness and exploitability in neoliberal times. They also orient their aspirations to social mobility toward cosmopolitan, individualized, and affluent late-modern lifestyles against the prevalence of conservative gender values and sexual mores at home. To capture this complex interplay, I introduced in chapter 4 the concept of "boditarian cosmopolitanism," referring to the embodied and tacit ways marginalized young migrant men and women challenge class-based, racialized, and sex-gendered restrictions on their spatial and social mobility. For many young people, accessing a different material world through migration allows them to be the kind of men or women they want to be, and this is a priority that shapes their understandings of agency and exploitation. Few of them migrate to survive. For the majority, the decision to migrate is the agencing of a mobile orientation, a way of starting a project of desired social mobility that has become unviable at home. This does not mean that all decisions lead to agentic mobile orientations; migratory projects and experiences are sometimes characterized by the impossibility of achieving the psychological and material resources that would enable migrants to fulfill their mobile orientations and to complete their ritual passage to adulthood. For instance, as explained in chapters 3 and 4, in young migrant men's abilities to navigate these deep, complex transformations, one can distinguish between "minor" mobilities and "errant" mobilities. The former are more agentic; the latter are characterized by the lack of psychological and socioeconomic resources to meet the needs and priorities that frame their mobile orientations.

Often the decision to migrate and/or work in the sex industry results not from the constraints posed by extreme poverty, but from an assessment of its potential implications in terms of both "security" and "mobility"—key factors in these migrants' agency (Ham 2017, 165). By working in the sex industry, migrants use conspicuous consumption to cope with contradictory regimes of subjectification brought about by the global convergence of late modernity and neoliberalism. In chapters 2, 3, and 4 I discussed how, in the post-social and objectualized scenarios of late modernity, subjectivities and moralities are socially monitored according to one's "success" as a conspicuous consumer (Winnubst 2012, 86), sanctioned by owning and displaying specific objects in relation to specific social performances. These dynamics are strategic for understanding the relationship between neoliberal commodification, social polarization, and how migrants express their agency within their mobile orientations. As I analyzed in chapters 6 and 7, by strategically selfrepresenting according to the trafficking, sexual-humanitarian biographical border, migrant women working in the global sex industry are attempting to avoid the whore stigma associated with being deported back home empty-handed. By "becoming victims" (Jaksic 2013) and translating their subjectivities according to sexual-humanitarian trafficking scripts (Giordano 2014), migrant female sex workers are trying to obtain both humanitarian protection and legal residence in the Global North. At the same time, when among peers and away from sexual-humanitarian biographical borders and institutions, they project the trafficking stigma—that is, the stigma of being seen as controlled, pimped, and/or trafficked within the sex industry—onto previous personal experiences and other individuals and groups of sex workers. Both of these discursive and performative practices allow them to selfrepresent and remain part of the normalized "world" of privileged consumption that has subjectified them as potential conspicuous consumers and successful entrepreneurs, with reference to different social settings and dynamics.

Although the young men and women whose life experiences inform this book come from different national settings, their mobile orientations are influenced by the same socioeconomic and macro-historical event: the "rupture of intelligibility" represented by the global onset of neoliberal onto-epistemology (Humphrey 2008). Moreover, as I described in the introduction, their migratory trajectories, sex-gendered selfrepresentations, and material cultures belong to two shared and intersecting transnational social fields and migration spaces: that between the European Union and Eastern Europe, and that between the European Union and (North/sub-Saharan) Africa. The notion of a "transnational social field" refers to the networks and social relationships through which "ideas, practices, and resources are unequally exchanged, organized, and transformed" (Levitt and Glick Schiller 2004, 1009). To analyze how migrants working in the sex industry manage contradictory, sex-gendered representations and roles across intersecting transnational social fields and migration spaces, in chapter 4 I introduced the geometrical concept of the fractal space through which they challenge normative life trajectories and patriarchal gender/sexual roles abroad without taking full public responsibility for their actions at home.

The convergence of all these different factors makes the experiences of migration and sex work analyzed in this book highly comparable. For instance, the fear of being stigmatized as a "failure" for having nothing to show was a current refrain within the narrated life histories of the migrants I interviewed. The necessity of avoiding at all costs the social humiliation of coming home "empty-handed" was a key factor in their understandings and experiences of exploitation. For most people, anything—including oppressive working conditions and abusive relationships—was better than being seen to "fail" according to hegemonic and commodified models of successful migrant selfhood. For instance, Alina's sense of humiliation (analyzed in chapter 9) emerged less in relation to the whore stigma and more in relation to her role as family provider. This orienting, existential priority is confirmed by previous studies of the impact of deportation on Nigerian women who used to work in the sex industry in Europe, which show that, in most cases, women are stigmatized primarily for having failed in their gendered role as family providers because "they did not come back with anything" (Ratia and Noterman 2012, 144). These considerations are important for my argument because they highlight how migrants' understandings and experiences of agency in the sex industry (and other sectors of employment) are embedded within existential priorities and needs that emerge in relation to a dynamic evaluation of "past experiences and a desire to achieve some improvement in the future" (Bastia and McGrath 2011). Strategic priorities for migrant sex workers include being able to provide for their families, achieving legal status, and owning/performing the objects that will ensure they are valued and accepted as "successful" by their families and peer groups, both at home and in the context of emigration. These connected priorities are part of their mobile orientations, and form the basis of the agencing decisions they make at different times in their lives.

These considerations and the research findings analyzed in this book challenge the usefulness of the concepts of trafficking and modern slavery for addressing migrant sex workers' experiences of agency and exploitation. They strongly suggest that only a labor-migration perspective recognizing and framing sex work as work can explain the complex and evolving understandings and experiences of agency of migrant and nonmigrant sex workers. They also point to the need for antitrafficking interventions to deprioritize their current law enforcement and state bordering priorities, and to accept migration and mobility as key factors structuring the experiences of agency and exploitation of the people they target (Segrave, Milivojevic, Pickering, et al. 2009, 202). These combined, evidence-based considerations mean that, given the scale of involvement of migrant sex workers in the sex industry worldwide, any policy and social intervention on sex work, and particularly those embedded in the sexual-humanitarian frameworks of antitrafficking and antislavery, will only have a chance of success if they are matched with prospective migrants' legal right to access the international labor market, which would reduce their socioeconomic vulnerability to exploitation by the people who facilitate their labor-migration trajectories (Bravo 2009). The multifaceted voices, experiences, and needs of sex workers informing this book also strongly suggest that the full decriminalization—that is, the repeal of all laws that criminalize both the sale and purchase of sexual services—is the most appropriate and least harmful policymaking framework, as it is consistent with an ethical and "integrative" approach that aims to "integrate the sex work sector into [the] societal, legal and institutional framework in order to protect those selling sex from harm" (Ostegren 2017, 15). These considerations are corroborated by the fact that the decriminalization of sex work was endorsed in 2015 by Amnesty International, which followed the earlier evidence-based positions of *The Lancet* (in 2014) and the Joint United Nations Programme on HIV/AIDS (in 2012). By highlighting the socioeconomic constraints that frame migrant sex workers' mobile orientations, my findings suggest that their agency can only be substantially enhanced by measures to counter the structural commodification and precarization of labor, including sex work, introduced by neoliberal politics and policies (O'Connell Davidson 2014). Also drawing on recent analyses of working conditions across decriminalized and regulated sex work environments (Ham 2017; Orchiston 2016), the research findings in this book suggest that decriminalization would be a fundamental but not sufficient first step to counter exploitative practices within the sex industry, and that a "more proactive approach" would be needed to improve the working conditions of migrant and non-migrant sex workers—but only through policies that they themselves have negotiated and that reflect their needs and priorities (Pitcher and Wijers 2014, 560).

While reviewing my own research and filmmaking for this book, I came to see more clearly how the methodological, ethical, and epistemological (agencing) decisions I made followed a heterogeneous approach that Paul Stoller (1992, 213) defines as both phenomenological and "radically empiricist": a "sensuous" heuristic practice that attempts to describe social life "from the perceptual orientation of the other" and "does not privilege theory over description, thought over feeling and sight over the 'lower senses' (touch, smell, taste)." Inspired by Stoller's "sensuous scholarship" (Stoller 1997), Jean Rouch's ethnofictional work, and Sara Ahmed's queer phenomenological approach, I have tried to challenge, analyze, and reproduce, together with my research participants, the selfrepresentations through which knowledge, subjectivities, and orientations happen within the neoliberal sexual-humanitarian onto-epistemology.

My intimate autoethnographic approach has allowed me to identify and analyze the affective, socioeconomic, and intersubjective dimensions informing the mobile orientations of migrant sex workers, whose needs and priorities challenge sexual-humanitarian moral panics and interventions. To understand the ambivalent experiences of agency and exploitation of migrants targeted by sexual humanitarianism, I challenged the onto-epistemological distinction between emic (culture-internal) concepts and the etic (culture-external) theories of observers, a distinction that usually characterizes ethnography. I did this by eliciting, acknowledging, and including research participants' own theorizations of vulnerability and agency within my analysis (Boellstorff 2011). In doing so, I attempted to develop a "southern theory" (Connell 2007) that uses emic understandings of agency and exploitation to analyze how participants negotiate the binarisms (e.g., vulnerability/agency, victim/trafficker) operationalized by sexual humanitarianism. I did this particularly through the method of ethnofictional filmmaking.

In sexual-humanitarian films and research, the complex fluidity of the relationships between sex workers and their agents, which I explored in chapters 7 to 9, falls victim to a neoliberal inflection of homogeneous thought, reducing the terms of intelligibility to false dichotomies of force and consent. These onto-epistemological binaries do not take into account research evidence showing that migrant women's experiences of agency, exploitation, and trafficking are framed by their abilities to navigate the fluid and complex sentimental and economic agreements they make with third-party agents in relation to evolving priorities and life circumstances. Rather than engaging with the complex conditions of agency and exploitation of migrants working in the sex industry, sexual-humanitarian organizations and policies operate on the basis of binary categories and rhetorical evidence supporting harmful social interventions and affective forms of governance that are undemocratic: they neither respect the rights nor respond to the needs of the majority of those they are supposed to support. I would like to explore the broader political significance of these dynamics a little further, as they express a dangerous affective and rhetorical erosion of the democratic polity's cognitive underpinnings at a global level. Artan Fuga's (1998) analysis of the relationship between a homogeneous cognitive framework and an authoritarian political order, which he elaborated in the context of the Albanian postcommunist transformation, can be seen as productive in this respect. According to Fuga, there is an intrinsic relationship between a cognitive order and a specific conception of political power, as a kind of social and political justice is reciprocally tied to a conception of truth (Fuga 1998, 28). At the center of his argument is the opposition between homogeneous thinking and heterogeneous thinking. Homogeneous thinking can be defined as a cognitive approach based on the principle of homogenization—that is, the appropriation of all of the conceptual space by one of the categories or perspectives involved in the process of intellectual confrontation (i.e., the debate about individual agency and social structure). On the other hand, heterogeneous thinking can be defined as a cognitive approach that starts from the acknowledgment of the value of difference and from the attempt to synthesize arguments produced by all of the categories or perspectives around which the debate is structured. According to Fuga, every philosophical logic operating with homogeneous categories legitimates authoritarian power; democracy has been characterized throughout the history of philosophy by heterogeneous conceptual structures.

Although Fuga's work analyzes the endurance of authoritarianism in postcommunist societies, it is also useful to capture a dangerous deterioration of democratic polity in contemporary neoliberal times. The latter are characterized by the "post-truth" cognitive, affective, and rhetorical simplification of complex social dynamics according to homogeneous, binary categories challenging democratic forms of "collaborative governance," which are based on the cognitively heterogeneous recognition of epistemologically dissonant arguments and evidence (Wagenaar, Amesberger, and Altink 2010, 263). One example is the simplistic, neo-abolitionist reduction of commercial sex to an issue of supply and demand according to neoliberal market rationality. These dynamics are representative of dangerous, wider sociocultural transformations that are destabilizing the cognitive, socioeconomic, and affective sustainability of contemporary democracies under the combined pressures of market fundamentalism and homogeneous thought. According to Wendy Brown (2015), the global hegemony of neoliberal governance is gradually undermining democracy, because the primacy of centralized laws and institutions in public life is being undermined by the extension of economic rationality to all social domains and activities, reframing human beings primarily as market actors. In the process, she argues, "liberty itself is narrowed to market conduct, divested of association with mastering the conditions of life, existential freedom, or securing the rule of the demos" (Brown 2015, 41).

Sexual-humanitarian onto-epistemology and global sentimentality play strategic roles in the neoliberalization of everyday life and the deterioration of the democratic polity in three interrelated respects. First, by promoting neo-abolitionist affective rhetoric over factual evidence, sexual-humanitarian global sentimentality fosters a homogeneous form of thought that directly undermines the sustainability of the democratic polity by systematically erasing the dissenting realities, experiences, and voices of the main social group whose exploitation it aims to fight: sex workers. Second, the homogeneous binaries of victimhood that characterize sexual-humanitarian onto-epistemology obfuscate the inequalities engendered by neoliberalism and protect those responsible for the precarization of global labor markets from facing their responsibility. Third, by disseminating selfrepresentations of extreme and stereotypical cases of victimhood, the affective politics that characterizes sexual-humanitarian global sentimentality triggers subconscious and protective dynamics of "projective disidentification" (Grotstein 1981, 2014), preventing people from the Global North from acknowledging their own increased exploitability and precariousness in neoliberal times.

My findings, writings, and films attempt to counter these dynamics by contextualizing the complexity of the agencing decisions of migrant (and nonmigrant) sex workers within the socioeconomic transformations encompassing the Global North and the rest of the world. By pushing the traditional boundaries of ethnofiction and using actors to represent true socio-anthropological characters and ethnographic interactions, I both acknowledge and challenge the "post-truth" rhetorical and affective merging of factual and fictional selfrepresentations that characterizes contemporary sexual-humanitarian times. In this respect, both my intimate autoethnographic approach and my ethnofictional filmmaking are a democratic, participative, and radically empiricist attempt to engage with the affective, sensuous, and intersubjective salience of socio-anthropological truth, in order to fulfill what Higgins (2016, 9) calls one of the most important social missions of science: "to provide the best information possible as the basis for public policy."

APPENDIX

Research Projects

Between 2004 and 2005, I conducted a one-year project funded by the Provence-Alpes-Côte d'Azure regional authority in France. This involved collecting eighty interviews with young migrant men selling sex and with people involved in social intervention initiatives targeting them Interviews were conducted in Albania, Belgium, France, Germany, Greece, Italy, Morocco, the Netherlands, Romania, and Spain. The project analyzed the psychological, social, and physical mobility of Albanian, Moroccan, and Romanian male migrant minors and young adults selling sex. The findings highlighted the difference between migration experiences characterized by psychological and social vulnerability and those marked by a higher degree of agency and recognition.

Between 2006 and 2008, I directed a research project funded by Save the Children on the relationship between the migration of minors (male and female) from Romania, their involvement in illegal activities, and the forms of social intervention addressing that interplay. The research analyzed the complex and conflicting ways migrant minors and social projects understood exploitation, vulnerability, and agency. It produced ninety-four interviews with migrant children and young people, their families, and stakeholders on their understandings and experiences of the exploitation of vulnerable migrant children, and original theorizations about the relationship between migration, agency, and vulnerability.

Between 2007 and 2009 I directed the two-year project *Migrant Workers in the UK Sex Industry*, funded by the UK's Economic and Social Research Council (ESRC). The project adopted an innovative, peer and community-based methodology as well as a migration studies framework to interview one hundred migrant women, men, and transgender people working in all of the main jobs and from the main countries of origin in the London sex industry. It produced evidence highlighting the variety of life and work experiences of migrants working in the sex industry and challenging hegemonic assumptions about the extent of trafficking.

In 2008 I directed a research project funded by the International Organization for Migration (IOM) that aimed to identify a psychosocial profile of male traffickers from Albania and Romania. The project produced thirty-three interviews with men working as agents in the Albanian and Italian sex industry both in and out of detention. The combined findings of the IOM and ESRC projects revealed the similarity of the socioeconomic backgrounds and circumstances of men and women involved as workers and agents/managers in the sex industry.

In 2010 I directed an evaluation of the services offered by the project SHOC to migrant sex workers in the London boroughs of Haringey and Enfield. The main aim of the project was to understand the extent of trafficking and exploitation within the migrant population working in the sex industry by undertaking qualitative interviews with thirty female sex workers.

Between 2014 and 2015 I directed a two-year project called *Emborders*, funded and hosted by Aix-Marseille University. This project challenged the scientific, documentary, and fictional representations produced by sexual humanitarianism through qualitative research and experimental filmmaking. It examined and compared the ways specific biographical borders were enforced by French and British sexual-humanitarian initiatives that targeted migrant sex workers as victims of trafficking and sexual minority asylum-seekers as potential refugees.

Filmography

Bouzid, Nouri. 1992. *Bezness*. 110 mins.
Mai, Nicola. 2010. *Comidas Rapidas—Fast Bites*. 5 mins.
Mai, Nicola. 2011. *Mother Europe*. 5 mins.
Mai, Nicola. 2012. *Normal*. 48 mins.
Mai, Nicola. 2013. *Samira*. 27 mins.
Mai, Nicola. 2016. *Travel*. 63 mins.
Moodysson, Lukas. 2002. *Lilya 4-Ever*. 109 mins.
Rouch, Jean. 1958. *Moi, un Noir*. 73 mins.
Rouch, Jean. 1967. *Jaguar*. 91 mins.
Ulmer, Bruno. 2006. *Welcome Europa*. 90 mins.

Most of Nicola Mai's films are available online at https://vimeo.com/users3467382.

NOTES

PREFACE

1. Joy, the fictional protagonist of my ethnofiction film *Travel*, is a character cowritten by eight Nigerian migrant women and me to express their shared histories of migration, sex work, and trafficking. The epigraph reproduces verbatim a comment made by one of the *Emborders* research participants. I provide more information about *Travel* and *Emborders* below.
2. The survey on the criminalization of clients was part of the project *Emborders: Problematising Sexual Humanitarianism through Experimental Filmmaking*, which I conducted while based at the Laboratory of Mediterranean Sociology at Aix-Marseille University between January 2014 and December 2015. The project compared the effects of humanitarian interventions targeting migrant sex workers and sexual minority asylum seekers in the United Kingdom (London) and France (Marseille/Paris). Its methodological approach combined participant observation, semi-structured qualitative interviews, and the production of two ethnographic films (ethnofictions).
3. As this book focuses on the relationship between migration and sex work, I use the terms *trafficking* and *sex trafficking* to refer exclusively to trafficking for the purposes of sexual exploitation, and not to forms of trafficking involving other sectors of employment for migrants.
4. For more information about the research projects I conducted, see the appendix.
5. I refer to third-party facilitators as *agents* and their work as *management*, rather than using terms such as *pimp* or verbs such as *to control*, which imply coercion and exploitation. The use of morally neutral terms such as *agent* and *management* is not meant to underestimate the ways in which some of these relations can be exploitative and abusive. It aims to create a discursive space within which the plurality of professional and personal relations developing between people working in the sex industry can become more visible; this is key to understanding the different degrees of agency involved.

INTRODUCTION

1. Throughout the book, all names of people (and sometimes places, if they might lead to identification) have been changed to guarantee the anonymity of research participants.

2. I refer to Karim/Samira as both "he" and "she," in order to convey the multiplicity of his sex-gendered subjectification.
3. Although Samira's complex sexual identification should be seen as belonging to the transgender spectrum, I use the term *transsexual* here because this was the term used both by Samira herself and in French law to adjudicate her asylum case.
4. For a more detailed discussion of the genealogy of my agencing decision to leave Italy, see Mai (2007).
5. I was born to a left-leaning family in the town of Modena, in the "red" Emilia Romagna region, which has been characterized by the strong and enduring cultural, political, and social hegemony of the left.
6. All films are documented in the appendix under the heading "Filmography."
7. "Straight" in this context refers to regular (i.e., not criminalized or stigmatized) work, rather than to the issue of sexual orientation.

CHAPTER ONE

1. The term *emic* refers to the analysis of social and cultural issues or processes from the perspective of the people directly involved.

CHAPTER TWO

1. The term *borgatari* refers to young Italians from Rome's peri-urban outskirts (*borgate*). Here it also refers to the young male sex workers portrayed in the films and novels of Pier Paolo Pasolini in the 1950s and 1960s.

CHAPTER THREE

1. By the terms *child migration* and *child prostitution*, I refer to the autonomous involvement of adolescents between the ages of fourteen and seventeen.
2. The film ultimately became Ulmer's *Welcome Europa* (2006).
3. Interviewees received a fifty-euro incentive to encourage their participation and to thank them for their contribution to the research.

CHAPTER FOUR

1. Some of the interviews, particularly those with Kurdish refugees, were undertaken directly by the film director.
2. Romania was not part of the European Union at the time.

CHAPTER FIVE

An earlier, shorter version of this chapter was published in the journal *Sexualities* (Mai 2017).

1. The expression also gave the title to the 1992 film *Bezness*, by Tunisian director Nouri Bouzid.
2. These estimates reflect the scale of the Tunisian tourist industry before terrorist attacks targeting tourists in 2015 caused a dramatic decrease in foreign visitors. One of the attacks took place in Sousse.
3. By referring to the time after Enver Hoxha, Albania's communist dictator, Fatjon is indicating the period that followed the collapse of the Albanian communist state.

CHAPTER SIX

1. This chapter draws on the findings and data produced by this project, which was funded by the Economic and Social Research Council (ESRC RES-062-23-137).

2. For instance, the empirical claims and dogmatic assumptions of leading neo-abolitionist scholars Melissa Farley, Sheila Jeffreys, and Janice Raymond have been thoroughly reviewed and convincingly debunked by American sociologist Ronald Weitzer (2012, 10–16). Weitzer provides details about how, in the context of a successful challenge to the constitutionality of Canada's laws addressing sex work in 2010, "the court downgraded the testimony of three antiprostitution witnesses (Melissa Farley, Janice Raymond, and Richard Poulin) because of their biases" (2012, 16). In the United Kingdom, the influential *Big Brothel* report on sex work clients carried out by the Poppy Project, a leading neo-abolitionist organization, was discredited by academics for its lack of ethical protocols and procedures, and for its weak methodology (Sanders, Pitcher, Campbell, et al. 2008).
3. A full transcript of the parliamentary debate is available online at http://www.publications.parliament.uk/pa/ld200809/ldhansrd/text/91103-0019.htm.

CHAPTER SEVEN

1. The *loverboy* term and concept have been particularly prominent in campaigns to prevent international trafficking from Romania and in awareness-raising campaigns against "internal trafficking" in the Netherlands and the United Kingdom.
2. I discuss the ethnofictional method and process that led to the production of *Travel* in chapter 9, which focuses on filmmaking.

CHAPTER EIGHT

1. Of the thirty-three interviews undertaken with men implicated in the arrangement and management of international sex work, nineteen interviews were with people in prison in Rome (two) and Albania (seventeen). The remaining interviews were with men on the outside who were or had been involved in the arrangement and management of sex work in Rome (seven) and Tirana (seven). Seven interviewees were Romanian (two of whom were in prison), the remaining twenty-four were Albanian (seventeen of whom were in prison in Albania). In addition, a Romanian, female third-party agent was also interviewed in the context of the research.

CHAPTER NINE

1. The passages in this section that analyze the production of *Travel* include excerpts from a previously published article (Mai 2016b).
2. As mentioned in the introduction, I use male and female pronouns to refer to Karim and Samira respectively. This usage reflects the fluidity of his/her sex-gendered subjectivity.
3. Algerian transsexuals are considered a social group under the 1951 Geneva Convention in French asylum law.
4. Both *Samira* and *Travel* were originally conceived as art-science installations composed of two large screens joined at a 120° angle, to maximize viewers' sensorial immersion in the situations being presented. Both installations were screened in a loop, which is also why the initial and last scenes have the same setting. The context for the production of the two installations was the *antiAtlas of Borders* project, which since 2012 has organized conferences and art exhibitions on the mutations of borders in contemporary times. The *antiAtlas of Borders* is led by a group of researchers, artists, and experts, including myself, and has actively participated in the production and diffusion of both *Samira and Travel*. For more information and the *antiAtlas of Borders*, its membership, and its activities, go to http://www.antiatlas.net/antiatlas-of-borders/.

5. Simoni (2013) analyzes the role of juju oaths in Ayelala temples in the agreements between prospective migrants and those who facilitate their migration and involvement in sex work abroad.

CONCLUSION

1. For an example of the understanding of the trafficking paradigm and neoliberal "managerial" governance as "depoliticizing" the issue of migration, see Anderson and Andrijasevic 2008.

REFERENCES

ACPO. 2010. *Setting the Record: The Trafficking of Migrant Women in the England and Wales Off-Street Prostitution Sector*. London: ACPO—Association of Chief Police Officers. Online at http://www.acpo.police.uk/documents/crime/2010/201008CRITMW01.pdf.

Adorjan, Michael, Tony Christensen, Benjamin Kelly, and Dorothy Pawluch. 2012. "Stockholm Syndrome as Vernacular Resource." *Sociological Quarterly* 53 (3): 454–74.

Agier, Michel. 2010. "Humanity as an Identity and Its Political Effects (A Note on Camps and Humanitarian Government)." *Humanity: An International Journal of Human Rights, Humanitarianism, and Development* 1 (1): 29–45.

Agustin, Laura. 2007. *Sex at the Margins: Migration, Labour Markets and the Rescue Industry*. London: Zed Books.

———. 2011. *Managing the Undesirables*. Oxford: Polity Press.

Ahmed, Sara. 2003. *Strange Encounters: Embodied Others in Post-Coloniality*. London: Routledge.

———. 2006. "Orientations: Towards a Queer Phenomenology." *GLQ* 12 (4): 543–74.

Altman, Dennis. 1996. "Rupture or Continuity? The Internationalization of Gay Identities." *Social Text* 14 (3): 77–94.

Amar, Paul. 2009. "Operation Princess in Rio de Janeiro: Policing 'Sex Trafficking,' Strengthening Worker Citizenship, and the Urban Geopolitics of Security in Brazil." *Security Dialogue* 40 (4–5): 513–41.

Anderson, Ben. 2009. "Affective Atmospheres." *Emotion, Space and Society* 2 (2):77–81.

Anderson, Bridget, and Rutvica Andrijasevic. 2008. "Sex Slaves and Citizens: The Politics of Anti-Trafficking." *Soundings* 40:135–45.

Anderson, Leon. 2006. "Analytic Autoethnography." *Journal of Contemporary Ethnography* 35 (4): 373–95.

Andrijasevic, Rutvica. 2007. "Beautiful Dead Bodies: Gender, Migration and Representation in Antitrafficking Campaigns." *Feminist* Review 86 (1): 24–44.

———. 2010. *Migration, Agency and Citizenship in Sex Trafficking*. Basingstoke, UK: Palgrave.

———, and Nicola Mai. 2016. "Editorial: Trafficking (in) Representations: Understanding the Recurring Appeal of Victimhood and Slavery in Neoliberal Times." *Anti-Trafficking Review* (7): 1–10. Online at http://www.antitraffickingreview.org/index.php/atrjournal/article/view/197/185.

Anzaldúa, Gloria. 1999. *Borderlands/La Frontera: The New Mestiza*. San Francisco: Aunt Lute Books.

Arsovska, Jana. 2015. *Decoding Albanian Organized Crime: Culture, Politics, and Globalization*. Oakland: University of California Press.

Ballauri, Elsa. 1997. "Prostitution, History, Causes, Reality." In *Prostitution: Society in Dilemma*, edited by Sevim Arbana and Elsa Ballauri, 1–31. Tirana: Useful to Albanian Women Association.

Barry, Kathleen. 1995. *The Prostitution of Sexuality*. New York: New York University Press.

Bastia, Tanja, and Siobhan McGrath. 2011. "Temporality, Migration and Unfree Labour: Migrant Garment Workers." Manchester Papers in Political Economy: Working Paper 6. Manchester: University of Manchester.

Battaglia, Debbora. 1995. "Problematizing the Self: A Thematic Introduction." In *Rhetorics of Self-Making*, edited by Debbora Battaglia, 1–15. Berkeley: University of California Press.

Bauman, Zygmunt. 2000. *Liquid Modernity*. Cambridge: Polity Press.

Bell, Daniel. 1976. *The Cultural Contradictions of Capitalism*. London: Cox and Wyman.

Bell, David, and Jon Binnie. 2000. *The Sexual Citizen: Queer Politics and Beyond*. Cambridge: Polity Press.

Belloumi, Mounir. 2010. "The Relationship between Tourism Receipts, Real Effective Exchange Rate and Economic Growth in Tunisia." *International Journal of Tourism Research* 12 (5): 550–60.

Benjamin, Jessica. 1988. *The Bonds of Love: Psychoanalysis, Feminism and the Problem of Domination*. New York: Pantheon Books.

———. 1998. *Like Subjects, Love Objects: Essays on Recognition and Sexual Difference*. New Haven, CT: Yale University Press.

Benoit, Cecilia, Bill McCarthy, and Mikael Jansson. 2015. "Stigma, Sex Work, and Substance Use: A Comparative Analysis." *Sociology of Health & Illness* 37 (3): 1–15.

Bergquist, Kathleen. 2015. "Criminal, Victim, or Ally? Examining the Role of Sex Workers in Addressing Minor Sex Trafficking." *Affilia: Journal of Women and Social Work* 30 (3): 314–27.

Berlant, Lauren. 2001. "The Subject of True Feelings: Pain, Privacy and Politics." In *Cultural Pluralism, Identity Politics and the Law*, edited by Austin Sarat and Thomas R. Kearns, 49–84. Ann Arbor: University of Michigan Press.

Bernstein, Elizabeth. 2007a. "The Sexual Politics of the 'New Abolitionism.'" *Differences: A Journal of Feminist and Cultural Studies* 18 (5): 128–51.

———. 2007b. *Temporarily Yours: Intimacy, Authenticity, and the Commerce of Sex*. Chicago: Chicago University Press.

———. 2010. "Militarized Humanitarianism Meets Carceral Feminism: The Politics of Sex, Rights, and Freedom in Contemporary Antitrafficking Campaigns." *Signs* 36 (1): 45–72.

———. 2016. "Redemptive Capitalism and Sexual Investability." In *Perverse Politics? Feminism, Anti-Imperialism, Multiplicity*, edited by Ann Shola Orloff, Raka Ray, and Evren Savci, 45–80. Bingley, UK: Emerald.

Bhabha, Homi. 1994. *The Location of Culture*. London: Routledge.

Blanchette, Thaddeus, and Ana Paula da Silva. 2012. "On Bullshit and the Trafficking of Women: Moral Entrepreneurs and the Invention of Trafficking of Persons in Brazil." *Dialectical Anthropology* 36 (1–2): 107–25.

Blee, Kathleen M. 1998. "White-Knuckle Research: Emotional Dynamics in Fieldwork with Racist Activists." *Qualitative Sociology* 21 (4): 391–99.

Boellstorff, Tom. 2011. "Queer Techne." In *Queer Methods and Methodologies: Intersecting Queer Theories and Social Science Research*, edited by Kath Browne and Catherine J. Nash, 215–30. Farnham, UK: Ashgate.

Bonaventura de Sousa, Santos. 2005. *Toward a New Legal Common Sense: Law, Globalization and Emancipation*. Cambridge: Cambridge University Press.

Boris, Eileen, and Rhacel Parreñas. 2011. "Introduction." In *Intimate Labors: Cultures, Technologies, and the Politics of Care*, edited by Eileen Boris and Rhacel Parreñas, 1–12. Stanford, CA: Stanford University Press.

Bourdieu, Pierre. 1986. "L'Illusion Biographique." *Actes de la Recherche en Sciences Sociales* 62 (1): 69–72.

Bowman, Glen. 1989. "Fucking Tourists: Sexual Relations and Tourism in Jerusalem's Old City." *Critique of Anthropology* 9 (2):77–93.

Bravo, Karen E. 2009. "Free Labor: A Labor Liberation Solution to Modern Trafficking in Humans." *Transnational Law and Contemporary Problems* 18 (3): 545–616.

Brennan, Denise. 2004. *What's Love Got to Do with It? Transnational Desires and Sex Tourism in the Dominican Republic*. London: Duke University Press.

Brents, Barbara, and Teela Sanders. 2010. "Mainstreaming the Sex Industry: Economic Inclusion and Social Ambivalence." *Journal of Law and Society* 37 (1): 40–60.

Brown, Wendy. 2015. *Undoing the Demos: Neoliberalism's Stealth Revolution*. New York: Zone Books.

Butler, Judith. 1999. *Gender Trouble: Feminism and the Subversion of Identity*. London: Routledge.

———. 2008. "Sexual Politics, Torture and Secular Time." *British Journal of Sociology* 59 (1): 1–23.

Cantù, Lionel. 2002. *The Sexuality of Migration: Border Crossings and Mexican Immigrant Men*. New York: New York University Press.

Çaro, Erka, Ajay Bailey, and Leo Van Wissen. 2018. "'I Am the God of the House': How Albanian Rural Men Shift Their Performance of Masculinities in the City." *Journal of Balkan and Near Eastern Studies* 20 (1): 49–65.

Castles, Stephen. 1995. "How Nation-States Respond to Immigration and Ethnic Diversity." *New Community* 21 (3): 293–308.

———, and Mark J. Miller. 2009. *The Age of Migration: International Population Movements in the Modern World*. Basingstoke, UK: Palgrave Macmillan.

Chapkis, Wendy. 2003. "Trafficking, Migration, and the Law: Protecting Innocents, Punishing Immigrants." *Gender & Society* 17 (6): 923–37.

Cheng, Sealing. 2010. *On the Move for Love: Migrant Entertainers and the US Military in South Korea*. Philadelphia: University of Pennsylvania Press.

———. 2011. "The Paradox of Vernacularization: Women's Human Rights and the Gendering of Nationhood." *Anthropological Quarterly* 84:475–505.

Cho, Seo-Young, Axel Dreher, and Eric Neumayer. 2013. "Does Legalized Prostitution Increase Human Trafficking?" *World Development* 41:67–82.

Chobeaux, François. 1996. *Les Nomades du Vide*. Arles: Actes Sud.

Chouliaraki, Lilie. 2013. *The Ironic Spectator: Solidarity in the Age of Post-Humanitarianism*. Oxford: Polity.

Chuang, Janie A. 2014. "Exploitation Creep and the Unmaking of Human Trafficking Law." *American Journal of International Law* 108 (4): 609–49.

Clifford, James, and George E. Marcus. 1986. *Writing Culture: The Poetics and Politics of Ethnography*. Berkeley: University of California Press.

Connell, Raewyn. 2007. *Southern Theory*. Oxford: Polity.

Connell, R. W., and J. W. Messerschmidt. 2005. "Hegemonic Masculinity: Rethinking the Concept." *Gender & Society* 19 (6): 829–59.

Constable, Nicole. 2009. "The Commodification of Intimacy: Marriage, Sex and Reproductive Labour." *Annual Review of Anthropology* 38:49–64.

Cusick, Linda, Hillary Kinnell, Belinda Brooks-Gordon, and Rosie Campbell. 2009. "Wild Guesses and Conflated Meanings? Estimating the Size of the Sex Worker Population in Britain." *Critical Social Policy* 29 (4): 703–19.

Das, Veena. 1998. "Wittgenstein and Anthropology." *Annual Review of Anthropology* 27: 171–95.

Davies, Nick. 2009. "Inquiry Fails to Find Single Trafficker Who Forced Anybody into Prostitution." *Guardian*. Last modified 20 October 2009. http://www.theguardian.com/uk/2009/oct/20/government-trafficking-enquiry-fails.

De Haas, Hein. 2007. "Turning the Tide? Why Development Will Not Stop Migration." *Development and Change* 38 (5): 819–41

Decena, Carlos Ulises. 2011. *Tacit Subjects: Belonging and Same Sex Desire among Dominican Immigrant Men*. Durham, NC: Duke University Press.

Deleuze, Gilles, and Félix Guattari. 1986. *Kafka: Toward a Minor Literature*. Minneapolis: University of Minnesota Press.

Denshire, Sally, and Alison Lee. 2013. "Conceptualizing Autoethnography as Assemblage: Accounts of Occupational Therapy Practice." *International Journal of Qualitative Methods* 12 (1): 221–36.

Ditmore, Melissa, and Marjan Wijers. 2003. "The Negotiations on the UN Protocol on Trafficking in Persons: Moving the Focus from Morality to Actual Conditions." *Nemesis* 4:79–88.

Doezema, Jo. 1998. "Forced to Choose: Beyond the Voluntary vs. Forced Prostitution Dichotomy." In *Global Sex Workers: Rights, Resistance, and Redefinition*, edited by Kamala Kempadoo and Jo Doezema, 34–50. New York: Routledge.

———. 2010. *Sex Slaves and Discourse Masters: The Construction of Trafficking*. London: Zed Press.

ECPAT. 2016. *Heading Back to Harm: A Study on Trafficked and Unaccompanied Children Going Missing from Care in the UK*. London: End Child Prostitution in Asian Tourism–UK.

Elliott, Anthony, and Charles Lemert. 2006. *The New Individualism*. London: Routledge.

Ellis, Carolyn, Tony E. Adams, and Arthur P. Bochner. 2010. "Autoethnography: An Overview." *Forum Qualitative Sozialforschung/Forum: Qualitative Social Research* 12 (1): 10. Online at http://nbn-resolving.de/urn:nbn:de:0114-fqs1101108.

Farley, Melissa. 2004. "Bad for the Body, Bad for the Heart: Prostitution Harms Women Even If Legalized or Decriminalized." *Violence Against Women* 10 (10): 1087–1125.

Fassin, Didier. 2005. "Compassion and Repression: The Moral Economy of Immigration Policies in France." *Cultural Anthropology* 20 (3): 362–87.

Fassin, Eric. 2010. "National Identities and Transnational Intimacies: Sexual Democracy and the Politics of Immigration in Europe." *Public Culture* 22 (3): 507–29.

Faubion, James. 1993. *Modern Greek Lessons*. Princeton, NJ: Princeton University Press.

Foucault, Michel. 1990. *The History of Sexuality. Vol. 2. The Use of Pleasure*. New York: Vintage Books.

Freise, Heidrun. 2013. "Ya l'Babour, Ya Mon Amour: Raï, Rap and the Desire to Escape." In *Music and Imagined Communities: Articulations of Self and Others in the Musical Realm*, edited by Magdalena Waligorska, 176–201. Cambridge: Cambridge University Press.

Frohlick, Susan. 2009. "Pathos of Love in Puerto Viejo, Costa Rica: Emotion, Travel and Migration." *Mobilities* 4 (3): 389–405.

Fuga, Artan. 1998. *L'Albanie entre la Pensée Totalitaire et la Raison Fragmentaire*. Paris: L'Harmattan.

GAATW. 2007. *Collateral Damage: The Impact of Anti-Trafficking Measures on Human Rights Around the World*. Bangkok: Global Alliance Against Traffic in Women.

Geertz, Clifford. 2001. *Available Light: Anthropological Reflections on Philosophical Topics*. Princeton, NJ: Princeton University Press.

Giami, Alain. 2001. "Counter-Transference in Social Research: Beyond George Devereux." Papers in Social Research Methods: Qualitative Series 7. London School of Economics, Methodology Institute. http://www.lse.ac.uk/methodology/pdf/qualpapers/giami-counter-transference2000a.pdf.

Giddens, Anthony. 1991. *Modernity and Self-Identity: Self and Society in the Late Modern Age*. Cambridge: Polity Press.

Giordano, Cristina. 2014. *Migrants in Translation: Caring and the Logics of Difference in Contemporary Italy*. Berkeley: University of California Press.

Gleeson, Kate. 2004. "Budging Sex: What's Wrong with the Pimp?" Paper presented at the Australasian Political Studies Association Conference, Adelaide, 29 September–1 October. Online at http://www.adelaide.edu.au/apsa/docs_papers/Others/Gleeson.pdf.

Grotstein, James. 1981. *Splitting and Projective Identification*. New York: Jason Aronson.

Grupo Davida. 2016. "Trafficking as a Floating Signifier: The View from Brazil." *Anti-Trafficking Review* (4): 161–66. Online at http://www.antitraffickingreview.org/index.php/atrjournal/article/view/97/118.

Guilhot, Nicolas. 2012. "The Anthropologist as Witness: Humanitarianism between Ethnography and Critique." *Humanity: An International Journal of Human Rights, Humanitarianism and Development* 3 (1): 81–101.

Guillemaut, Françoise. 2008. "Sexe, Juju et Migrations: Regard Anthropologique sur les Processus Migratoires de Femmes Africaines en France." *Recherches Sociologiques et Anthropologiques* 39 (1): 11–26.

Gutton, Philippe, and Linda Slama. 1994. "Essai de Psychopathologie de l'Errance." *Adolescence* 23:49–71.

Hage, Ghassan. 2009. "Waiting Out the Crisis. On Stuckedness and Governmentality." In *Waiting*, edited by Ghassan Hage, 97–106. Melbourne: Melbourne University Press.

Hall, Stuart. 1996. "Introduction: Who Needs Identity?" In *Questions of Cultural Identity*, edited by Stuart Hall and Paul Du Gay, 1–17. London: Routledge.

Ham, Julie. 2017. *Sex Work, Immigration and Social Difference*. London: Routledge.

Harvey, David. 2005. *A Brief History of Neoliberalism*. Oxford: Oxford University Press.

Hemmings, Clare. 2012. "Affective Solidarity: Feminist Reflexivity and Political Transformation." *Feminist Theory* 13 (2): 147–61.

Hernández-León, Rubén. 2008. *Metropolitan Migrants: The Migration of Urban Mexicans to the United States*. Berkeley: University of California Press.

Herzfeld, Michael. 2004. *The Body Impolitic: Artisans and Artifice in the Global Hierarchy of Value*. Chicago: Chicago University Press.

———. 2005. *Cultural Intimacy: Social Poetics and the Nation State*. London: Routledge.

Hesford, Wendy S. 2011. *Spectacular Rhetorics: Human Rights Visions, Recognitions, Feminisms*. Durham, NC: Duke University Press.

Higgins, Kathleen. 2016. "Post-Truth: A Guide for the Perplexed." *Nature* 540:9.

Hoefinger, Heidi. 2011. "'Professional Girlfriends': An Ethnography of Sexuality, Solidarity and Subculture in Cambodia." *Cultural Studies* 25 (2): 244–66.

———. 2013. *Sex, Love and Money in Cambodia*. London: Routledge.

hooks, bell. 1995. *Killing Rage: Ending Racism*. New York: Henry Holt.

Horning, Amber, and Anthony Marcus. 2017. "Introduction: In Search of Pimps and Other Varieties." In *Third Party Sex Work and Pimping in the Age of Anti-Trafficking*, edited by Amber Horning and Anthony Marcus, 1–14. Cham, Switzerland: Springer International Publishing.

Howard, Neil. 2017 *Child Trafficking, Youth Labour Mobility and the Politics of Protection*. Basingstoke, UK: Palgrave Macmillan.

Hubbard, Phil. 2012. "Afterword: Exiting Amsterdam's Red Light District." *City: Analysis of Urban Trends, Culture, Theory, Policy, Action* 16 (1–2): 195–201.

Humphrey, Caroline. 1995. "Creating a Culture of Disillusionment: Consumption in Moscow, a Chronicle of Changing Times." In *World Apart: Modernity through the Prism of the Local*, edited by Daniel Miller, 43–68. London: Routledge.

———. 2008. "Reassembling Individual Subjects: Events and Decisions in Troubled Times." *Anthropological Theory* 8 (4): 357–80.

Jackson, Michael. 1998. *Minima Ethnographica: Intersubjectivity and the Anthropological Project*. Chicago: University of Chicago Press.

Jaksic, Milena. 2013. "Devenir Victime de la Traite." *Actes de la Recherche en Sciences Sociales 198 (3)*: 37–48.

Jeffreys, Sheila. 1997. *The Idea of Prostitution*. North Melbourne: Spinifex.

Jiménez, Mercedes. 2003. *Buscarse la Vida: Analisis Transnacional de los Procesos Migratorios de los Menores Marroquíes en Andalucía*. Madrid: Fundación Santa María.

———. 2004. "Análisis Transnacional de los Procesos Migratorios de los Menores de Origen Marroquí." Paper presented at the Fourth Conference on Immigration, Girona, Spain, 10–13 November 2004.

Jobe, Alison. 2008. "Sexual Trafficking: A New Sexual Story?" In *Gender and Interpersonal Violence: Language Action and Representation*, edited by Karen Throsby and Flora Alexander, 66–82. Basingstoke, UK: Palgrave Macmillan.

———. 2010. *The Causes and Consequences of Re-Trafficking: Evidence from the IOM Human Trafficking Database*. Geneva: International Organization for Migration.

Kay, Richard. 2014. "Fawn Faces Fight Over £45m Soho Clean-up." *Daily Mail*. Last modified 4 December 2014. Online at http://www.dailymail.co.uk/columnists/article-2517839/RICHARD-KAY-Fawn-faces-fight-45m-Soho-clean-up.html.

Kempadoo, Kamala, and Jo Doezema, eds. 1998. *Global Sex Workers: Rights, Resistance, and Redefinition*, New York: Routledge.

———, Jyoti Sanghera, and Bandana Pattanaik, eds. 2005. *Trafficking and Prostitution Reconsidered: New Perspectives on Migration, Sex Work and Human Rights*. Boulder, CO: Paradigm.

Kingston, Sarah. 2014. "The Police, Sex Work, and Section 14 of the Policing and Crime Act 2009." *Howard Journal of Criminal Justice* 53 (3): 255–69.

Knorr Cetina, Karin. 1997. "Sociality with Objects: Social Relations in Postsocial Knowledge Societies." *Theory, Culture and Society* 14 (4): 1–30.

Koikkalainen, Saara, and David Kyle. 2015. "Imagining Mobility: The Prospective Cognition Question in Migration Research." *Journal of Ethnic and Migration Studies* 42 (5): 759–76.

Kulick, Don, and Margaret Wilson, eds. 1995. *Taboo: Sex, Identity and Erotic Subjectivity in Anthropological Fieldwork*. London: Routledge.

La Cava, Gloria, and Raffaella Nanetti. 2000. *Albania: Filling the Vulnerability Gap*. Tirana, Albania: World Bank.

Lambevski, Sasho A. 1999. "Suck My Nation: Masculinity, Ethnicity and the Politics of (Homo)sex." *Sexualities* 2 (4): 397–419.

Latour, Bruno. 2004. "Why Has Critique Run Out of Steam? From Matters of Fact to Matters of Concern." *Critical Inquiry* 30 (2): 225–48.

———. 2005. *Reassembling the Social: An Introduction to Actor-Network-Theory*. Oxford: Oxford University Press.

Lăzăroiu, Sebastian, and Monica Alexandru. 2003. *Who Is the Next Victim? Vulnerability of Young Romanian Women to Trafficking in Human Beings*. Bucharest: International Organization for Migration.

Lee, Catherine. 2012. "Prostitution and Victorian Society Revisited: The Contagious Diseases Acts in Kent." *Women's History Review* 21 (2): 301–16.

Leman, Johan, and Steff Janssens. 2008. "The Albanian and Post-Soviet Business of Trafficking Women for Prostitution." *European Journal of Criminology* 5 (4): 433–51.

Lerum, Kari, Kiesha McCurtis, Penelope Saunders, and Stéphanie Wahab. 2012. "Using Human Rights to Hold the US Accountable for Its Anti-Sex Trafficking Agenda: The Universal Periodic Review and New Directions for US Policy." *Anti-Trafficking Review* (1): 81–87. Online at http://www.antitraffickingreview.org/index.php/atrjournal/article/view/24/26.

Levitt, Peggy, and Nina Glick Schiller. 2004 "Conceptualizing Simultaneity: A Transnational Social Field Perspective on Society." *International Migration Review* 38 (3): 1002–39.

Levy, Jay. 2014. *Criminalising the Purchase of Sex: Lessons from Sweden*. London: Routledge.

Lewis, Hannah, Peter Dwyer, Stuart Hodkinson, and Louise Waite. 2015. "Hyper-Precarious Lives: Migrants, Work and Forced Labour in the Global North." *Progress in Human Geography* 39 (5): 580–600.

Lindquist, Johan. 2007. "Of Maids and Prostitutes: Indonesian Female Migrants in the New Asian Hinterlands." In *Postcolonial Disorders*, edited by Mary-Jo DelVecchio Good, Sandra Teresa Hyde, Sarah Pinto, and Byron J. Good, 218–37. Berkeley: University of California Press.

———. 2010. "Images and Evidence: Human Trafficking, Auditing, and the Production of Illicit Markets in Southeast Asia and Beyond." *Public Culture* 22 (2): 223–36.

Loizos, Peter. 1993. *Innovation in Ethnographic Film*. Manchester: Manchester University Press.

———. 1997. "First Exits from Observational Realism: Narrative Experiments in Recent Ethnographic Films." In *Rethinking Visual Anthropology*, edited by Marcus Banks and Howard Morphy, 81–104. New Haven, CT: Yale University Press.

Luibhéid, Eithne. 2002. *Entry Denied: Controlling Sexuality at the Border*. Minneapolis: University of Minnesota Press.

MacDougall, Douglas. 2003. "Beyond Observational Cinema." In *Principles of Visual Anthropology*, edited by Paul Hockings, 115–32. New York: Mouton de Gruyter.

Mahdavi, Pardis. 2014. *From Trafficking to Terror*. New York: Routledge.

Mahmood, Saba. 2005. *The Politics of Piety: The Islamic Revival and the Feminist Subject*. Princeton, NJ: Princeton University Press.

Maher, Lisa, Thomas Crewe Dixon, Pisith Phlong, Julie Mooney-Somers, Ellen Stein, and Kimberly Page. 2015. "Conflicting Rights: How the Prohibition of Human Trafficking and Sexual Exploitation Infringes the Right to Health of Female Sex Workers in Phnom Penh, Cambodia." *Health and Human Rights Journal* 17 (1): 102–113.

Mai, Nicola. 2001a. "Transforming Traditions: A Critical Analysis of the Trafficking and Exploitation of Albanian Girls in Italy." In *The Mediterranean Passage: Migration and New Cultural Encounters in Southern Europe*, edited by Russell King, 258–78. Liverpool: Liverpool University Press.

———. 2001b. "'Italy Is Beautiful': The Role of Italian Television in the Albanian Migratory Flow to Italy." In *Media and Migration: Constructions of Mobility and Difference*, edited by Russell King and Nancy Wood, 95–109. London: Routledge.

———. 2002. "Between Losing and Finding Oneself: The Role of Italian Television in the Albanian Migration to Italy." PhD diss., University of Sussex.

———. 2003. "The Cultural Construction of Italy in Albania and Vice Versa: Migration Dynamics, Strategies of Resistance and Politics of Mutual Self-Definition across Colonialism and Post-Colonialism." *Modern Italy* 8 (1): 77–94.

———. 2004a. "Albanian Masculinities, Sex Work and Migration: Homosexuality, AIDS and Other Moral Threats." In *National Healths: Gender, Sexuality and Health in a Cross-Cultural Context*, edited by Michael Worton and Nana Wilson-Tagoe, 45–58. London: UCL Press.

———. 2004b. "Looking for a More Modern Life . . . : The Role of Italian Television in the Albanian Migration to Italy." *Westminster Papers in Communication and Culture* 1 (1): 3–22.

———. 2005. "The Albanian Diaspora in the Making: Media, Transnational Identities and Migration." *Journal of Ethnic and Migration Studies* 31 (3): 543–61.

———. 2007. "Errance, Migration and Male Sex Work: On the Socio-Cultural Sustainability of a Third Space." In *Places We Share: Migration, Subjectivity, and Global Mobility*, edited by Susan Ossman, 97–120. Lanham, MD: Lexington Books.

———. 2008. *Opportunities and Challenges for Social Intervention Aimed at Migrant Minors*. Rome: Save the Children–Italy.

———. 2009a. "Between Minor and Errant Mobility: The Relation between the Psychological Dynamics and the Migration Patterns of Young Men Selling Sex in the EU." *Mobilities* 4 (3): 349–66.

———. 2009b. *Migrant Workers in the UK Sex Industry: Final Policy-Relevant Report*. London: London Metropolitan University, Institute for the Study of European Transformations. Online at http://cice.londonmet.ac.uk/iset/research-units/iset/projects/esrc-migrant-workers.html?8810F8AC-060C-A7FC-7F15-A583EB86BCE8.

———. 2010. "The Politicisation of Migrant Minors: Italo-Romanian Geopolitics and EU Integration." *Area* 42 (2): 182–9.

———. 2011. "Tampering with the Sex of 'Angels': Migrant Male Minors and Young Adults Selling Sex in the EU." *Journal of Ethnic and Migration Studies* 37 (8): 1237–52.

———. 2012. "The Fractal Queerness of Non-Heteronormative Migrants Working in the UK Sex Industry." *Sexualities* 15 (5–6): 570–85.

———. 2013. "Embodied Cosmopolitanisms: The Subjective Mobility of Migrants Working in the Global Sex Industry." *Gender, Place and Culture* 20 (1): 107–24.

———. 2014. "Between Embodied Cosmopolitism and Sexual Humanitarianism: The Fractal Mobilities and Subjectivities of Migrants Working in the Sex Industry." In *Borders, Mobilities and Migrations: Perspectives from the Mediterranean in the 21st Century*, edited by Virginie Baby-Collins and Lisa Anteby-Yemini, 175–92. Brussels: Peter Lang.

———. 2015. "Surfing Liquid Modernity: Albanian and Romanian Male Sex Workers in Europe." In *Men Who Sell Sex: Global Perspectives*, edited by Peter Aggleton and Richard Parker, 27–41. Abingdon, UK: Routledge.

———. 2016a. "Assembling Samira: Understanding Sexual Humanitarianism Through Experimental Filmmaking." *antiAtlas Journal* 1. Online at https://www.antiatlas-journal.net/01-assembling-samira-understanding-sexual-humanitarianism-through-experimental-filmmaking/.

———. 2016b. "'Too Much Suffering': Understanding the Interplay between Migration, Bounded Exploitation and Trafficking Through Nigerian Sex Workers' Experiences." *Sociological Research Online* 21 (4): 13; doi: 10.5153/sro.4158.

———. 2017. "Mobile Orientations: An Autoethnography of Tunisian Professional Boyfriends." *Sexualities* 20 (4): 482–96.

———, and Cristiana Paladini. 2013. "Flexible Circularities: Integration, Return and Socio-Economic Instability within the Albanian Migration to Italy." In *Circular Migration between Europe and Its Neighbourhood*, edited by Anna Triandafyllidou, 42–68. Oxford: Oxford University Press.

Mandelbrot, Benoit. 1982. *The Fractal Geometry of Nature*. New York: W. H. Freeman.

Marcus, Anthony, Amber Horning, Ric Curtis, Jo Sanson, and Efram Thompson. 2014. "Conflict and Agency among Sex Workers and Pimps: A Closer Look at Domestic Minor Sex Trafficking." *Annals of the American Academy of Political and Social Science* 653 (1): 225–46.

———, Jo Sanson, Amber Horning, Efram Thompson, and Ric Curtis. 2016. "Pimping and Profitability: Testing the Economics of Trafficking in Street Sex Markets in Atlantic City, New Jersey." *Sociological Perspectives* 59 (1): 46–65.

Marcus, George E. 1995. "Ethnography in/of the World System: The Emergence of Multi-Sited Ethnography." *Annual Review of Anthropology* 24:95–117.

Marques, Olga. 2010. "Choice-Makers and Risk-Takers in Neo-Liberal Liquid Modernity: The Contradiction of the 'Entrepreneurial' Sex Worker." *International Journal of Criminology and Sociological Theory* 3 (1): 314–32.

Massad, Joseph A. 2007. *Desiring Arabs*. London: University of Chicago Press.

Massoumi, Brian. 2002. *Parables for the Virtual*. Durham, NC: Duke University Press.

McLennan, William. 2014. "It's Back to Work as Soho 'Walk-up Flat' Closed During Police Raids Is Allowed to Reopen." *West End Extra*. Last modified 24 March 2014. Online at http://www.westendextra.com/news/2014/mar/it's-back-work-soho-'walk-flat'-closed-during-police-raids-allowed-reopen.

Mezzadra, Sandro. 2010. "The Gaze of Autonomy: Capitalism, Migration, and Social Struggles." In *The Contested Politics of Mobility: Borderzones and Irregularity*, edited by Vicky Squire, 121–42. London: Routledge.

———, and Brett Neilson. 2013. *Border as Method, or the Multiplication of Labor*. Durham, NC: Duke University Press.

Mitchell, Gregory. 2016. *Tourist Attractions: Performing Race and Masculinity in Brazil's Sexual Economy*. Chicago: University of Chicago Press.

Montgomery, Heather. 2011. "Defining Child Trafficking and Child Prostitution: The Case of Thailand." *Seattle Journal for Social Justice* 9 (2): 775–811.

Monsutti, Alessandro. 2007. "Migration as a Rite of Passage: Young Afghans Building Masculinity and Adulthood in Iran." *Iranian Studies* 40 (2): 167–185.

Moore, Henrietta. 1994. *A Passion for Difference: Essays in Anthropology and Gender*. Bloomington: Indiana University Press.

Mullin, Frankie. 2016. "Are the Soho Brothel Raids Really About Saving Sex Workers?" *Vice*. Last modified 27 October 2016. Online at https://www.vice.com/sv/article/5gqdbb/operation-lanhydrock-soho-chinatown-sex-worker-raids.

Musto, Jennifer. 2013. "Domestic Minor Sex Trafficking and the Detention to Protection Pipeline." *Dialectic Anthropology* 37:257–76.

———. 2016. *Control and Protect: Collaboration, Carceral Protection and Domestic Sex Trafficking in the United States*. Berkeley and Los Angeles: University of California Press.

Nair, Parvati. 2007. "Voicing Risk: Displacement and Relocation in Spanish-Moroccan

Raï." In *Popular Music, National Identity and the Politics of Location: Between the Local and the Global*, edited by Ian Biddle and Vanessa Knights, 65–80. London: Ashgate.

Najmabadi, Afsaneh. 2013. *Professing Selves: Transsexuality and Same-Sex Desire in Contemporary Iran*. Durham, NC: Duke University Press.

Nencel, Lorraine. 2005. "Feeling Gender Speak." *European Journal of Women's Studies* 12 (3): 345–61.

O'Brien, Erin. 2016. "Human Trafficking Heroes and Villains: Representing the Problem in Anti-Trafficking Awareness Campaigns." *Social & Legal Studies* 25 (2): 205–224.

O'Connell Davidson, Julia. 2005. *Children in the Global Sex Trade*. Cambridge: Polity Press.

———. 2013. "Troubling Freedom: Migration, Debt, and Modern Slavery." *Migration Studies* 1 (2): 176–95.

———. 2014. "Let's Go Outside: Bodies, Prostitutes, Slaves and Worker Citizens." *Citizenship Studies* 18 (5): 516–32.

O'Neill, Maggie. 1997. "Prostitute Women Now." In *Rethinking Prostitution: Purchasing Sex in the 1990s*, edited by Graham Scambler and Annette Scambler, 3–28. London: Routledge.

———. 2001. *Prostitution and Feminism: Towards a Politics of Feeling*. Cambridge: Polity Press.

———. 2010. *Migration, Asylum and Community*. Bristol: Policy Press.

———. 2011. "Participatory Methods and Critical Models: Arts, Migration and Diaspora." *Crossings: Journal of Migration and Culture* 2 (1): 13–37.

———, and Jane Scoular. 2008. "Legal Incursions into Supply/Demand: Criminalising and Responsibilising the Buyers and Sellers of Sex in the UK." In *Demanding Sex: Critical Reflections on the Regulation of Prostitution*, edited by Vanessa Munro and Marina della Giusta, 13–34. Farnham, UK: Ashgate.

Orchiston, Alice. 2016. "Precarious or Protected? Evaluating Work Quality in the Legal Sex Industry." *Sociological Research Online* 21 (4): 12; doi: 10.5153/sro.4136.

Osgood, Jayne. 2014. "Playing with Gender: Making Space for Post-Human Childhood(s)." In *Early Years Foundations: An Invitation to Critical Reflection*, edited by Janet Moyles, Jane Payler, and Jan Georgeson, 191–202. Milton Keynes, UK: Open University Press.

Ossman, Susan. 2013. *Moving Matters: Patterns of Serial Migration*. Stanford, CA: Stanford University Press.

Ostegren, Petra. 2017. "From Zero-Tolerance to Full Integration: Rethinking Prostitution Policies." DemandAT Working Paper 10. Online at http://www.demandat.eu/sites/default/files/DemandAT_WP10_ProstitutionPoliciesTypology_June2017_0.pdf.

Oude Breuil, Brenda C. 2008. "'Precious Children in a Heartless World'? The Complexities of Child Trafficking in Marseille." *Children & Society* 22 (3): 223–34.

Padilla, Mark. 2007. *Caribbean Pleasure Industry: Tourism, Sexuality and AIDS in the Dominican Republic*. Chicago: University of Chicago Press.

Pandolfo, Stefania. 2007. "'The Burning': Finitude and the Politico-Theological Imagination of Illegal Migration." *Anthropological Theory* 7 (3): 329–63.

Papadopoulos, Dimitris, Niamh Stephenson, and Vassilis Tsianos. 2008. *Escape Routes: Control and Subversion in the 21st Century*. London: Pluto Press.

Park, Robert E., and Ernest W. Burgess. 1967. *The City: Suggestions for the Investigation of Human Behavior in the Urban Environment*. Chicago: University of Chicago Press.

Parreñas, Rhacel S. 2011. *Illicit Flirtations: Labor, Migration and Sex Trafficking in Tokyo*. Stanford, CA: Stanford University Press.

Pattegay, Patrice. 2001. "L'actuelle construction, en France, du problème des jeunes en errance: Analyse critique d'une catégorie d'action publique." *Déviance et Société* 25 (3): 257–77.

Peano, Irene. 2013. "Bondage and Help: Genealogies and Hopes in Trafficking from Nigeria to Italy." In *Slavery, Migration and Contemporary Bondage in Africa*, edited by Joel Quirk and Darshan Vigneswaran. Trenton, NJ: Africa World Press. Online at http://www.academia.edu/4498855/Bondage_and_help_Genealogies_and_hopes_in_trafficking_from_Nigeria_to_Italy#.

Perry, Georgina. 2012. "Sex Work and the London 2012 Olympics: How Was It for You?" *Trafficking Research Project*, 14 September. http://thetraffickingresearchproject.wordpress.com/2012/09/14/sex-work-and-the-london-2012-olympics-how-was-it-for-you/.

Pheterson, Gail. 1993. "The Whore Stigma: Female Dishonor and Male Unworthiness." *Social Text* (37): 39–64.

———. 1996. *The Prostitution Prism*. Amsterdam: Amsterdam University Press.

Phillips, John. 2006. "Agencement/Assemblage." *Theory, Culture & Society* 23:108–9.

Pitcher, Jane and Marjan Wijers. 2014. "The Impact of Different Regulatory Models on the Labour Conditions, Safety and Welfare of Indoor-Based Sex Workers." *Criminology and Criminal Justice* 14 (5): 549–64.

Plambech, Sine. 2014. "Between 'Victims' and 'Criminals': Rescue, Deportation, and Everyday Violence among Nigerian Migrants." *Social Politics: International Studies in Gender, State & Society* 21 (3): 382–402.

———. 2016. "Sex, Deportation and Rescue: Economies of Migration among Nigerian Sex Workers." *Feminist Economics* 23 (3): 134–59.

Platt, Lucy, Pippa Grenfell, Chris Bonell, Sarah Creighton, Kaye Wellings, John Parry, and Tim Rhodes. 2011. "Risk of Sexually Transmitted Infections and Violence among Indoor-Working Female Sex Workers in London: The Effect of Migration from Eastern Europe." *Sexually Transmitted Infections* 87 (5): 377–84.

Plummer, Ken. 1995. "Telling Sexual Stories in a Late Modern World." *Studies in Symbolic Interaction* 18:101–20.

Pœrregaard, Karsten. 1997. "Imagining a Place in the Andes." In *Siting Culture*, edited by Karen Fog Olwig and Kirsten Hastrup, 39–58. London: Routledge.

Pratt, Mary Louise. 1991. "Arts of the Contact Zone." *Profession*, 33–40.

Probyn, Elspeth. 1993. *Sexing the Self: Gendered Positions in Cultural Studies*. London: Routledge.

Rabinow, Paul. 1977. *Reflections on Fieldwork in Morocco*. Berkeley: University of California Press.

Rancière, Jacques. 2004. "Who Is the Subject of the Rights of Man?" *South Atlantic Quarterly* 103 (2/3): 297–310.

———. 2006. *The Politics of Aesthetics: The Distribution of the Sensible*. London: Bloomsbury Press.

Ratia, Emma, and Catrien Noterman. 2012. "'I Was Crying, I Did Not Come Back with Anything': Women's Experiences of Deportation from Europe to Nigeria." *African Diaspora* 5 (2): 143–64.

Raymond, Janice. 2004. "Prostitution on Demand: Legalizing the Buyers as Sexual Consumers. *Violence Against Women* 10 (10): 1156–86.

Ricoeur, Paul. 1969. *Le Conflit des Interpretations*. Paris: Éditions du Seuil.

Roman, Denise. 2007. *Fragmented Identities: Popular Culture, Sex and Everyday Life in Postcommunist Romania*. Lanham, MD: Lexington.

Rose, Nikolas. 1996. *Inventing Our Selves: Psychology, Power and Personhood*. Cambridge: Cambridge University Press.

Rouch, Jean. 2003. *Ciné-Ethnography*. Minneapolis: University of Minnesota Press.

Salvation Army. 2016. *Supporting Adult Victims of Modern Slavery: Update on the Fifth Year of the Salvation Army's Victim Care and Coordination Contract*. London: Salvation Army–UK.

Sanchez Taylor, Jacqueline. 2006. "Female Sex Tourism: A Contradiction in Terms?" *Feminist Review* 83:42–59.

Sandberg, Sveinung. 2009. "Gangster, Victim or Both? The Interdiscursive Construction of Sameness and Difference in Self-Presentation." *British Journal of Sociology* 60 (3): 523–42.

Sanders, Teela. 2004. "Controllable Laughter: Managing Sex Work Through Humour." *Sociology* 38 (2): 273–91.

Sanders, Teela, Jane Pitcher, Rosie Campbell, Belinda Brooks-Gordon, Maggie O'Neill, Jo Phoenix, Phil Hubbard, et al. 2008. "An Academic Response to Big Brothel." Manchester: Network of Sex Work Projects. Online at http://www.uknswp.org/wp-content/uploads/AcademicResponseBigBrothelFinSept2008.pdf.

Sanders-McDonagh, Erin, Magali Peyrefitte, and Matt Ryalls. 2016. "Sanitising the City: Exploring Hegemonic Gentrification in London's Soho." *Sociological Research Online* 21 (3): 3; doi: 10.5153/sro.4004.

Schapendonk, Joris, Ilse van Liempt, and Bas Spierings. 2014. "Travellers and Their Journeys: A Dynamic Conceptualisaton of Transient Migrants' and Backpackers' Behaviour and Experiences on the Road." *Migration Studies* 3 (1): 49–67.

Schuster, Liza, and Nassim Majidi. 2015. "Deportation Stigma and Re-migration." *Journal of Ethnic and Migration Studies* 41 (4): 635–52.

Schwandner-Sievers, Stephanie. 2000. "The Enactment of 'Tradition': Albanian Construction of Identity, Violence and Power in Times of Crisis." In *Anthropology of Violence and Conflict*, edited by Bettina E. Schmidt and Ingo W. Schröder, 97–120. London: Routledge.

———. 2010. "Between Social Opprobrium and Repeat Trafficking: Chances and Choices of Albanian Women Deported from the UK." In *Human Trafficking, Human Rights and Non-Standard Migration: Australian, European and South-East Asian Perspectives*, edited by Leslie Holmes, 95–115. Cheltenham: Edward Elgar.

Segrave, Marie, Sanja Milivojevic, and Sharon Pickering. 2009. *Sex Trafficking: International Context and Response*. Cullompton, UK: Willan Publishing.

Shah, Svati. 2013. "Brothels and Big Screen Rescues: Producing the Idea of 'Prostitution in India' Through Documentary Film." *Interventions: International Journal of Postcolonial Studies* 15 (4): 549–66.

———. 2014. *Street Corner Secrets: Sex, Work and Migration in the City of Mumbai*. Durham, NC: Duke University Press.

Shih, Elena. 2015. "The Anti-Trafficking Rehabilitation Complex: Commodity Activism and Slave-Free Goods." Open Democracy. Online at https://www.opendemocracy.net/beyondslavery/elena-shih/antitrafficking-rehabilitation-complex-commodity-activism-and-slavefree-goo.

Sigona, Nando, and Jennifer Allsopp. 2016. "Mind the Gap: Why Are Unaccompanied Children Disappearing in Their Thousands?" Open Democracy. Online at https://www.opendemocracy.net/5050/nando-sigona-and-jennifer-allsopp/mind-gap-why-are-unaccompanied-children-disappearing-in-thous.

Simoni, Vanessa. 2013. "'I Swear an Oath': Serments d'allégeances, coercitions et stratégies migratoires chez les femmes nigérianes de Benin City." In *Prostitution Nigériane:*

Entre rêves de migration et réalités de la traite, edited by Bénédicte Lavaud-Legendre, 33–60. Paris: Editions Khartala.
Sismondo, Sergio. 2017. "Post-Truth?" *Social Studies of Science* 47 (1): 3–6.
Sjøberg, Johannes. 2008. "Ethnofiction: Drama as a Creative Research Practice in Ethnographic Film." *Journal of Media Practice* 9 (3): 229–42.
Skeggs, Beverley. 2004. *Class, Self, Culture*. London: Routledge.
Skilbrei, May-Len, and Charlotta Holmström. 2013. *Prostitution Policy in the Nordic Region*. Farnham, UK: Ashgate.
Soja, Edward. 2000. *Postmetropolis: Critical Studies of Cities and Regions*. Oxford: Blackwell.
Souter, James. 2008. "Emancipation and Domination: Human Rights and Power Relations." *In-Spire Journal of Law, Politics and Societies* 3 (2): 140–50.
Stallaert, Cristiane. 1998. *Etnogénesis y Etnicidad en España: Una Aproximación Histórico-Antropológica al Casticismo*. Barcelona: Proyecto A Ediciones.
Stoller, Paul. 1992. *The Cinematic Griot: The Ethnography of Jean Rouch*. Chicago: University of Chicago Press.
———. 1997. *Sensuous Scholarship*. Philadelphia: University of Pennsylvania Press.
Stone, Sandy. 1992. "The *Empire* Strikes Back: A Posttranssexual Manifesto." *Camera Obscura* 10 (229): 150–76.
Suchland, Jennifer. 2013. "Double Framing in *Lilya 4-Ever*: Sex Trafficking and Postsocialist Abjection." *European Journal of Cultural Studies* 16 (3): 362–76.
Sykes, Gresham M., and David Matza. 1957. "Techniques of Neutralization: A Theory of Delinquency." *American Sociological Review* 22 (6): 664–70.
Tabaku, Arben. 2008. "Ethnic Albanian Rings of Organized Criminals and the Trafficking and Smuggling of Human Beings: An International, Regional and Local Perspective." *Seer: Journal for Labour and Social Affairs in Eastern Europe* 11 (1): 99–109.
Tapinc, Huseyin. 1992. "Masculinity, Femininity and Turkish Male Homosexuality." In *Modern Homosexualities: Fragments of Gay and Lesbian Experiences*, edited by Ken Plummer, 39–49. London: Routledge.
Tarrius, Alain. 2000. *Les nouveaux cosmopolitismes: Mobilités, identités, territoires*. Paris: Editions de l'Aube.
Taussig, Michael. 1993. *Mimesis and Alterity: A Particular History of the Senses*. London: Routledge.
Taylor, Diane, and Mark Townsend. 2014. "Mariana Popa Was Killed Working as a Prostitute: Are the Police to Blame?" *Guardian*. Last modified 19 January 2014. Online at http://www.theguardian.com/society/2014/jan/19/woman-killed-prostitute-police-blame.
Telegraph. 2016. "97 Nail Bar Workers Arrested in Crackdown on 'Barbaric' Modern Slavery." *Telegraph*. Last modified 28 December 2016. Online at http://www.telegraph.co.uk/news/2016/12/28/97-nail-bar-workers-arrested-incrackdown-barbaric-modern-slavery/.
Ticktin, Miriam. 2011. *Casualties of Care: Immigration and the Politics of Humanitarianism in France*. Berkeley: University of California Press.
———. 2017. "A World without Innocence." *American Ethnologist* 44 (4): 577–90.
Travis, Alan. 2008. "Anti-Trafficking Law Will Be Hard to Police, Says Met Commander." *Guardian*. Last modified 10 December 2008. http://www.theguardian.com/politics/2008/dec/10/sex-trafficking-law-enforcement.
UN General Assembly. 2000. "Protocol to Prevent, Suppress and Punish Trafficking in Persons, Especially Women and Children, Supplementing the United Nations Convention Against Transnational Organized Crime." Online at http://www.refworld.org/docid/4720706c0.html.

Vance, Carol S. 2012. "Innocence and Experience: Melodramatic Narratives of Sex Trafficking and the Consequences for Law and Policy." *History of the Present* 2 (2): 200–210.

Veblen, Thorstein. 1899. *Theory of the Leisure Class: An Economic Study in the Evolution of Institutions*. New York: Macmillan.

Wagenaar, Hendrik, Helga Amesberger, and Sietske Altink. 2010. *Designing Prostitution Policy. Intention and reality in Regulating the Sex Trade*. Bristol: Policy Press.

Wacquant, Loïc. 2009. *Punishing the Poor: the Neoliberal Government of Social Insecurity*. Durham, NC: Duke University Press.

Walby, Kevin. 2010 "Interviews as Encounters: Issues of Sexuality and Reflexivity When Men Interview Men about Commercial Same Sex Relations." *Qualitative Research* 10 (6): 639–57.

Walters, William. 2010. "Foucault and Frontiers: Notes on the Birth of the Humanitarian Border." In *Governmentality: Current Issues and Future Challenges*, edited by Ulrich Bröckling, Susanne Krasmann, and Thomas Lemke, 138–64. London: Routledge.

Webber, Frances. 2012. *Borderline Justice*. London: Pluto Press.

Weitzer, Ronald. 2007. "The Social Construction of Sex Trafficking: Ideology and. Institutionalization of a Moral Crusade." *Politics and Society* 35 (3): 447–75.

———. 2012. *Legalizing Prostitution: From Illicit Vice to Lawful Business*. New York: New York University Press.

———. 2014. "New Directions in Research on Human Trafficking." *Annals of the American Academy of Political and Social Science* 653 (1): 6–24.

Werbner, Pnina. 2006. "Vernacular Cosmopolitanism." *Theory, Culture and Society* 23 (2–3): 496–98.

Wetherell, Margaret. 2013. "Feeling Rules, Atmospheres and Affective Practice: Some Reflections of the Analysis of Emotional Episodes." In *Privilege, Agency and Affect*, edited by Claire Maxwell and Peter Aggleton, 221–39. Basingstoke, UK: Palgrave Macmillan.

Whitehead, Ann. 2007. "Independent Child Migration: Issues and Context." Paper presented at Workshop on Independent Child Migrants: Policy Debates and Dilemmas, London, 12 September. Online at http://www.unicef.org/socialpolicy/files/Workshop_on_Independent_Child_Migrants.pdf.

Whyte, Jessica. 2012. "Human Rights: Confronting Governments? Michael Foucault and the Right to Intervene." In *New Critical Legal Thinking*, edited by Matthew Stone, Illan Rua Wall, and Costas Douzinas, 12–31. London: Routledge.

Wilson, Ara. 2004. *The Intimate Economies of Bangkok: Tomboys, Tycoons and Avon Ladies in the Global City*. Berkeley: University of California Press.

Winnubst, Shannon. 2012. "The Queer Thing about Neoliberal Pleasure: A Foucauldian Warning." *Foucault Studies* (14): 79–97.

Young, Iris Marion. 2002. "Lived Body vs. Gender: Reflections on Social Structure and Subjectivity." *Ratio* 15 (4): 410–28.

Young, Robert. 1995. *Colonial Desire*. London: Routledge.

Zelizer, Viviana. 2005. *The Purchase of Intimacy*. Princeton, NJ: Princeton University Press.

Zetter, Roger. 1999. "Reconceptualizing the Myth of Return: Continuity and Transition Amongst the Greek-Cypriot Refugees of 1974." *Journal of Refugee Studies* 12 (1): 1–22.

Zhang, Sheldon. 2009. "Beyond the 'Natasha' Story: A Review and Critique of Current Research on Sex Trafficking." *Global Crime* 10 (3): 178–95.

Zheng, Tiantian. 2014. "Migrant Sex Workers and Trafficking in China." In *Human Trafficking Reconsidered: Rethinking the Problem, Envisioning New Solutions*, edited by Kimberly Kay Huang and Rhacel Salazar Parreñas, 139–48. New York: International Debate Education Association.

INDEX

The research participants are at the heart of this book. To enable the reader to trace their trajectories through its pages, individuals are indexed by pseudonym under the heading "participants."

abolitionism. *See* neo-abolitionism
actor network theory, 51
actors, 173–76, 181, 183
affect, 21–22, 93–94, 109–11, 196–98. *See also* humor; irony; love; sentimentality
agencing, 9–10, 48–52, 190–91
agency, ix–xv, 169–70
Ahmed, Sara, 9–10, 178, 195
Albania, viii–ix, 33–40, 143–56, 162–64
Albanian sex workers, 8, 33–34, 37–40, 44–45, 112–13
Albanian third-party agents, 142–56, 158–59, 162–64
Alexandru, Monica, 164
Algeria, 5–6, 10–11
Algerian sex workers, 5–6, 8–9, 177–81
Amnesty International, 194
Amsterdam, 74–79, 88–89
antiAtlas of Borders, 203n4
Athens, 73, 86
authoritarianism, 196–97
autoethnography, xv, 12–13, 22–24, 195
Ayelala, 184, 204n5

Bauman, Zygmunt, 51, 158
Berlant, Lauren, 4, 115, 189
Bernstein, Elizabeth, 99
bezness, 92–93, 202n1 (chap. 5)
biographical borders, xii–xiii, 1–2; trafficking, 116–23, 131–32, 140–41, 177, 185–87, 192; transgender, 5–6, 177–81
boditarianism, 80–81, 88, 191
Boris, Eileen, 104
bounded exploitation, xii, 99, 138–40, 186–87
brothel workers, 27–28, 106–7, 111–14, 118, 133–37
Brown, Wendy, 197
Bus de Femmes, 181–83

Canada, 203n2 (chap. 6)
children. *See* minors
Chouliaraki, Lilie, 115, 119
clients: as allies, 123; criminalization, ix, xii, 107–10, 201n2; female, 91–105; scripts, 23–24, 93–94, 104
consumption, 9, 51, 60–61, 94, 192. *See also* objectualization
critical trafficking studies, 31
Crowley, Matthew, 174–75
curb-crawling, 111

Dante Alighieri, 142
Das, Veena, 20
debt bondage. *See* bounded exploitation
decisions, xi, 49–50. *See also* agencing
decriminalization, ix, 194–95
De Haas, Hein, 103
Deleuze, Gilles, 9, 61, 82
documentary, 4, 15, 53, 56, 126, 178. *See also* ethnofiction
drugs, 28–30, 40, 44, 59, 88–89

Eastern European sex workers, 133–38. *See also* Albanian sex workers; Lithuanian sex workers; Moldovan sex workers; Romanian sex workers
Economic and Social Research Council (United Kingdom), 199–200
economic necessity discourse, 28, 44–47, 77, 80, 83, 147
Emborders, 1–2, 14–15, 139, 177, 200
English Collective of Prostitutes, 113
erotic subjectivity, 13, 26–27, 47
errant mobility, xiii, 53, 56, 72–73, 80–88, 191–92. *See also* minor mobility
ethnofiction, xv, 13–15, 19, 116–17, 171–87, 195, 197–98; *Comidas Rapidas*, 14, 61–65, 173; *Mother Europe*, 14, 96–97, 100–102; *Normal*, 14–15, 117, 125, 150–51, 172, 174–76; *Samira*, 14–15, 176–81, 203n4; *Travel*, 14–15, 138–40, 176–77, 181–87, 203n4
Europe, migrants' images of, 71–73, 77, 85–86

Farley, Melissa, 203n2 (chap. 6)
fathers, 83, 95–96, 102–3
fiction, 4, 8, 126–27, 173. *See also* ethnofiction
film, 4, 56, 126–27, 200. *See also* ethnofiction
Foucault, Michel, 42–43
fractals, xiv, 81–82, 193
France, xii, 5–6, 53, 82–83, 178–87, 199
free/forced dichotomy, xi, 25–26
"fucking queers," 42–47, 63–64, 79–80
Fuga, Artan, 196

gambling, 155–56
gender. *See* masculinity; selfrepresentation
Geneva Convention (1951), 182, 203n3 (chap. 9)
gentrification, xi–xii, 111–14, 190
Gibson, Allan, 107
Giles Foreman Centre for Acting, 174–75
Glick Schiller, Nina, 16
Global North, xi, 4, 54, 168, 188–89
global sentimentality. *See* sentimentality
Greece, 42–43, 87
Guattari, Félix, 9, 61, 82
Gutton, Philip, 83

harragas, 93, 105
Hemmings, Clare, 7
Higgins, Kathleen, 198
Hoefinger, Heidi, 91–92
homophobia, 10–12, 33–34, 83
homosexuality, 8, 11–13, 26–28, 34, 42–43, 180. *See also* "fucking queers"
Howarth, Valerie, 110
humor, 59, 64, 120. *See also* irony

identity. *See* selfrepresentation
indenture. *See* bounded exploitation
International Organization for Migration, 38, 143, 200
intersubjectivity, 20–22
intimate autoethnography. *See* autoethnography
irony, 22, 119–22, 124–25, 145–46. *See also* humor
Italy, 5, 33, 37, 40–41, 87, 157; author's background, 11–12, 202n5; prisons, 142–44. *See also* television, Italian

Jeffreys, Sheila, 203n2 (chap. 6)
Jiménez, Mercedes, 54, 63
Jobe, Allison, 8
Joint United Nations Program on HIV/AIDS, 194
juju oaths, 184, 204n5

Lambevksi, Sasho, 43
Lancet, The, 194
Lăzăroiu, Sebastian, 164
Levitt, Peggy, 16
lies, 22, 28, 118
Lilya 4-Ever, 126–27
liquid modernity, 47, 51–52, 115, 158, 162, 190
Lithuanian sex workers, 27–29, 135–37
Loizos, Peter, 183
London, 27–29, 111–14, 133, 200
London Metropolitan Police, 107, 111–12
London Olympics (2012), 111
love: cultural scripts, 104; performance of, 92–93, 97–99; trafficking, 123–25, 127–29, 133, 135–38, 147–50, 156–59
loverboy discourse, 127, 203n1 (chap. 7)
Luibhéid, Eithne, 80

madams, 140, 184. *See also* third-party agents
madonna/whore dichotomy, 146–48
Mahmood, Saba, 10
Marseille, 5–6, 56
masculinity, 42–48, 73, 83–88, 93, 155, 158–59. *See also* "fucking queers"
Matza, David, 131
melomentary, 126, 177
Migrant Workers in the UK Sex Industry, 18, 107–8, 199–200
migratory project, xiii, 51
Miller, Susan, 107, 109–10
mimicry, 61
minor mobility, xiii, 82, 85, 89, 191–92. *See also* errant mobility
minors, 49, 53–56, 74, 82–84, 168–70, 202n1 (chap. 3); unaccompanied, 53–54, 62, 157
Mitchell, Gregory, 93
mobile orientation, xiii–xiv, 9–10, 51, 190–91
Modern Slavery Act (2015) (United Kingdom), 113
Moldova, 118
Moldovan sex workers, 117–22
Moodysson, Lukas, 126–27
moral gentrification, xi–xii, 111–14, 190
moral panic, x, 4, 191
Moroccan sex workers, 57–73, 87, 93
Morocco, 57, 71–72
mothers, 83–86, 97–98, 147
multisited ethnography, 15. *See also* research methods

Natasha script, 126–27
National Asylum Court (France), 182, 185
national moralities, 8–9, 39, 43–44
National Referral Mechanism (United Kingdom), 106, 113–14, 132
neo-abolitionism, ix–xii, 8, 108–11, 165–66, 203n2 (chap. 6). *See also* sexual humanitarianism
neoliberalism, xi, 2–4, 50–52, 54–55, 188–98
Netherlands, 74–79, 88–89
neutralization techniques, 130–31, 145–47, 154
Nigeria, 139, 184–85, 193, 204n5
Nigerian sex workers, xi–xii, 138–40, 148, 181–87, 193
North Africa, 41, 43, 68. *See also* Algeria; Morocco; Tunisia

objectualization, 9, 55, 60, 85, 160, 192. *See also* consumption
Office for Protection of Refugees and Stateless People (France), 179, 182, 184

Palermo Protocol, ix–x
Paris, 14. *See also* France
parliamentary debate (United Kingdom), 109–11
Parreñas, Rhacel, 104
participants: Abdel, 63–64; Adrian, 156–62, 174–75; Ahmed, 91–105; Alexander, 87; Alina, 106, 117–22, 132, 167–68, 170; Alketa, 135; Altin, 29–30, 45; Anca, 124–25, 132–33; Arben, 44–45; Besnik, 148–56, 162; Candy, 123–33, 160; Catalin, 168–70; Cesar, 160–61; Ciprian, 75–78, 88–89, 102–3; Claudiu, 77–78, 84–85; Daniela, 137; Dorina, 160–61; Eduard, 46–47; Fatjon, 20, 33, 38–40, 49, 102; Fatmir, 158–59; Florin, 49–50, 76–79, 84–85, 89, 102–3; Fouad, 94–96, 101–2; Ida, 35–36; Ivana, 91, 99–101; Jessica, 134–35; Joy, vii, 138–40, 183–87, 201n1 (preface); Karim/Samira, 1, 5–6, 8–11, 177–81, 202n2 (introduction); Katerina, 138; Lucy, 75; Mirela, 112; Ovidiu, 87–88; Samir, 62–63; Tarek, 59–72, 85, 102; Tatiana, 135–36; Tracy, 27–29; Valbona, 112–13; Viorica, 124–25, 130–33
Pasolini, Pier Paolo, 12, 202n1 (chap. 2)
pimps. *See* third-party agents
Plummer, Kenneth, 7
Policing and Crime Act (2009) (United Kingdom), 107–11
Popa, Mariana, 111
Poppy Project, 203n2 (chap. 6)
postcommunism, 50–51, 102–3, 196; Albania, 34–37, 39, 149–64, 202n3 (chap. 5); Moldova, 118
poststructuralism, 6–7
post-truth, 114–16

prison, 72, 121, 128, 142–45, 153–55, 203n1 (chap. 8)
professional fiancés, 91–105, 156. *See also* love
projective improvisation, 183
prostitution, terminology, 25
psychoanalytic theory, 83–86
psychosocial profiling, 143–44, 164

Raymond, Janice, 203n2 (chap. 6)
refugee status, 5–6, 33, 177–79, 182–85. *See also* minors: unaccompanied
research methods, 15–16, 20–28, 30–32, 108, 143–44, 203n1 (chap. 8). *See also* autoethnography; ethnofiction
Roma (people), 57, 59–60, 157
Romania, 131, 160–61
Romanian migrants, 57–58. *See also* Romanian sex workers
Romanian sex workers: female, 123–35; male, 8, 40, 46–47, 49–50, 75–79, 87–89, 168–69
Romanian third-party agents, 146–47, 156–64
Rome, 33, 40–49, 73, 202n1 (chap. 2)
Rouch, Jean, 172–73

Salvation Army, 106
Sarafidis, Karl, 181
Save the Children, 199
Schiller, Nina Glick, 16
Scotland, Patricia, 109
secularism, 189
selfrepresentation, 6–9; contradictory, 21, 28–30, 85–86, 103–4; preferred, 24–30, 44–47, 64, 83, 108, 171; sex-gendered, 4–5, 8–9; youth, 61. *See also* biographical borders; masculinity
sentimentality, 4, 114–16, 169, 189
Seville, 56–73, 76–77
sex-gendered. *See* selfrepresentation
sex industry, terminology, 16, 24–25, 143, 201n5
Sexual Health On Call (SHOC), 133, 200
sexual humanitarianism, vii–xvi, 2–4, 188–98; affective rhetoric, 109–11, 114–16, 196–98; global governance, x–xi, 2–3, 115–16, 188–90; humanitarian media complex, 4, 126, 173
sexual stories, 7–8, 23–26
Sex Work Trilogy, 14–15
Shah, Svati, 41
Shih, Elena, 115
SHOC (Sexual Health On Call), 133, 200
silences, 22, 28. *See also* lies
Simoni, Vanessa, 204n5
slavery, 50, 113–14, 165
Soho, 27–29, 111–14
Soho Estates, 113–14
Sousse, 91–105, 202n2 (chap. 5)
southern theory, 195
Spain, 56–73, 76–77, 87
stealing, 44–45, 49, 59, 76, 79, 157
stigma. *See* trafficking; whore stigma
Stockholm syndrome, 165
Stoller, Paul, 195
Swedish model, ix, xii, 107–10, 201n2
Sykes, Gresham M., 130–31

Tapinc, Huseyin, 43
Taussig, Michael, 61
television, Italian, 34–37, 94, 157
theater, 174, 181–82
third-party agents, 117, 134–66, 169, 184, 195–96, 201n5, 203n1 (chap. 8). *See also* trafficking
tourism, 77–79, 91–105, 202n2 (chap. 5)
trafficking: Albanian stereotypes, 37, 150; antitrafficking raids, 106–7, 112–18, 123; child, 53–56, 169–70; critical trafficking studies, 31; discourse, ix–x, 115–17, 136, 164–66, 203n1 (chap. 7); "first time" stories, 121, 167–68, 170; immigration control, 2–3, 113–14, 166, 194; liquid, 156–66, 195–96; prevalence and statistics, 31–32, 106–9; relational dynamics, 125–38, 157–66; retrafficking, 165; stigma, 134–36, 140–41, 192; support for victims, 132, 165–66, 181–83; use of term, 201n3. *See also* biographical borders; third-party agents
Trafficking in Persons Report (United States), x
transnational social field, 16, 193
trans people, 5–6, 8–11, 75–76, 83–85, 177–81, 202n2–3 (introduction)
Tunisia, 91–105
Tunisian professional fiancés, 91–105

United Kingdom, 11–12, 17–18, 27–28, 106–14, 117–38, 203n2 (chap. 6)
United Nations Convention Relating to the Status of Refugees (1951), 182, 203n3 (chap. 9)
United Nations Palermo Protocol, ix–x
United States, x, 116, 169

Vance, Carole, 126
violence: antimigrant, 68; domestic, 120; sex work as, ix–x; against sex workers, 108, 111–12, 147–58, 161–63

Weitzer, Robert, 203n2 (chap. 6)
whore stigma, 13, 131, 134, 160–61, 192

Young, Iris Marion, 4

Lightning Source UK Ltd.
Milton Keynes UK
UKHW041822030119
334938UK00001B/4/P